세계조리학

World Cuisine

World Cuisine

세계조리학

유상훈 Sanghun Yoo 지음

(주)교 문 사

PREFACE

항공수단과 인터넷의 발달로 나라 간의 인적교류가 활발해지고 세계의 다양한 식문화가 유입되면서 식탁에도 국제화 바람이 일어나고 있다. 기하급수적으로 국내 외국인 거주자 수가 늘어남에 따라 우리나라에도 양식, 중식, 일식뿐 아니라 인도, 동남아 및 터키 레스토랑이 늘어나고 있으며 많은 관심을 끌고 있다.

국제화 사회를 맞이하여 국내 및 세계 각국에서 조리인력도 점차 많이 요구되고 있지만 국내에는 기능적인 전문 인력에 비해, 세계 각국의 사람들과 현장실무에서 레시피를 이해하고 소통할 수 있는 전문 인력이 부족하다. 현장에서는 실무자 간의 의사소통 못지않게 업무능력에 있어서 레시피를 이해하고 실행에 옮기는 것이 중요한 부분이다.

필자는 다년간 해외에서 생활하며 다양한 현지의 식문화 및 음식을 접하면서 세계 각국의 음식에 많은 관심을 갖고 있었다. 또한 대학에서 다년간 '조리실무영어'를 강의하면서 한 학기 분량에 적합한 교재의 필요성을 느끼고 본 교재를 서술하게 되었다.

이 교재는 세계로 뻗어나갈 예비 조리인을 위해서 현장실무에서 흔히 쓰이는 단어들을 토대로 미국, 중국, 프랑스, 그리스, 이탈리아, 태국, 일본 등 각 나라별 대표적인 음식의 레시피를 선별해 다양한 식재료와 조리법을 알 수 있도록 설명하였다. 또한 간결한 문체를 사용하여 대학에서 영어레시피를 처음 접해 보는 학생들도 부담 없이 접근할 수 있도록 쉽게 집필하였다.

책의 구성이 전체적으로는 복잡해 보일 수도 있지만, 식재료, 계량, 만드는 방법의 순서가 매 레시피마다 똑같이 반복되므로 쉽게 익힐 수 있다. 다양한 인터넷 영상물 및 학습자료를 이용하면 더 효율적인 학습효과를 기대할 수 있다.

큰 꿈을 안고 조리에 첫발을 내디딘 미래의 쉐프들에게 좋은 길잡이가 되길 바란다.

2012년 12월

저자 일동

CONTENTS

MOROCCO 187

RUSSIA 211

AMERICA

World Cuisine

AMERICA still has among its favorite dishes porterhouse steak, hot southern-style drop biscuits, roast beef, Thanksgiving turkey and apple pie—some of the down-home dishes included in a list of personal favorites jotted down by Mark Twain as he returned from a tour of Europe in the late 1870s. Throughout his career, this giant of American literature passionately rooted for American home cooking, both at home and abroad. However, the national cuisine has changed in many ways since Mark Twain's time.

Unfortunately, since the time of World War II, American food has been treated as the "whipping boy" of the culinary world in general. Classed as either two-minute pre-packed technology or plain "junk", the food of the United States has been subjected to the damning criticism once reserved for English food.

This dishes which are the foundations of today's fast-food empires have clearly evolved in America. However, much more importantly, the ethnic diversity and regional bounty have also produced a varied cuisine ranging from the wonderful Mexican-influenced cuisine of Texas and the Southwest, the legendary Creole cooking of Louisiana with its nuances of Spain, France and Africa, the simple, hearty dishes of New England, to the *Mittel Europa* tastes of Illinois and Wisconsin. And New York is practically the world in miniature as far as restaurants are concerned: nearly every ethnic taste is catered to, from Afghanistan to Zanzibar.

The "mixing pot" origins of American cooking have produced a national cuisine that is not only diverse but that also transcends its antecedents. Often the American ingredients were such a vast improvement on their "Old Country" counterparts that many transported dishes were not only adapted but changed irrevocably. The big creamy cheesecake that developed from smaller European ideas has become a world favorite. The American pies—pumpkin, apple, lemon meringue, key lime and pecan—are yardsticks of pie-making. And American bakers have produced a dazzling array of cake recipes that has few equals anywhere in the world.

Another feather in America's cap is the invention of so many of the labor-saving gadgets without which modern life would be a hard day at the grindstone. Proudly first "Made in the USA" were the apple peeler, the hand-cranked ice cream freezer, the high-speed blender, the electric juicer and countless other everyday kitchen items the world now takes for granted.

American regional cooking has leapt into the late twentieth century with a bang. Throughout the 1980s and into the 90s, chefs across the country have taken the old regional cuisines and zapped them with characteristic flair.

In Boston, the "new" New England cuisine blends Yankee ingredients with the overtones of the city's large Mediterranean communities in such dishes as salt cod cakes with saffron and leek sauce.

The revamped Southwestern cuisine now found in Texas and New Mexico has us tucking into lobster frijoles with an equally light-handed salsa.

The "new" California cuisine changes its image weekly, depending on which chef is holding sway : an offshoot of Pacific Rim and Cal Ital could see you enjoying ingredients as diverse as daikon, rocket and fat scallops dressed with truffle oil on the same plate.

The Pilgrim Fathers' landing at Ply-mouth Rock is branded on the American consciousness as the event that heralded the birth of the nation but that unique culinary event—the Thanksgiving Day dinner—didn't become a national symbol until after the Civil War. The idea can be traced back to the Pilgrim Fathers' early feast, but the turkey at the center of the table today looks nothing like its seventeenth-century ancestor. Nowadays everyone's dream Thanksgiving repast is a succulent fat turkey, served up with chestnut stuffing, squash, creamed onions, cranberry sauce and sweet potatoes, and finished off with pumpkin pie. Although the early settlers made do with a tougher bird, the first Thanksgiving Dinner boasted roast duck, goose, lobster, eel pie and venison, additions most modern-day cooks forgo.

Southern cooking is nostalgic even for those who have had no experience of it. To many, it is the definitive American style. No wonder that the first American cookbook—The Compleat Housewife—was published in Virginia in 1742. Like all American regional styles, Southern cooking is a mixture of influences. Here a barebones structure of the original English, Irish, Scottish and French ways was over-laid with the influence of Africa and built on the great quarter of poultry, fish, corn and pork in the guises of straight meat, cured ham, spareribs, fatback and crackling. The many Southern recipes containing corn—corn fritters, corn bread, corn biscuits, corn grits—are living testimony to the ingenuity of American cooks.

But the city that spells fabulous American food to people all over the world is New Orleans. You can only find bad food here if you're really looking. "N' Awlins" food has a vivacity that stems from its various roots in French genius, Spanish spice, Native American herbs and the culinary skills of black city and plantation cooks. Creole and Cajun cooking are the two main strands—one is fragrantly explicit, the other down-to-earth and jumping. William Makepeace Thackeray, the English writer, called New Orleans the city "where you can eat and drink the most and suffer the least."

In his wonderful book *It Gives Me Great Pleasure*, the legendary English photographer Cecil Beaton noted "More and more in American restaurants, advertising is taking over the menu. You are sold on the meal before you have even started." These days, with the growing American interest in fine food, the smell and taste of it is all that you need.

CLAM CHOWDER AND CORN BREAD

In 1602 the Native Americans introduced clams to the colonists in Massachusetts Bay and taught them how to bake the clams in the ground with hot rocks. Gradually the colonists incorporated clams(and other local foods) into their own style of cooking, and now clam chowder is synonymous with New England cuisine. Corn bread is another traditional food, with many states proud of their regional recipe. It can be served at every meal, from baked at dinner, to crumbled in milk and topped with syrup for breakfast.

CLAM CHOWDER

SERVES 4

If fresh clams are unavailable, canned or frozen ones can be substituted.

Ingredient

1 ¼ lbs (625g) shelled clams, cleaned
2oz (60g) bacon or speck
2 large potatoes, peeled and diced
1 cup (4oz / 125g) all-purpose (plain) flour
2 ½ cups (20 fl oz / 625mL) milk
4 dry crackers, broken into pieces and soaked in a little milk
1 ¼ cups (10 fl oz / 300mL) cold water
1 large onion, sliced
Salt and pepper, to taste
1 ¼ cups (10 fl oz / 300mL) boiling water
¼ cup (2oz / 60g) butter
Finely chopped parsley, for garnish, optional

Method

1 Place the clams in the cold water. Heat to boiling, and cook the clams for 1 minute. Strain, and retain the water. Chop the hard clams flesh into dice and keep aside the soft portions.
2 Cook the bacon and onion in a small pan until the onion has softened.
3 Parboil the potatoes.
4 Arrange half the potatoes in a layer in the base of a large saucepan and top with the diced clams. Season with salt and pepper. Sprinkle some flour on top, then add another layer of potatoes and sprinkle on more flour. Pour in the boiling water and boil for 20 minutes.
5 Add the milk, soft clam flesh and boil for 3 minutes. Add the milk-soaked crackers.
6 Blend together 1 tablespoon of flour with a little of the reserved clam liquid. Heat the remainder of the clam liquid to boiling, add the flour mixture and stir until it thickens. Stir into the chowder just before serving.
7 Garnish, if desired, and serve.

CORN BREAD

SERVES 8

This tasty and sturdy bread is a great accompaniment for soups and casseroles. The addition of a higher than usual proportion of flour ensures that the corn bread will be lighter than the old-fashioned versions.

Ingredient

1 ½ cups (6oz /185g) all-purpose (plain) flour
1 cup (5oz / 155g) cornmeal
½ teaspoon salt
2 eggs, lightly beaten
⅓ cup (3oz / 90g) butter, melted
1 tablespoon baking powder
1 tablespoon sugar
½ teaspoon chili powder, optional
1 ¼ cups (10 fl oz / 300mL) milk
½ cup (3oz / 90g) fresh corn kernels

Method

1 Preheat the oven to 350°F (180℃).
2 In a large bowl, sift the flour and baking powder together, then stir in the cornmeal, sugar, salt and chili powder, if using.
3 Beat the eggs into the milk with the melted butter and stir in the cornmeal mixture. Mix only until combined, and then fold in the corn kernels.
4 Spoon the batter into a well-buttered 8 inches (20cm) baking pan and bake in the oven for 45 to 50 minutes, or until the bread springs back when lightly touched in the center with a fingertip.
5 Remove from the oven and turn onto a wire rack. Allow to cool slightly, then cut into wedges and serve at once.

SWEETCORN Corn, also known as maize, is the only indigenous cereal crop of America. Drawings on the tombs of pre-Incan civilizations show that wild grasses from which today's corn is descended were cultivated by the Peruvian Indians. Both Columbus and Cortés were introduced to corn by the American Indians and took the variety developed for the table, is rich in starch and vitamin C. Sweetcorn can be cooked on the cob in boiling water or on a barbecue. The kernels can be dried and ground to make cornmeal and cornstarch(cornflour). Sweetcorn also yields corn oil, which is widely used in cooking, and popcorn, made by puffing the small, hard kernels. Sweetcorn is best bought in brine, creamed, or frozen.

Wine Notes

The partner for this dish is a full-bodied, dry white.

FRANCE : Muscadet from the Loire is famous as a shellfish wine. The sur lie (unfiltered) examples have the most character.

USA : Try a Fume Blanc—Sonoma Country boasts many fine examples.

AUSTRALIA : A Hunter Valley or Margaret River Semillon would be an excellent choice.

NEW ZEALAND : Try a crisp Sauvignon Blanc from Marlborough or Hawkes Bay.

CORN AND BACON MUFFINS

Muffins have been around since recipe books were first written in America, and corn muffins have always been popular. Corn was a basic food of the Native Americans. They introduced it to the early settlers who, altogether they had brought wheat and rye seed with them from Europe, found that corn grew much more easily. Corn quickly became part of the colonists' diet, and it continues to play an important part in American cooking. These muffins can be eaten as a snack or as an accompaniment to soups and salads.

MAKES ABOUT 18

Muffins are best eaten the day they are made, but they may be successfully frozen in plastic bags or containers. To use, remove from the bags or container and thaw. Reheat in a moderate oven (350°F / 180℃) for 15 to 20 minutes, until the muffins are heated through.

Ingredient

1 cup (4oz / 125g) all-purpose (plain) flour
1 cup (5oz / 155g) cornmeal
Salt and pepper, to taste
2 slices (rashers) lean bacon, diced
1 cup (8 fl oz / 250mL) milk
1 egg
1 tablespoon plus 1 teaspoon baking powder
1 teaspoon sugar
⅓ cup (3oz / 90g) butter
1 scallion (spring onion), finely chopped

Method

1 Preheat the oven to 420°F (220℃).
2 Sift together the flour and baking powder into a bowl, and then stir in the cornmeal, sugar, salt and pepper.
3 Heat the butter in a small pan and sautéthe bacon and scallion until lightly cooked. Set aside to cool.
4 Beat together the milk and egg mixture into the cornmeal and flour mixture and mix lightly for about 1 minute.
5 Spoon the butter into well-greased muffin cups and bake for 15 to 20 minutes, or until risen and golden.
6 Serve warm.

CORNMEAL Cornmeal is processed from corn (maize), and can be either yellow or white. White cornmeal is finer and keeps longer than the yellow, but almost all of the skin and germs of the grain are lost; along with some of the flavor. Cornmeal is used mainly to make cornbread, pancakes and muffins. It should be stored dry. While cornmeal will last for months; keep yellow cornmeal will last for months; keep yellow cornmeal in the refrigerator and use it more quickly.

Wine Notes

A straightforward, full-flavored dry while is the best choice of wine. A good beer is another alternative.

FRANCE : Choose a while from the South, where the character is full and obvious, such as Chais Baumiére Chardonnay from Edna Valley; Chamisal and Leeward produce interesting examples.

AUSTRALIA : Select a McLaren Vale Chardonnay made using fully ripe fruit and new oak from Pirramimma or Hugo.

NEW ZEALAND : Choose a Marlborough Sauvignon Blanc.

BOSTON BAKED BEANS

Dried beans came from England with the early Americans settlers and were a major part of their diet during those first long winters. This traditional dish has been modified to suit modern palates without losing its essential character. Black molasses has been replaced with the lighter variety and fat salt bacon has been replaced with lean pork shoulder. Originally the baked beans would have simmered for many hours over a wood-fired stove and, to give the best still need this long cooking time.

SERVES 4

The old-fashioned but reliable way to tell whether dried beans have soaked long enough is to blow on one. If the skin bursts, the beans are ready to be cooked.

Ingredient

2 ½ cups (1lb / 500g) dried navy (haricot) beans
12oz (375g) piece of smoked pork shoulder
¼ teaspoon peppercorns
½ cup (4 fl oz / 125mL) light molasses or treacle
3 teaspoons dry mustard
10 cups (80 fl oz / 2.4L) water
2 bay leaves
2 white onions, thickly sliced
3 tablespoons dark brown sugar
1 teaspoon salt

Method

1 Soak the beans in cold water for up to 12 hours. Drain well and cover with fresh cold water. Heat to boiling then reduce heat and simmer until the skins have softened and the beans are slightly tender.
2 Drain and rinse the beans.
3 Place the 10 cups of water in a large heavy pot and add the beans, pork, bay leaves and peppercorns. Heat to boiling then reduce heat to low, cover the pot and simmer for 1 hour.
4 Remove the pork from the pot and set aside.
5 Drain the beans, reserve the liquid and discard the bay leaves.
6 Preheat the oven to 325°F (165℃).
7 Cut the pork into 1 inch (2.5cm) cubes.
8 In a large casserole, combine the sliced onions, molasses, sugar, mustard and salt.
9 Add the beans and 4 cups of the reserved cooking liquid and mix in the pork cubes.
10 Cover the casserole and back the beans in the oven for 5 hours, or until tender, stirring occasionally.
11 Add a little more of the bean cooking liquid from time to time, if necessary, and stir in lightly.
12 Uncover the casserole and bake the beans for an additional 20 to 30 minutes, or until the liquid has reduced and thickened.

MUSTARD Mustard is a condiment made from the seeds of a plant in the Brassica family. There are three varieties of seed: black (which is spicy), brown (less so), and white (which is more bitter and pungent). The seeds are crushed and then mixed with a liquid to produce a sharp pungent condiment. Mustard seeds have been widely used since biblical times. In the eighteenth century a merchant from Dijon, France, named Jean Naigeon created mustard by mixing black and brown seeds with verjuice (the unfermented juice of grapes), and this has remained the base for the famous Dijon mustard ever since. The French mustards are considered milder than the bright yellow English ones, which can be stingingly hot. American mustards too are milder than the English. Most kinds of mustard are sold as ready-made paste in jars, and area vailable in supermarkets. It is, however, possible to buy hot English mustard in powder form. Add water to make a paste and then leave for 10 minutes to allow its piquancy to develop. It should be made fresh when needed as it loses its flavor with prolonged exposure to air. Mustard should be stored in a cold place, preferably the refrigerator. There are many exotic flavors of mustard available today as the condiment grows in popularity.

Wine Notes

This dish could be served with a light dry red, a rosé or a rich aromatic white wine. Indulge in your preferred wine style.

FRANCE : Try a Loire Rosé, such as Cabernet d' Anjou.

USA : Choices include a Merlot, made in the lighter style, or a Californian Barbera.

AUSTRALIA : Select a commercial Shiraz that is not too heavy or overbearing in style.

ITALY : Bardolino, from the Veneto region in Italy's northeast corner, would appeal. It is usually at its best when it is fresh and young.

CALIFORNIA PIZZA

Americans soldiers become great fans of pizza while they were stationed in Italy during World War II, and they popularized the inexpensive dish when they returned home. Whereas in Italy pizza was a simple creation of dough (sometimes pastry) with a tomato-based topping, in the United States pizza has since found a place not only as a fast food, but it has also been elevated to gourmet status with exotic versions. The choice of topping is limitless with the variety of food combinations available.

SERVES 6

A pizza stone or a pizza tray with a perforated base gives a desirable crispness to the crust. If you are using a stone, you will need a peel, which is a wooden, spade-shaped implement used to transfer the unbaked pizza to the heated stone.

Ingredient

CRUST

¾ cup (6 fl oz / 180mL) lukewarm water
⅓ cup (1 ½ oz / 45g) whole wheat flour
½ teaspoon salt
2 teaspoons active dry yeast
3 tablespoons olive oil
2 cups (8oz / 250g) unbleached all-purpose (plain) flour, sifted

TOPPING

¾ cup (6 fl oz / 180mL) thick tomato puree
2 tablespoons virgin olive oil
3 slices (rashers) lean bacon or ham, cut into matchsticks
1 small red bell pepper (capsicum), halved and seeded
1 tablespoon vinaigrette dressing
Fresh ground black pepper, to taste
3 tablespoons chopped stuffed green olives
2 large tomatoes, sliced and drained well on paper towels
¾ cup (3oz / 90g) grated Mozzarella or Fontina cheese
½ avocado, cut into cubes or sliced
1 tablespoon shredded basil leaves

Method

1 Mix together ¼ cup (2 fl oz / 60mL) of the water, the yeast and whole wheat flour in a bowl and mix well. Leave the mixture to rise in a warm place for 20 to 30 minutes.
2 Add the remaining water, olive oil, salt and flour, and mix well with a wooden spoon. Turn out onto a floured board and knead until soft and a little sticky. Ifnecessary add a little more flour to the board while kneading.
3 Knead the dough for an additional 15 minutes, or until soft and pliable.
4 Place the tough in an oiled bowl, cover with a cloth and leave to rice in a warm spot for about 45 minutes.
5 Shape into a ball, then roll out into a round and place on a lightly oiled pizza tray.
6 Preheat the oven to 425℉ (220℃).

7 Mix together the tomato puree and the olives. Brush the pizza crust generously with olive oil and spread the tomato puree mixture over it. Arrange the tomato slices evenly on top and sprinkle over the ham and cheese. Bake for 30 to 35 minutes, or until the pizza has risen slightly. Reduce heat and cook for an additional 20 minutes, or until pizza is cooked through.

8 While the pizza is cooking, broilthe red pepper until well charred, place in a plastic bag and leave for 15 minutes before peeling off the skin and cutting flesh into strips.

9 Arrange the red pepper and the avocado on the cooked pizza. Mix together the vinaigrette dressing, basil leaves and black pepper and pile onto the cook pizza.

10 Cut into wedges and serve at once.

YEAST Yeast has been used to leaven dough for at least 6000 years, since the time Egyptian bakers had discovered that their bread had accidently trapped wild yeast cells in the air. By the late nineteenth century yeast was an essential kitchen ingredient, and was readily available in grocery stores. Yeast is a fungus that feeds on sugar and produces carbon dioxide and alcohol. It is the carbon dioxide that is responsible for making dough rise. The gluten in the flour traps the gas and the desired shape is formed. When the risen dough is placed in a hot oven the yeast is killed, which prevents a too open and coarse texture from being produced. Fresh yeast can be purchased at health food stores or bakers and must be kept refrigerated and used within a week. Active dry yeast is sold in most supermarkets and can be stored for several months at room temperature. Apart from the wide variety of breads, sweet dough like croissants, English muffins and brioches, and savory ones such as pizza, all get their lift from yeast.

Wine Notes

Most people find that a simple, medium to full-bodied red is ideal with pizza.

FRANCE : The soft, full-bodied reds of Côtes-du-Rhône would strike the right balance.

USA : A reasonably priced Napa Valley Cabernet or Cabernet Merlot would be fine.

AUSTRALIA : Choose a Shiraz (even a young one) from almost any region, although McLaren Vale and Coonawarra are particularly good.

ITALY : The attractive red wine of Abruzzi, Montepulciano d'Abruzzo, would be an excellent choice with pizza.

FRIED GREEN TOMATOES

In prehistoric times the tomato grew as a weed in the Central American corn fields, but by the time of the Spanish invasion it was recognized as a plant of value. Until the very successful movie, Fried Green Tomatoes, few cooks outside America were familiar with this dish, long beloved in the American South. It is a useful way to use the first tomatoes of the year, before they are truly ripen on the vine before summer ends.

SERVES 6

Cooks disagree as to whether sugar should be included in this dish. A small quantity is added here, but it is a personal choice.

Ingredient

1 ½ cups (8oz / 250g) cornmeal
1 teaspoon sugar, optional
3 lbs (1.5kg) large green tomatoes, thickly sliced
½ cup (2oz / 60g) all-purpose (plain) flour
¼ cup (2 fl oz / 60mL) oil, for frying
Salt and pepper, to taste

Method

1 Mix together the cornmeal, flour and sugar, if using. Press both sides of each tomato slice firmly but gently into the mixture.
2 Pour some of the oil into a heavy-based pan and heat to moderately hot. Place a few tomato slices in the pan and fry until golden brown, about 2 minutes. Turn over and cook the other side. Do not fry too many tomatoes at the same time or the oil will cool too much.
3 Remove the tomatoes from the pan, drain on paper towels, and sprinkle with salt and pepper.

Wine Notes

A challenging recipe to match with wine; Sauvignon Blanc would be interesting.

FRANCE : Choose a varietal Sauvignon Blanc from the South or a Sancerre from the Loire Valley.

USA : Try a Sauvignon or Fumé Blanc from a good Sonoma Country vineyard.

AUSTRALIA : Some of the best Sauvignon Blanc comes from Western Australia. Try an example from Margaret River; or perhaps an excellent Verdelho from the same region.

NEW ZEALAND : A Marlborough Sauvignon Blanc would be the ideal choice.

TEXAS CHILI

In a state where there are more head of cattle than people, it is not surprising that beef plays a major part in the region's cooking. The influence of their nearest southern neighbor—Mexico—shows the inclusion of chili peppers and beans in the plain dishes brought by the first settlers. The original Texas chili was probably made using dried meat, with beans added only as an optional extra. If fresh or dried beef was not available, almost any meat would be used—sometimes even snake meat!

SERVES 8

Texas Chili may be simmered for considerably longer than 1 hour, if desired, as long as the heat is kept low. In fact, the longer it cooks, the more the flavor develops. It is a fine dish to make a day ahead and reheat. Some cooks add ketchup or Worcestershire sauce for extra zest.

Ingredient

3 tablespoons lard (fork fat) or oil
½ garlic clove, finely chopped
1 ¼ cups canned tomatoes, drained and chopped
½ teaspoon salt
Freshly ground black pepper, to taste
1 teaspoon chili powder (more or less to taste)
½ cup chopped onion
2 lbs (1kg) lean ground (minced) beef
3 cups cooked dried kidney or canned kidney beans
1 bay leaf

Method

1 Heat the lard in a heavy saucepan over moderate heat, add the onion and garlic and cook until just soft. Add the meat and stir-fry until cooked through.
2 Add all the remaining ingredients and mix well. Cover and simmer for 1 hour or longer.
3 Serve very hot. If desired, garnish with chopped onion, grated cheese and shredded lettuce.

Wine Notes

Long Star, a Texas beer, is great with Tex-Mex food. As for wines, choose a full-bodied, spicy red.

FRANCE : Try a Crozes-Hermitage or Châteauneuf-du-Pape from Rhône Valley, both full, soft and spicy reds.

USA : A Californian Syrah or Mourvédre would be excellent.

AUSTRALIA : Choose a peppery Victorian or South Australian Shiraz.

HUNGARY : The world-famous Egri Bikavér (Bill's Blood), made to match the pepper and spice of Hungarian food, would be perfect.

BARBECUED SALMON CUTLERS

Salmon is considered the king of fish in the cuisines of many geographically unrelated areas: Scandinavia, Russia, Britain, New Zealand and the United States. Salmon was long an integral element in the diet of the Native Americans of the Northwest. In fact, the fish was present in such abundance that in some Indian language there was no other word for fish. Salmon is naturally flavorful and needs only the simplest seasonings; this recipe relies on lemon, pepper and herbs.

SERVES 6

Salmon fillets may be substituted for the cutlets. If lemon balm is not available, sprinkle each fish cutlet with 1 ½ tablespoons of lemon juice and tuck 2 sprigs of dill down each side.

Ingredient

6 salmon cutlets (steaks)
1 teaspoon lemon thyme leaves
1 lemon, thinly sliced
1 bunch lemon balm
1 lemon, cut into wedges, for garnish
¼ cup (2oz / 60g) butter, melted
½ teaspoon seasoned pepper or freshly ground black pepper
Lemon thyme, lemon balm or dill, for garnish

Method

1 Butter 3 sheets of foil large enough to hold 2 salmon cutlets each. Place 2 cutlets on each, then brush with the melted butter and sprinkle with the lemon thyme leaves and seasoned pepper. Arrange the lemon slices on top. Tuck clumps of the lemon balm down each side of the cutlets. Wrap the foil loosely around the fish.
2 Place the fish parcels on a grill (hotplate) over a heated barbecue and cook for 10 to 15 minutes, or until the fish flakes when touched with a fork.
3 To serve, remove from the foil, place on individual plates with vegetables, and garnish with lemon thyme and lemon wedges.

LEMON THYME Lemon thyme (Thymus citriodorus) is less well known than garden thyme, but both have been used for centuries for their flavor and scent. The Ancient Egyptians employed thyme in their embalming process, and the ancient Greeks extracted its oil (thymol) to use as incense. Lemon thyme has smaller leaves than garden thyme and when used in cooking it imparts a distinctive citrus tang. It combines well in some meat and veal dishes, and with shellfish and chicken. The fresh herb is available from larger supermarkets and specially stores. It can be kept in a basin of cold water in the refrigerator for up to a week. Dried lemon thyme is also readily available.

Wine Notes

A clean well flavored white seems the most appropriate style.

FRANCE : A Chassagne Montrachet or Premier Cru Chablis would be a fine choice.

USA : Select an elegant Chardonnay from the Pacific Northwest region.

AUSTRALIA : Choose a Tasmanian Chardonnay; Heemskerk is one of the best.

NEW ZEALAND : Try a Sauvignon Blanc from the Gisborne or Hawkes Bay district.

CHICKEN GUMBO WITH OKRA

Gumbo, that archetypal dish of Louisiana, and New Orleans in particular, is a mixture between a soup and stew, but is justifiably famous in its own right. There are many versions of gumbo—vegetable, fish, poultry, meat—but okra is a standard ingredient. Brought to American by African slaves, okra has a long history, featuring heavily in the cooking of India and other eastern countries. In this classic Cajun dish, okra is used as a thickening agent as well as for its flavor.

SERVES 4~5

If fresh okra is not available, look for the canned variety. Drain before using.

Ingredient

1 roasting chicken, about 2 ½ lbs, cut into serving portions
3 tablespoons flour
2 white onions, finely chopped
5 cups (40 fl oz / 1.26L) hot water
Salt and pepper, to taste
3 tablespoons lard (pork fat) or salad oil
1 cup chopped ripe tomatoes
1 cup sliced okra
5 scallions (spring onions), finely chopped

Method

1 Sprinkle the chicken pieces with salt and pepper.
2 Heat the lard in a pan over fairly high heat, add the chicken pieces, and fry for about 30 minutes, turning often to prevent burning and sticking.
3 When the chicken pieces have browned, move them to one side of the pan. Add the flour and stir until browned, then add the onion and okra.
4 Gradually add about half the hot water, stirring well with each addition.
5 Add the chopped scallions, and the remainder of the water. Adjust the seasoning and simmer for about 1 hour. The gumbo should have quite a lot of liquid when it has finished cooking; add more water, as required, during cooking.
6 Serve with boiled rice and boiled sweet potatoes.

OKRA A seed-bearing, green pod of the mallow family, okra is native to northeastern Africa and is an essential ingredient of Greek, Middle Eastern, Cajun, Caribbean and South American cookery. Also known as ladies' fingers, bamia and gumbo, okra (Abelmoschus esculentus) is best used when very young, before the seeds are completely formed. The can also be steamed, sautéed, braised, and used in salads or as an accompaniment to rice or meat dishes.

Wine Notes

While wine with plenty of flavor would complement this dish.

FRANCE : Choose an Alsace white; perhaps a spicy, full-bodied Tokay or Pinot Gris.

USA : Look for a Sauvignon Blanc-Semillon blend from Napa Valley area.

AUSTRALIA : A Barossa Valley Semillon, soft but flavorsome and rich, would be an ideal choice.

NEW ZEALAND : Try one of the distinctive, pungent Chardonnays from Gisborne or Hawkes Bay.

SOUTHERN FRIED CHICKEN

Fried chicken is perhaps the best known of Southern dishes, and with good reason —perfect crispness on the outside and melting tenderness inside make for a delicious dish. It was traditionally cooked with bacon fat, rather than lard, for the added flavor. However, these days less cholesterol-laden oils are generally used. Chicken breasts would not have been the original typical cut, but using this tender portion of the chicken ensures that cooking is even and the flesh doesn't dry out.

SERVES 6

Although this recipe seems simple, it requires careful attention. The temperature of the cooking fat is critical: too hot and the coating will burn before the flesh cooks; too cool and the chicken will absorb too much fat and the dish will be greasy. The trick is to heat the oil to about 375°F (190℃) in a heavy pan and to cook the chicken as quickly as possible. Do not flour the meat until you are ready to cook, or the coating will be soggy rather crisp and golden.

Ingredient

⅔ cup (3oz / 90g) all-purposed (plain) flour
½ teaspoon salt
Light oil, for frying
½ teaspoon dried sage
⅓ teaspoon freshly ground black pepper
3 large whole chicken breasts, split and skin removed

Method

1 Sift the flour, sage, salt and pepper onto a tray.
2 Heat the oil in a large heavy-based pan.
3 While the oil heats, dip the chicken into the flour, ensuring it is evenly coated. Shake off any excess.
4 Place the chicken breasts in the hot oil, then cover the pan and cook for 10 minutes. Turn the breasts over and cook, uncovered, for a further 10 to 15 minutes or until cooked through. The time will depend upon the thickness of the breasts.
5 Drain the chicken on paper towels and serve at once.

SAGE Sage is a perennial herb (Salvia officinalis), marries well with marjoram and thyme to make what is known as mixed herbs. It is readily available. Fresh sage leaves will keep for up to a week in the refrigerator, while dried sage, if stored in an airtight container away from sunlight, will last for several months.

Wine Notes

Serve a round, reasonably full-bodied dry white wine with this dish.

FRANCE : Try a style such as Macon-Villages, which is usually harmonious with simply prepared white meats.

USA : Choose one of California's innumerable good-quality Chardonnays.

AUSTRALIA : A Barossa Semillon would be a good choice.

NEW ZEALAND : A Hawkes Bay Chardonnay should provide the right combination of flavor and body for this dish.

BARBECUED SPARERIBS

Americans have been using the term "barbecue" since the early 1700s. And now, its popularity has spread worldwide. Traditionally, spareribs were covered and cooked over a slow fire for about an hour and a half, with the sauce added afterwards. However many cooks enjoy the meat with the sauce cooked on—try ways and choose for yourself. Although this is described as a barbecue recipe, it also cooks well in the oven, which is useful if you live in an area with inclement weather.

SERVES 4

Recipes for barbecued spareribs vary. Some call for short ribs of beef; some call for marinating overnight or for several hours and, if preferred, this method may be followed here by using the sauce as the marinade.

Ingredient

2 lbs (1kg) pork spareribs, neatly trimmed
1 large onion, chopped
1 tablespoon Worcestershire sauce
1 tablespoon brown sugar
½ teaspoon salt
2 tablespoons oil or 1oz (30g) lard (pork fat)
2 tablespoons red wine vinegar
Juice of 2 lemons
⅔ cup (5 fl oz / 169mL) chili sauce
1 teaspoon paprika

Method

1 Preheat the oven to 400°F (200℃).
2 Place the spareribs in a baking dish, cover with aluminum foil or cooking parchment, and bake in the oven for 15 minutes.
3 While the meat is cooking, heat the oil or melt the lard in a small saucepan over moderate heat and cook the onion until it is brown. Add the other ingredients and simmer for 15 minutes.
4 Remove the foil or parchment from the ribs and pour the sauce over them.
5 Reduce the oven temperature to 375°F (190℃) and bake the ribs for about 1 hour, basting them often. Add a little hot water of beef stock if the liquid begins to dry up.
6 To serve, place the ribs on a serving platter and spoon the remaining sauce over them.

WINE VINEGAR Wine vinegars are made from champagne, sherry, white wines and red wines that have been subject to bacterial activity. Traditional vinegars may also be flavored with herbs such as tarragon and basil. Balsamic vinegar, made from the Trebbiano grape and aged in a series of barrels made of different woods, has a sweetness and depth not found in other vinegars. White wine vinegar is used most often in sauces and for marinades, while red wine vinegar is best in beef and lamb recipes. All make delicious dressings when mixed with olive oil. Wine vinegars are readily available in supermarkets, though some of the more exotic herb-flavored varieties may only be found in specialty food shops.

Wine Notes

A soft, spicy red is a great partner for this dish.

FRANCE : Choose from the Rhône Valley reds, such as Gigondas, Cornas and Crozes-Hermitage.

USA : A Californian Zinfandel would be excellent.

AUSTRALIA : Choose a blend of Cabernet, Shiraz and Merlot, especially one from Coonawarra.

ITALY : Try a Barbera or Dolcetto from Piedmont.

THANKSGIVING ROAST TURKEY

Turkey bones have been found in an Indian refuse heap that dates from 3000 BC, and the European settlers who arrived later happily continued the tradition of enjoying them. Since the days of the Pilgrim Fathers, turkey has played an important role in the celebration of Thanksgiving Day. However, the farmed turkeys of today are quite different from those earlier birds, which weighed as much as 40 pounds (18 kilograms). The domesticated turkeys have more breast meat and the flesh is tenderer.

SERVES 10~12

If fresh herbs are not available, substitute dried herbs but reduce the quantity by half.

Ingredient

- ⅓ cup (3oz / 90g) butter
- 2 celery stalks, sliced
- 1 teaspoon thyme leaves
- 1 tablespoon finely sliced sage leaves
- 4 cups (1 lb / 500g) coarse corn bread crumbs or whole wheat bread crumbs
- 1 tablespoon grated orange zest
- 16 lbs (8kg) turkey (save neck and giblets for stock)
- Melted butter
- 3 tablespoons light (pouring) cream
- 1 large onion, finely chopped
- ¾ cup (3oz / 90g) peeled, finely chopped fresh chestnuts
- 3 tablespoons chopped parsley
- 1 egg, beaten
- ½ cup (2oz / 60g) diced ham
- Stock (see recipe)
- Salt and pepper, to taste
- 3 tablespoons port

Method

1. Preheat the oven to 400°F (200℃).
2. To make the stuffing, melt the butter in a large pan. Cook the onion, celery, chestnuts, thyme and sage over moderate heat until the onion softens, stirring from time to time. Stir in the parsley.
3. Place the corn bread crumbs in a large bowl and mix in the onion and chestnut mixture. Stir in the beaten egg, diced ham and orange zest, and mix in enough stock to moisten. Season with salt and pepper.
4. Fill the cavity of the turkey with the stuffing and truss the turkey with kitchen twine. Brush generously all over with melted butter and place in a large baking dish.
5. Roast the turkey in the oven for 30 minutes. Reduce heat to 325°F (165℃) and brush over again with butter. Cook for an additional 3 ½ hours, basting from time to time with the pan juices. If the breast skin begins to brown too early, cover with aluminum foil to prevent burning. When the turkey is cooked (when juices from the thigh run clear when tested), remove from the baking dish and keep warm while preparing the gravy.

6 Drain the juices from the baking dish and skim off any excess fat. Pour the juices into a saucepan and add sufficient stock to bring up to about 2 cups (16 fl oz / 500mL). Add the port and heat to boiling. Cook until reduced by one third.
7 Add the cream, adjust seasoning if necessary and reheat without boiling.
8 Spoon onto carved turkey portions.

STOCK

For a really rich flavor, simmer the stock down to 1 ½ cups.

Ingredient

Turkey neck and giblets
5oz (155g) chicken giblets, diced
2 stalks celery, sliced
Few sprigs parsley
1 chicken carcass
1 carrot, chopped
1 small onion, chopped
Salt and pepper

Method

1 Combine all the ingredients in a large saucepan and cover with water. Simmer for at least 1 hour, or until the flavor has developed.
2 Strain, reserving the liquid. Refrigerate overnight, and then remove any fat that has risen to the surface.

SPICED SWEET POTATOES

SERVES 6

If peeling the sweet potatoes in advance, soak them in cold water to which a little lemon juice has been added. This will stop them from discoloring.

Ingredient

4 golden sweet potatoes, peeled.
¾ cup (6 fl oz / 180mL) apple cider
¼ teaspoon ground cinnamon
⅓ teaspoon ground cloves
¼ cup (2oz / 60g) butter
½ cup (3oz / 90g) dark brown sugar
¼ teaspoon ground nutmeg
2 tablespoons orange juice

Method

1 Cook the sweet potatoes in simmering water until barely tender.
2 Cut them into thick slices. Heat the butter in a pan, add the sweet potato slices and cook for several minutes, or until lightly browned on each side.
3 Combine the cider, sugar, spices and orange juice in a small saucepan and cook until syrupy. Pour the syrupy over the sweet potatoes in the pan and cook foranother 5 to 8 minutes over moderately high heat, ensuring that they do not burn.
4 Spoon onto a serving platter.

CRANBERRY SAUCE WITH ORANGE

MAKES ABOUT 4 CUPS

Do not use an aluminum saucepan to prepare this sauce.

Ingredient

1 ¾ cups (14oz / 440g) sugar
½ cup (4 fl oz / 125mL) water
4 cups fresh or frozen cranberries
¾ cup (6 fl oz / 180mL) fresh orange juice
3 cloves
Julienned zest of 1 large orange

Method

1. Combine the sugar, orange juice, water and cloves in a small saucepan and heat to boiling. Reduce heat a little and cook for 5 minutes, or until the sugar dissolves.
2. Add the cranberries and cook over moderately high heat for 5 minutes.
3. Add the julienned orange peel and cook for another 2 to 3 minutes.
4. Remove from heat and cool to room temperature.
5. Spoon into a bowl to serve.

CRANBERRIES Cranberries (Vaccinium macrocarpum) are native to both Europe and North America, although the species found in the United States is larger and less acidic than those in Europe. In America, cranberry sauce is the quintessential condiment for Thanksgiving turkey. Apart from sauces and jellies, cranberries are delicious in breads, pies and muffins, chutneys and relishes, pudding and mousses. Fresh cranberries are harvested in the fall. Frozen cranberries are an excellent substitute, however, ready-made cranberry sauce and jellies are readily available.

Wine Notes

White and red can both find favor with turkey.

FRANCE : Full-bodied Beaujolais such as Chénas or Moulin-à-vent will provide soft, lively flavor without hard tannins.

USA : An Oregon Pinot Noir would be a delicious choice, being fairly light in weight but with berry and "game" flavors, typical of this variety.

AUSTRALIA : Choose a good Sparkling Burgundy from the Great Western District—superb with roast turkey.

NEW ZEALAND : Try a North Island Merlot, from Hawkes Bay or Gisborne.

MISSISSIPPI MUD CAKE

The cocoa bean, from which all cocoa and chocolate products are made, was so important in Aztec society that it was used as currency. Although Spanish explorers sent samples home in the early 1500s, it took another century for the development of cocoa powder, and chocolate bars were not made until the 1800s. Both ingredients add their richness to the Mississippi Mud Cake. The reason for the name of this cake is not known, although it has been speculated that the appearance of the mixture was the inspiration.

SERVES 8

If preferred, an equal amount of milk plus a teaspoon of vanilla may be substituted for the bourbon.

Ingredient

1 cup (8oz / 250g) unsalted butter
1 ¾ cups (14oz / 450g) superfine (caster) sugar
⅓ cup (3 fl oz / 90mL) bourbon
2 cups (8oz / 250g) all-purpose (plain) flour
¼ cup (1oz / 30g) plus 1 tablespoon cocoa powder
1 tablespoon confectioners' (icing) sugar
5oz (155g) bittersweet chocolate, cut into chunks
1 cup (8 fl oz / 250mL) freshly brewed strong hot coffee
⅓ teaspoon baking powder
3 eggs, lightly beaten

Method

1 Preheat the oven to 350°F (180℃).
2 Prepare a 9 inches (24cm) spring form pan by lining the base with wax (grease proof) paper and buttering the sides. Set aside.
3 Place the butter, chocolate, sugar and coffee in a large bowl or in the top half of a double boiler and position over simmering water, stirring constantly until chocolate melts and the mixture is quite smooth.
4 Leave to cool slightly, and then mix in the bourbon.
5 Sift together the flour, baking powder and ¼ cup of the cocoa powder. Gradually stir into the chocolate mixture.
6 Add the beaten eggs, mixing gently but thoroughly.
7 Pour the mixture (which will be quite liquid) into the prepared pan and bake for 1 hour.
8 Reduce heat to 300°F (150℃) and bake for an additional 30 minutes, or until a cake tester comes out clean.
9 Allow the cake to cool before releasing the sides and removing from the pan.
10 Combine the remaining cocoa powder and the confectioners' sugar and dust over the cake before serving.

BOURBON Bourbon is a member of the whiskey family and gets its name from Bourbon County in Kentucky where it was first produced. The earliest written mention of whiskey comes from fifteenth-century Scotland. Then, as now, it was a distillation from barley that had been malted (that is, soaked, germinated, roasted and crushed). In North America, migrants from Scotland and Ireland brought with them their traditional water of life, usquebaugh, and whiskey production started in the eighteenth century. Again, it was based on malted grain, but also used the local crop, bourbon from other whiskeys. Originally called Kentucky whiskey, this corn liquor became popular throughout the South. At one time it was the beverage served at most social occasions, even resulting in a following for moonshine, the illegally home-brewed bourbon. Today regulations dictate that for a whiskey to be called bourbon it must contain at least 51 percent corn and it must be aged for a minimum of two years in new charred oak barrels. As with all whiskeys, it is used to make a cocktail such as a Manhattan or an Old-Fashioned of the famous Mint Julep of the South. However, bourbon also has a place in the kitchen. Its hint of sweetness allows it to partner desserts, especially those prepared with chocolate. Bourbon also adds a bite to a dish when used judiciously, and it turns out in sauces, cakes and even in icecream.

Wine Notes

Avoid "dessert" wines with chocolate desserts.

A rich and heavy wine or liqueur would be most suitable.

FRANCE : The orange of the classic and versatile Grand Marnier would combine wonderfully with chocolate. Crème-de-Grand Marnier would also be worth trying.

USA : Try an Orange Muscat sweet wine from the Central Valley in California.

AUSTRALIA : A very old Rutherglen Liqueur Tokay would be interesting.

Mexico : Kahlúa, the delicious coffee liqueur most often associated with Mexico, would be an excellent choice.

PECAN PIE

The pecan nut tree is native to America's South, and the people there have been enjoying its fruits for centuries. Pecan pie is surely one of America's most beloved desserts, and is said to have been created in a small logging town outside New Orleans, in Louisiana. There are advertising signs all over the little town of Slidell boasting different versions of their own culinary delight, and during the pecan season in the fall there is a regular stream of tourists seeding out the local delicacy.

SERVES 8~10

If the pecans are browning too quickly, place a piece of aluminum foil lightly over the top of the pie as it cooks. Crème fraîche, though not a traditional accompaniment, makes a beautiful replacement for the usual scoop of cream, balancing out the sweetness of the pie.

Ingredient

PASTRY

1 ½ cups (6oz / 185g) all-purpose (plain) flour
1 ½ tablespoons sugar
⅓ teaspoon salt
1 tablespoon heavy (thick) cream, chilled little
½ cup (4oz / 125g) unsalted butter, chilled and diced
1 egg yolk
Chilled water

FILLING

3 eggs
1 cup (8oz / 250mL) corn syrup or golden syrup
1 teaspoon vanilla extract (vanilla essence)
About 1 cup (5oz / 155g) pecan halves
1 cup (8oz / 250g) sugar
1 tablespoon butter, softened
1 cup (4oz / 125g) chopped pecans

Method

1 Preheat the oven to 350°F (180℃).
2 To make the pastry, place the flour, butter, sugar and salt in the bowl of a food processor and pulse on and off until the mixture resembles bread crumbs.
3 With the motor still running, add the egg yolk and cream and process only until the mixture begins to "lump." Add a tiny amount of chilled water, only enough to form dough that holds together when pressed with the fingertips.
4 Scoop the dough onto a piece of plastic wrap, wrap and refrigerate until firm.
5 Lightly butter a 9 inches (23cm) spring form pan or a small pie pan and set aside. Roll the pastry to fit into the base and about 1 ¼ inches (3cm) up the side of the pan.
6 Press the pastry evenly into base and sides and return to the refrigerator while preparing the filling.
7 To make the filling, beat together the eggs, sugar, syrup, butter and vanilla extract. Stir in the chopped pecans and pour the mixture carefully into the chilled base.

8 Arrange the pecan halves in concentric circles on top of the filling until the whole surface is covered.

9 When the pastry is crisp and golden brown and the filling is just firm to the touch, turn off heat and leave in the oven for 10 to 15 minutes before cooling on a wire rack in the pan.

10 Remove the pie from the pan and allow it to become quite cold before cutting it into slices. If desired, it can be served with cream or icecream.

Wine Notes

Serve a light, but sweet, fortified wine with this rich pie.

FRANCE : Try a fortified Muscat from the South, or perhaps the sparkling liqueur from the Champagne region.

USA : A sweet white perhaps in the Madeira or White Port style, would be suitable.

AUSTRALIA : A liqueur Tokay or Frontignac will provide a good match.

SPAIN : An old oloroso cherry, rich but not overly heavy, would be an excellent choice.

BOSTON CREAM PIE

Despite its name, Boston Cream Pie is a cake, not a pie. It is made by sandwiching a cream filling between two layers of yellow cake, then adding a chocolate glaze. The chocolate glaze became part of the traditional recipe in the 1800s, an innovation from the kitchen of Parker House, one of America's oldest hotels. The concept of using vegetable oil instead of butter in cakes was introduced in America in the early 1920s by the appropriately named Harry Baker.

SERVES 10

Do not assemble the cake until shortly before serving.

Ingredient

CAKE
2 large eggs
1 cup (8oz / 250g) superfine (caster) sugar
⅓ cup (3 fl oz / 90 mL) vegetable oil
1 ½ teaspoons vanilla extract (vanilla essence)
2 cups (8oz / 250g) all-purpose (plain) flour
2 ½ teaspoons baking powder pinch of salt
1 cup (8 fl oz / 250mL) milk

CREAM FILLING
1 cup (8 fl oz / 250mL) whipping cream
1 teaspoon vanilla extract (vanilla essence)
1 egg white, optional
2 tablespoons (1oz / 30g) confectioners' (icing) sugar

CHOCOLATE GLAZE
½ cup (3oz / 90g) semisweet chocolate, chopped
3 tablespoons butter

Method

1 Preheat the oven to 350°F (180℃).
2 Lightly butter and flour two round 9 inches (26cm) cake pans.
3 Separate the eggs, placing the whites and yolks in separate bowls.
4 In another bowl, sift together the flour, two-thirds of the sugar, the baking powder and salt.
5 Beat the egg whites with an electric mixer until soft peaks form. Gradually beat in the remaining sugar and continue beating until the mixture stiffens. Set aside.
6 Add the egg yolks, oil and half the milk to the flour mixture and beat until smooth, using a spatula to scrape the side of the bowl from time to time.
7 Add the remaining milk and the vanilla extract and beat until just mixed.
8 Carefully fold the egg whites into the mixture and pour into the prepared pans.
9 Bake the cakes for 20 to 25 minutes, or until the center springs back when gently touched with a fingertip.
10 Cool the cakes in the pans for 5 minutes, and then turn them onto wire racks to cool completely.
11 Meanwhile, prepare the cream filling.

12 In a small bowl, beat the cream until it holds a soft peak.
13 Add the confectioners' sugar and vanilla extract and continue beating until the mixture is stiff.
14 Lightly beat the egg white, if using, and fold into the cream.
15 To make the glaze, heat the chocolate and butter in the top section of a double boiler and stir until the mixture is melted and smooth.
16 To assemble, spread the cream filling on one layer of cake, place the second layer over the filling and use a spatula to spread the warm chocolate glaze smoothly over the top.

Wine Notes

This is a very sweet, and only a very sweet wine could match it. A rich fortified style is a must.

FRANCE : Try a vin doux naturel from the Languedoc-Roussillon district.

USA : Choose a fortified Muscat or Madeira-style from California.

AUSTRALIA : A liqueur Okay or Frontignac from Rutherglen in Nort-East Victoria would be delicious.

PORTUGAL : Malmsey Madeira would be perfect.

CHINA

World Cuisine

CHINA hit the food headlines in the early 1960s, the New York Times ran an article entitled "Mao's Great Crime Against Cuisine". It accused Chairman Mao of destroying the "world's best, most richly diversified cuisine." Fortunately much of popular journalism is more a reflection of its own time than an accurate prediction for the future. Gastronomy has always been at the very center of Chinese national life, so much so that the Chinese equivalent of "How are you?" is "Have you eaten rice today?" Nowadays, the food of Hong Kong, Taiwan and Singapore may be better than that of mainland China but the reason is straight wealth. The roots of one of the world's oldest cuisines remain as vigorous as ever.

The very size of China makes discussion of its cuisine, in anything smaller than an encyclopedic tome, rather difficult. Regional differences and the great diversity that distinguishes Chinese cooking must be grossly simplified.

Indigenous northern cooks are responsible for inventing delicate wheat pancakes, like those served with Peking Duck. Noodles were also invented in the north, and the noodles shops of Beijing and Xian still produce some of the best examples of the region's great culinary creations. Dumplings and steamed buns are also a popular staple food, especially the meat filled "pot-sticker" variety.

T'sing, a soy bean paste that brings out the full flavor of any ingredient with which it is cooked, is a popular condiment in northern cooking. The liberal use of garlic and scallions (spring onions) is a hallmark of Shandong cuisine. Beijing is also the home of Pa Ssi Ping K' U, the caramel-covered apple dish popularized in the West as "toffee apples." Other specialties of northern cooking include meat in aspic, the hair vegetables (a freshwater algae), monkey's head (a fist-sized tree mushroom), and sweet and sour carp.

Shanghai and its neighboring cities in the Yangtze River valley are still glorious pockets of grand cuisine. Shanghai cooks are noted for their red-cooked dishes like pork shoulder or spareribs braised in a soy sauce marinade, and rock candy, a special type of sugar that produces a shiny sauce with a mellow flavor. Hangzhou boasts the best dark-red cured hams, while Suzhou, at one time the haunt of scholars, artists and poets, is famous for "squirrel fish." The climate of eastern China is lush and humid, and therefore the growing season extends year round. Wheat, corn, rice and sweet potatoes are the major crops. The Yangtze River abounds in shad and carp, which are used extensively in the local cuisine. Although duck, chicken and pork are the flavored meats of the region, it was in eastern China that vegetarianism became an art form. Bamboo shoots, cabbage, melons, squash and mustard greens form the basis of a huge array of very refined meatless dishes.

The area is also the greatest rice-producing region in China and all rice-based products, such as rice wine and vinegar, are very popular. Although in most of China they usually eat boiled or steamed rice, in Shanghai, green vegetables are often combined to make the regional specialty, Chao fan (fried rice). Rice is also used as a stuffing for chickens and ducks, and to produce luscious puddings of glutinous rice.

The keynote of eastern Chinese cuisine is delicacy. The hot and spicy seasonings associated with the cooking of Hunan and Szechwan are totally absent. The main flavorings are mellow soy sauce, chao hsing (rice wine)and often black vinegar. The distinctive black Chinkiang vinegar is used widely in the seafood dishes in the eastern seaboard. The excellence of chao hsing wine has produced a whole repertoire of "drunken" dishes using chicken, crap, prawns and spareribs.

The traditional cooking techniques of eastern China are red-cooking, steaming, stir-frying, quick simmering and poaching. Because of the region's abundance of fresh foods of the highest quality, the simple cooking methods of the area evolved in such a way as to bring out the natural flavors of the main ingredients. The subtlety of eastern Chinese cuisine is being enjoyed by an ever-increasing audience.

The cooking of Guangzhou (formerly Canton) is the most subtle, refined cuisine in China. The strong point of Cantonese classic cooking is its heavy reliance on the blending of natural flavors of ultra-fresh ingredients rather than on seasoning. Because of this philosophy, the Cantonese are renowned for their quick-cooking techniques like quick-dipping and quick-boiling of fresh foods such as seafood and vegetables. Stir-frying was perfected in Guangzhou and steaming is another preferred cooking method, the food emerging in a succulent state.

Cantonese cuisine lays claim to being the most varied and ingenious in China. Indispensable in the Cantonese kitchen are black beans, soy sauce, oyster sauce, salt fish, prawn paste, crab, Chinese sausage, roast pork, cilantro (coriander), broccoli and water chestnuts. Tropical fruits are also widely used.

Szechwan and Hunan cooking first became well known in the West in the 1970s.

Szechwan is the great heartland of China and embraces the region known as the "rice bowl" . The leitmotifs of Szechwan cooking are onions, scallions, garlic, ginger, pepper, chilies, peanuts, and sesame seeds and oil. These, used with soy sauce, soy paste, bean curd and fermented black beans, are the soul of Szechwan cooking, while steaming, frying and stir-frying food until it is somewhat crusty are typical Szechwan techniques.

Like Szechwan cooking, Hunan food can be hot and highly spiced. To thicken sauces, the chefs of Hunan use the process of rapid reduction. In spite of the fame of the Szechwan peppercorn, the Hunanese take the lead in the pepper stakes, but contrary to popular opinion, both Szechwan and Hunan possess countless mild dishes.

Fujian, in the deep South, was once considered a culinary backwater. The region's cooking style developed relatively late, with a heavy emphasis on the local seafood.

China, heading as it is towards a booming economic future in the twenty-first century, remains a mixture of strange contradictions. Today's China is a Marxist society on the one hand; on the other, it is moving at an enormous pace towards consumerism, personal profit and individual incentive. As far as food is concerned, for quality and diversity it remains one of the most fascinating places on earth.

CHA SHAO PAO HE CHUEN JUEN

Steamed Pork Buns and Spring Rolls

In China, informal meetings often take place in teahouses, and while alcohol is available, tea is more commonly drunk. An entire cuisine of sweet and savory has evolved for such informal gatherings, and spring rolls and steamed buns are two popular choices. Most teahouse dishes make excellent appetizers in the Western sense, particularly accompanied by condiments such as soy, plum or chili dipping sauce.

CHA SHAO PAO

Steamed Pork Buns

SERVES 6

Cook the buns in several batches to allow them plenty of room in the steamer.

Ingredient

DOUGH

3 cups (12oz / 375g) all-purpose (plain) flour
½ teaspoon salt
1 teaspoon rice wine vinegar
1 tablespoon baking powder
½ cup lard (pork fat)
Approximately ¾ cup (6 fl oz / 180mL) water

FILLING

1 tablespoon sesame oil
2 scallions (spring onions), chopped
1 tablespoon dark soy sauce
1 teaspoon cornstarch (corn flour)
8oz (250g) cold roast pork, finely chopped
1 garlic clove, finely chopped
2 teaspoon sugar

Method

1 To make the dough, sift the flour, baking powder and salt into a large bowl. Rub in the lard until it is well mixed. Stir in the vinegar and enough water to form stiff dough. Knead lightly and allow the dough to stand for about 20 minutes.
2 Heat the oil in a skillet and add the remaining filling ingredients. Stir-fry for about 5 minutes, until the mixture is hot and has thickened slightly.
3 Remove from heat and cool.
4 Divide the dough into 12 pieces and shape each into a ball. Roll out each boll to form a 6 inches (15cm) wide circle on a lightly floured board. Place a tablespoon of the dough with water and bring to the center. Fold the pastry over the filling and pinch the edges together to seal.
5 Place each bun on a square of greased wax (greaseproof) paper and place in a steamer.
6 Cover and steam for about 20 minutes.

CHUN JUEN

Spring Rolls

SERVES 6

These delicious rolls are popular throughout China and may be served as a main course or appetizer. They may be served with a variety of dipping sauces, such as soy, plum or chili. You can buy spring roll wrappers in any Asian supermarket, often in the frozen food section.

Ingredient

6 dried Chinese mushrooms
8oz (250g) ground (minced) pork
¾ cup (3 ½ oz / 100g) sliced bamboo shoots
1 ¼ cups (3 ½ oz / 100g) bean sprouts
1 teaspoon dark soy sauce
2 teaspoons cornstarch (cornflour)
1 egg, beaten
1 tablespoon peanut oil
3 cups (6oz / 185g) shredded Chinese cabbage
½ cup (2oz / 60g) chopped water chestnuts
1 teaspoon sugar
1 teaspoon Chinese rice wine or dry sherry
18 small spring roll wrappers
Oil, for deep-frying

Method

1. Place the mushrooms in a bowl, cover with boiling water and allow to stand for 20 minutes. Squeeze excess water from the mushrooms and chop them finely.
2. Heat the peanut oil in a wok, add the pork and stir-fry until it has changed color, about 5 minutes.
3. Add the mushrooms, cabbage, bamboo shoots, water chestnuts, bean sprouts and sugar and stir-fry for 3 minutes.
4. Combine the soy sauce, rice wine and cornstarch and stir this into the pork and vegetables. Stir until the filling has thickened, then remove from heat and allow to cool.
5. To make the spring rolls, place one wrapper on a board with a corner facing you. Place one heaped tablespoon of the cooled filling about one-third up from the corner. Fold the corner up and over the filling and fold in the sides. Brush the top corner with a little beaten egg and roll up to form a neat parcel. Brush the edges with the beaten egg to seal.
6. Deep-fry the spring rolls until crisp and golden brown and drain on paper towels.
7. Serve them with bowls of sauce of your choice for dipping.

CHINESE WATER CHESTNUTS Chinese water chestnuts (Trapa spp.) are not nuts at all but the bulbs of wild rushes that grow in Southeast Asia. They grow prolifically in waterholes that are not being used for rice-growing or fish farming. They are about the size of walnuts and have a prickly brown coating that can be difficult to peel when fresh. Water chestnuts feature in Asian cuisine, particularly in Chinese and Vietnamese dishes, and are used mainly for their crunchy texture. They can be added to most dishes that call for a nutty consistency. Sliced or silvered, water chestnuts are used in stir-fries and in stuffing, and are often mixed with other vegetables, such as bamboo shoots. They can also be coarsely chopped and combined with finely diced meat or fish to form meatballs or fishballs. Flour made from water chestnuts is used in Chinese kitchens as thickening agent in a manner similar to cornstarch (cornflour). Fresh raw or boiled roasted water chestnuts can be eaten as a snack, like popcorn. They are also served fresh as a dessert, or they can be candied. In ancient China water chestnuts were prescribed for their cooling properties; today they are still eaten as a cooling snack in summer. Chinese water chestnuts are available fresh, principally from Asian food stores. Once peeled, they must be kept in water in the refrigerator and used within 3 or 4 days. It is far easier to buy canned water chestnuts, which are readily available. Store in the refrigerator in an airtight container; use them within a week.

Wine Notes

A rich dry white such as a Chardonnay would be a good choice.

FRANCE : Choose a Village White Burgundy, such as Chassagne Montrachet or Meursault.

USA : Try a non-wooded Chardonnay from the Pacific Northwest or one from the cooler Californian areas such as the Russian River Valley or the Sonoma-Green Valley district.

AUSTRALIA : Select a Chardonnay from the Yarra Valley or the Mornington Peninsula in Victoria.

NEW ZEALAND : Choose a good quality Chardonnay from Gisborne or Hawkes Bay.

HUN TUN TANG

Wonton Soup

Wonton soup is another example of a teahouse snack—a dish that is eaten is informal surroundings while meeting friends and sipping tea. It is most popular in the area around Guangzhou. Extra fine dough must be used. When added to a soup, wontons (literally translated as "swallowed clouds") should be light enough to float on the surface of the hot liquid. This recipe produces a delicately flavored soup.

SERVES 6

Wonton wrappers are available from Asian grocery stores. The wontons may be assembled some time in advance and chilled until ready to cook.

Ingredient

11oz (345g) ground (minced) pork
2 tablespoons Chinese rice wine or dry sherry
1 egg, beaten
½ teaspoon cornstarch (cornflour)
5 cups (40 fl oz / 1.25L) rich chicken stock
½ cup fresh watercress springs
½ teaspoon finely shredded ginger
2 scallions (spring onions), chopped
¼ cup (2 fl oz / 60mL) light soy sauce
1 teaspoon sesame oil
30 wonton wrappers
1 cup straw mushrooms
1 scallion (spring onion), finely chopped

Method

1 Combine the pork, scallions, rice wine, half the soy sauce, the egg, sesame oil and cornstarch in a bowl.
2 Place a teaspoon of this mixture in the center of a wonton wrapper. Lift the corners up to meet each other, and holding the corners, press firmly above the filling, to seal. Repeat the process with the remaining filling and wonton wrappers.
3 Fill a large saucepan with water and heat to boiling. Cook the wontons, in batches, in the boiling water until they rise to the surface, about 2 to 3 minutes.
4 Remove with a slotted spoon.
5 Heat the chicken stock to boiling and add the remaining soy sauce, the mushroom, wontons, watercress, scallion and ginger. Heat through for 2 minutes.
6 Serve at once.

WATERCRESS Watercress (Nasturtium officinale) is an aquatic plant from the mustard family, valued for its peppery taste. In Asia it thrives in paddyfields and water-ways. It is mainly used raw in salads and as a garnish. Cooked, it makes delicious soups that taste equally good hot or cold. Store it in the vegetable drawer of the refrigerator. Use it within a couple of days of purchase.

Wine Notes

A chilled fino sherry marries well with this soup, but there is a case for a light, fruity white.

FRANCE : Choose a light, slightly tart Sylvaner from Alsace.

USA : A vanity like Colombard from the Napa Valley or Sonoma County would provide the right balance of zippy flavor without excessive body or acidity.

AUSTRALIA : Try a chilled fino sherry (from Angoves, Seppelts, or Mildara, among others).

SPAIN : The delicious, tangy manzanilla sherry goes perfectly with delicate soups such as this.

CUONG YOU BING

Green Onion Cakes

All the cuisines of Asia boast a home-grown pancake or griddle bread, like the naan and parathas in India, lumpia in Philippines, and hoppers from Sri Lanka. In China there are the pancakes that wrap the famous crispy Peking Duck and these Green Onion Cakes. They have an enticing aroma and are often sold as a snack from wayside stands in Szechwan. They can also be eaten with a traditional Chinese dipping sauce.

SERVES 8

Don't replace the lard with other shortening as the lard is critical for achieving the characteristic crispness of these cakes.

Ingredient

4 cups (1 lb / 500g) all-purpose (plain) flour, sifted
2oz (60g) lard (pork fat), softened
1 cup (8 fl oz / 250mL) chilled water
Oil, for cooking

FILLING

12 scallions (spring onions), each cut into 16 pieces
2 teaspoons sesame oil
¼ teaspoon salt
2 teaspoons lard (pork fat)

Method

1 Combine the flour and cold water in a large bowl and mix thoroughly. Add the softened lard and mix firmly with your hands until the dough is smooth.
2 Transfer the dough to a lightly floured board and knead for about 5 minutes, or until smooth and elastic. Roll the dough into a 12 inches (30cm) length, then cut it into 8 pieces. Cover lightly with a cloth and leave for 20 minutes.
3 Press the dough portions into rounds. Roll thinly into ovals 10 inches (25cm) long.
4 Combine all the filling ingredients in a small bowl and mix well. Spread some of the filling down the center of each pastry oval, then roll it up to make a long roll. Squeeze the dough at the ends to seal, then coil in a spiral. Gently flatten each cake.
5 Place enough oil in a large pan to cover the base generously. When the oil is hot, cook the cakes one at a time over moderate heat. When one side is golden brown, after about 3 minutes, turn carefully and cook the second side. Keep warm while the other cakes are cooked.
6 Serve hot.

Wine Notes

Serve this dish with a lightish crisp dry white.

FRANCE : Choose an Entre-Deux-Mers with mild acidity and fresh melony flavor.

USA : Try a Chenin Blanc from a winery such as Parducci (of Mendocino) or Sutter Home (in the Napa Valley).

AUSTRALIA : Select a lively South Australian Colombard from Primo Estate or Ingoldby.

NEW ZEALAND : Try a crisp zesty Semillon, such as Nobilo or DeRedcliffe from the North Island.

XIA QIU

Crystal Shrimp

Although stir-frying is commonly thought of as a means of combining one or more varieties of meat with thinly sliced vegetables and seasonings, there are stir-fry dishes that feature only one main ingredient. These dishes are only minimally seasoned, to allow the full flavor of the meat, or the shrimp in this recipe, to come through. This approach to stir-frying gives great clarity of flavor and is known as "crystal."

SERVES 4

Asian grocery stores sell flower-shaped cutters for vegetables. If ginger wine is not available, use 2 tablespoons of dry sherry and ½ teaspoon shredded ginger instead.

Ingredient

24 raw shrimp (prawns), shelled and deveined
¼ teaspoon freshly ground white pepper
2 tablespoons sesame oil
1 carrot, sliced and cut into flower shapes
2 tablespoons ginger wine
6 scallions (spring onions)
1 teaspoon finely chopped ginger

Method

1 Cut a deep slit into each shrimp along the vein line. Combine the ginger wine, pepper and shrimp and marinate for 10 to 15 minutes.
2 While the shrimp are marinating, cut 2 of the scallions into julienne strips 2 inches (5cm) long. Place in a bowl of iced water and leave to curl while the other ingredients are being cooked.
3 Chop the remaining 4 scallions into 1 inch (2.5cm) lengths.
4 Heat the oil in a wok or skillet and stir-fry the shrimp and their marinade with the ginger and the chopped scallions. Cook only a few minutes, until the shrimp flesh is opaque and just firm.
6 Serve immediately, garnished with the carrot flowers and curled scallions.

Wine Notes

A dish noted for its purity and subtlety of flavor needs a wine to reflect this. Choose a dry white which avoids strong oak or very pungent varietal character.

FRANCE : Muscadet from the Loire Valley is the perfect shellfish wine.

USA : Try a clean fruity Chenin Blanc or Colombard from the Napa Valley or Sonoma County.

AUSTRALIA : Look for a Classic Dry White from Evans and Tate or Vasse Felix from Western Australia, or for St Huberts or Lilydale in Victoria.

NEW ZEALAND : Choose one of the crisp, smoothly flavored blends from Coopers Creek or Babich in the North Island.

QUING ZHENG YU

Steamed Whole Fish with Ginger

Given China's long coastline and its many rivers and lakes, it is not surprising that fish plays an important part in the country's cuisine. Whole fish from the ocean, such as sea bass, or freshwater fish like carp, often feature as the final savory platter at a formal dinner or banquet, as the fresh taste of the fish refreshes the diner's palate. Seasonings should be used to enhance, and not smother, its natural flavor.

SERVES 4

The most efficient way to grate ginger is with a special bamboo ginger grater. They are quite inexpensive, and are sold by Asian supermarkets.

Ingredient

2 lb (1kg) very fresh whole fish, cleaned and scaled
½ teaspoon salt
1 ¾ inches (4cm) piece fresh ginger, grated
1 tablespoon sesame oil
1 tablespoon light soy sauce
1 tablespoon Chinese rice wine or dry sherry
½ teaspoon freshly ground black pepper
6 scallions (spring onions), cut into 1 inch (2.5cm) pieces
cilantro (coriander) leaves, for garnish

Method

1 Make 3 diagonal cuts into each side of the fish, sprinkle with the rice wine and marinate for 10 minutes. Rub the fish inside and out with the salt and pepper.
2 Combine all the remaining ingredients except the cilantro leaves. Spoon half the mixture inside the fish, and the remainder on top.
3 Place the fish on a large serving plate and garnish with the cilantro leaves.

GINGER Ginger is the root or rhizome of the ginger plant (Zingiber officinale). Originally a native of Asia, it is now grown throughout the world's tropical regions. It was one of the first spices taken to Europe. In modern European cuisines it is used in drinks, such as ginger ale, in cakes, and is preserved in syrup or sugar. In Asia ginger is an important spice. It forms one of the basic ingredients of curries, and in China it is grated fresh into marinades, cooked in stir-fries and soups and is essential in fish dishes. It is found in many forms: fresh, powdered, dried, crystallized and preserved. All these will last indefinitely, except for fresh ginger, which stored in a cool place will keep for up to 2 months.

Wine Notes

A wine of some subtlety is best to emphasize the natural flavors in Chinese seafood dishes.

FRANCE : Try a premier cru Chablis.

USA : Choose a Semillon or Semillon-Sauvignon Blanc from the Pacific Northwest, or from one of the cooler California "appellations" such as Russian River Valley.

AUSTRALIA : Select a Semillon or Semillon-Sauvignon Blanc blend, particularly from Margaret River region in Western Australia.

NEW ZEALAND : Try a Chardonnay from Gisborne or Marlborough.

NINGMENG JI

Lemon Chicken

In the subtropical south of China, particularly around Guangzhou (formerly Canton), fruit is plentiful. So, naturally, fruit and fruit juices are used more often in Cantonese -style cooking than in other parts of China. Sweetness and sharpness are well balanced in this version of Lemon Chicken. There are many variations of this popular dish, both from different regions of China and in the West.

SERVES 4

If a more piquant flavor is desired, garnish with lemon wedges or sprigs of cilantro or watercress.

Ingredient

1 lb (500g) chicken breast fillets, skinned
1 ½ tablespoons cornstarch (cornflour)
2 egg whites, lightly beaten
¼ cup (2 fl oz / 60mL) peanut oil

SAUCE
⅓ cup (3 fl oz / 90mL) plus 1 tablespoon chicken stock
2 tablespoons honey
1 tablespoon Chinese rice wine or dry sherry
2 teaspoons cornstarch (cornflour)
Juice of 1 lemon
1 tablespoon light soy sauce
1 garlic clove, finely chopped

Method

1 Cut the chicken fillets into strips. Combine the egg whites and cornstarch and coat the chicken strips with the mixture. Chill for about 20 minutes.
2 Heat the oil in a wok or skillet and cook the chicken strips in batches, stirring often to prevent sticking. When they begin to brown, remove from the pan and drain on paper towels. Keep warm.
3 Place all the sauce ingredients except the 1 tablespoon of stock and the cornstarch in a small saucepan and stir to combine. Heat to boiling, reduce heat and simmer for about 5 minute. Mix together the cornstarch and extra chicken stock and stir into the sauce until it thickens slightly.
4 Add the chicken strips to the sauce and toss to coat evenly. Spoon onto a platter and serve with steamed rice and stir-fried vegetables.

RICE WINE Chinese rice wine (shao hsing) is golden in color and has a taste reminiscent of malt whiskey. Chinese writings through the centuries have recorded the making of rice wine. It is a vital ingredient in many Chinese dishes. It is also used as a marinade and is added to stir-fry recipes. Chinese rice wine is also drunk warm as an accompaniment to the meals. Stored in a cool dark place, it will keep for a long period of time, but its flavor will lessen with age.

Wine Notes

This dish is best accompanied by a white wine of crisp acidity, with length of flavor. It should not be too full bodied.

FRANCE : Select a white Bordeaux, principally a blend of Semillon and Sauvignon Blanc.

USA : Try a Semillon or Chardonnay from Washington State; avoid a very okay Chardonnay if possible.

AUSTRALIA : Choose a Semillon from the Hunler Valley; it has the required crispness.

ITALY : Try one of the elegant, understated Chardonnays from the northeastern region such as Trentino(Alto Adige)

SHA GHO DOUFU

Hot pot of Tofu and Vegetable

Over 5000 year ago Emperor Sung Loong Sze discovered the medicinal properties of herbs which he brewed in clay pots. By the time of the Sia Sung and Chan Dynasties the clay pot had become the standard cooking container. It was believed that as clay is a natural substance, it would retain the nutritious quality, tenderness and flavor of the food, particularly important with vegetarian dishes like this one.

SERVES 4

This dish is often served at the table from the pot in which it is cooked. Before an earthenware pot 10 which it is cooked. Before an earthenware pot can be used for cooking, it must be soaked in water for 12 hours and then allowed to dry. If you don't have a pot, use a saucepan and then transfer to another dish for serving.

Ingredient

12 dried Chinese mushrooms
6 cups (48 fl oz / 1.5L) vegetable stock or wafer
I celery stalk, sliced diagonally
4 scallions (spring onions), cut into I inch (2.5cm) lengths
3 tablespoons light soy sauce
1oz (30g) black (cloud ear) fungus, cut into bite-sized pieces
2 carrots, sliced
½ cup sliced bamboo shoots
1 lb (500g) tofu, diced

Method

1. Cover the dried mushrooms and black fungus with boiling water and leave them to stand for 30 minutes. Drain well.
2. Pour the stock or water into an earthenware pot and heat to boiling. Stir in the mushrooms, black fungus, celery and carrots and simmer for about 10 minutes.
3. Add all the remaining ingredients and simmer for an additional 10 minutes.
4. Serve immediately.

A fairly dry Riesling is a good accompaniment for this dish.

FRANCE : Try one of the Alsatian Rieslings.

USA : Choose from the lovely Johannisberg Rieslings from Washington State or from Monterey or Santa Barbera. (J. Lohr Winery and Firestone Vineyards both make good examples.)

AUSTRALIA : Try a Rhine Riesling from the Clare Valley in South Australia or Mitchelton in Victoria. Both areas produce wines with fragrant varietal bouquet and persistent acidity.

GERMANY : Choose a Kabinett or spatlese nesling in 1he trocken style; the wehlen and Johannisberg vineyards produce good examples.

LIANG BAN MIAN

Cold spicy noodles

For centuries in China wheat was eaten only by those who were unable to afford rice or millet. But during the Han era (206 BC~AD 220) flour milling was introduced and wheat and noodles came into their own. Today noodles are still very popular in China, either on their own or mixed with other ingredients. This noodles recipe is from Szechwan, the home of spicy food; it is a refreshing summer dish.

SERVES 4

Sesame paste (also known as tahini) is sold in supermarkets and health food shops.

Ingredient

1 lb (500g) thin egg noodles

SAUCE

3 tablespoons sesame paste
2 tablespoons light soy sauce
3 small red chilies, finely shredded
2 teaspoon sesame oil
1 tablespoon toasted sesame seeds
4 garlic cloves, finely chopped
1 tablespoon rice vinegar
2 teaspoon sugar
½ teaspoon salt
2 scallions (spring onions), finely chopped

Method

1 Cook the egg noodles in boiling salted water. Rinse them under cold running water until cold, about 3 minutes, and drain.
2 Combine all the sauce ingredients and whisk together well.
3 Toss the cooked noodles with the sauce and serve.

Wine Notes

This dish combines beautifully with a fairly dry Riesling.

FRANCE : Alsace is the stronghold of Riesling in France and its dry but aromatic quality is perfect.

USA : Choose a Johannisberg Riesling from the Pacific Northwest.

AUSTRALIA : Try a Rhine Reisling from the Clare-Watervale district; they are firm but fragrant and fruity.

GERMANY : Try a trocken (dry) style Riesling from the Mosel fo Rheingau.

NIURU, XILANHUA, YAOGUO HE FEN

Rice Noodles with Beef, Broccoli and Cashews

The essence of stir-fry is the speed of the cooking method, which ensures the fresh flavors, are not lost. The best way to achieve this is in a wok-invented by the Chinese almost 2000 years ago. In this recipe, as in many stir-fried dishes, a number of ingredients are cooked together to create a unique blending of flavors. Rice sticks are thin noodles made fro ground rice, and are a speciality of southern China.

SERVES 4

Cook the broccoli until just tender-the Chinese like their vegetables crunchy and still brig green. Chinese broccoli has a long thin stalk which is also used.

Ingredient

8oz (250g) rice stick noodles
2 tablespoons Chinese rice wine or dry sherry
2 teaspoons honey
approximately 2 tablespoons peanut oil
2 cups broccoli florets
1 small red bell pepper (capsicum), cut into Julienne strips
2 tablespoons dark soy sauce
1 tablespoons oyster sauce
1 lb (500g) rump steak, cut into strips
½ cup (4oz / 125g) cashew nuts
3 scallions (spring onions), cut into 1 inch (2.5cm) pieces

Method

1 Soak the rice noodles in a bowl of warm water for 20 minutes and drain well.
2 Combine the soy sauce, rice wine, oyster sauce and honey in a bowl. Add the meat strips and stir well. Allow to marinate for at least 30 minutes
3 Heat the peanut oil in a wok and stir-fry the cashew nuts until golden brown. Remove the nuts and drain on paper towels.
4 In the same pan, stir-fry the meat and its marinade in two batches, until it is almost cooked through. Remove from the heat and keep warm. Add a little more oil to the pan if needed and stir-fry the broccoli for about 2 minutes.
5 Return the meat to the wok and add the scallions, bell pepper, cashews and rice noodles. Gently stir the ingredients over moderate heat for about 5 minutes.
6 Serve immediately with a little extra soy sauce, if necessary.

CASHEW NUTS The cashew nut (Anacardium occidentale), native to South America, was taken to Asia by Portuguese explorers about five hundred years ago. The nut flourished there and became an ingredient in the local cuisines. In the West cashew nuts are mainly eaten as a snack or added to salads. In Asia the nuts are used extensively in cooking : for example, in curries and particularly in Chinese stir-fries. Cashew nuts, both salted and unsalted, are readily available.

SICHUAN LA JIAO NIUROU

Szechwan Stir-Fry Beef with Hot Pepper

There is no record of exactly when stir-frying originated, though historians are sure it was being used by AD 100. It is a relatively uncomplicated and quick form of cooking, unlike many of the more elaborate Chinese methods, and therefore it is believed to have been used by field-workers who needed quick hot food to complement the rice brought from home. There are many stir-fry recipes from Szechwan, a province known for its spicy cuisine.

SERVES 6

It Is easier to cut the meat if it is partially frozen. Make sure you use a very sharp knife.

Ingredient

2 lb (1kg) rump steak, well trimmed of fat
10 large dried red chilies
2 tablespoons Chinese rice wine or dry sherry
2 carrots, cut into julienne strips
4 fresh long red chilies, cut into fine shreds
1 cup (8 fl oz / 250mL) peanut oil
3 tablespoons dark soy sauce
1~2 teaspoons sugar, to taste
3 celery stalks, cut into julienne strips

Method

1. Cut the meat into very thin slices, then cut these into very fine shreds.
2. Heat the oil in a wok and stir-fry the meat over medium-high heat for 10 minutes, or until quite dry and crispy. Drain on paper towels.
3. Pour off all but 2 tablespoons of the oil from the wok and stir-fry the dried chilies for 1 to 2 minutes. Remove and discard the chilies.
4. Mix together the soy sauce, rice wine and sugar.
5. Add the soy sauce mixture and the meat to the work and stir-fry for 5 minutes. Add the remaining ingredients and cook for 4 minutes, or until the vegetables are just tender.
6. Serve with noodles or steamed rice.

PEANUT OIL Peanut oil is extracted from the peanut or groundnut (Arachis hypogaea). The peanut was native to South America but was taken to other parts of the world by Portuguese traders. It is now one of the main cash crops in the world's tropical regions. It is widely used in cooking, and in margarine and the canning industry. It is very stable at high temperatures and has faint nutty overtones. It also complements salad dressings. Oil from the cold pressing is greatly prized in many countries for its nuttier flavors.

Wine Notes

An aromatic white such as Gewurztraminer will complement this dish most successfully.

FRANCE : Gewurztraminer from Alsace, with its rich aromatic quality, is an obvious choice.

USA : Try one of the fine Californian Gewurztraminers from winemakers such as Firestone Vineyards, Phelps, Lazy Creek and Navarro.

AUSTRALIA : Choose a Gewurztraminer from Tim Knappstein (Clare Valley), Piper's Brook (Tasmania) or Delatite (central Victoria).

HUNGARY : Select a white wine such as Keknyelu, Furmint or Szurkebarat.

CHA SHAO HE CHAO FAN

Cantonese Roast Pork Strips and Fried Rice

Cha shao, which originated m Guangzhou (formerly Canton), is one of the most commonly served pork dishes in China. The meat is only mildly seasoned but is enhanced when served with a variety of dipping sauces or with Chao fan. Chao Fan, one of the most popular and best known Chinese dishes in the West, is considered a snack in China, where it was created as a way to use up leftover rice.

CHA CHAO

Cantonese Roast Pork Strips

SERVES 6

This meat can also be served cold. It keeps well, and leftover pieces are often sliced and stirred through noodles and rice dishes to make them more filling.

Ingredient

2 lb (1kg) lean loin of pork
2 tablespoons red bean sauce
2 tablespoons Chinese rice wine or dry sherry
1 tablespoon sesame paste
¼ cup (2 fl oz / 60mL) light soy sauce
2 tablespoons sugar
1 teaspoon five-spice powder
2~3 drops red food coloring

Method

1 Using a cleaver or very sharp knife, cut the pork into 4 long strips. Arrange m a single layer in a large shallow dish.
2 In a small bowl, combine all the remaining ingredients. Blend well.
3 Pour the soy sauce mixture over the meat. Leave to marinate for about 30 minutes. Baste frequently.
4 Preheat the oven to 450°F (230℃).
5 Place the meat on a rack fitted into a roasting pan. Bake for 30 minutes, basting occasionally with the remaining marinade then turn the meat over and bake for an additional 15 minutes. It is cooked when clear juices run when a skewer is inserted.
6 Slice the meat into smaller pieces before serving to reveal the tender center.

CHAO FAN

Fried Rice

SERVES 6

If desired, replace the pork, soy sauce and sugar with 6oz (185g) of sliced Cha Shao.

Ingredient

6oz (185g) pork, cut into strips
½ teaspoon sugar
2 onions, finely chopped
⅓ cup button mushrooms, sliced
2 eggs, lightly beaten
1~2 tablespoons soy sauce, optional
1 ½ tablespoons dark soy sauce
⅓ cup (3 fl oz / 90mL) vegetable oil
⅓ cup green peas
2oz (60g) ham, diced
2 cups long-grain rice, cooked, then chilled
¼ cup finely julienned red bell pepper (capsicum)

Method

1 Combine the pork, soy sauce and sugar in a small bowl and set aside.
2 Heat 2 tablespoons of the oil in a large wok or skillet and saute the onions for 1 minutes.
3 Add the peas, mushrooms and ham and saute for another minute, Push these ingredients to the side of the wok, and add another 2 tablespoons of oil.
4 Pour in the beaten eggs and cook until set, then break the eggs into small pieces with a spatula and push to the other side of the wok.
5 Add the remaining oil and the pork and stir-fry 3 minutes.
6 Add the rice and stir over moderate heat until all ingredients are well combined and the rice is hot.
7 Add the soy sauce to taste, if desired, and serve hot, garnished with the julienned bell pepper.

CHINESE SOY SAUCE Soy (or soya) sauce is made from the fermented soya bean (Glycine max). Yeast and brine are added to the natural fermentation of the soya beans and wheat, and the resulting mash is then aged for two years before being processed and bottled. Soy sauce has been used in Chinese cooking for 3000 years. By the tenth century the Japanese had adopted and adapted soy sauce to their palate, and today soy sauce is an indispensable part of all Asian cuisines. This versatile sauce enlivens the ingredients to which it is added. There are various types of soy sauce but within Chinese cooking the light and dark sauces predominate. Light soy sauce is thinner and is normally used with poultry and vegetable dishes where the colors and flavors of the ingredients should not be overpowered. Dark soy sauce complements beef and other dark meat dishes. The sauces are used in marinades, stir-fries and soups, and are also used as a condiment. Soy sauce is widely available, but the more unusual varieties may only be found in Asian food stores.

Wine Notes

A fruity red of the Beaujolais style would be a good choice here.

FRANCE : Choose a good Beaujolais-a-Vent or Chenas.

USA : Try a soft Californian Merlot or one of the Gamays.

AUSTRALIA : Select a lighter Shiraz, such as the Wynns Ovens Valley.

ITALY : Try a young Dolcetto d'Alba or Barbera d'Asti from the Piedment region.

BEIJING KAO YA

Peking Duck

Unlike chicken, which is considered everyday food in China, the duck, regarded as a symbol of purity and fidelity is served at times of celebration. Peking Duck is thought to have originated in the imperial kitchens of the thirteenth-century Ming Dynasty, but the cooking method probably owes its origins to the spit-roasting techniques of the nomadic Mongolians. The proper preparation of Peking Duck requires a minimum of two days.

BEIJING KAO YA

Peking Duck

SERVES 6

Look for a well-shaped duck with long neck attached for this dish. There should be no marks or holes in the skin.

Ingredient

3 ½ lb (1.75kg) whole duck
1 cup (8 fl oz / 250mL) water
3 tablespoons honey
18 scallions (spring onions)
Chinese Pancakes (see recipe)
1 tablespoon lemon juice
3 tablespoons dark soy sauce
¼ cup (2 fl oz / 60mL) Chinese rice wine or dry sherry
hoisin sauce

Method

1 Close the cavity in the duck using a skewer or needle and thread. Pinch and pull the skin all over the duck to loosen it from the flesh.
2 Fill a large pot with water and heat to boiling. Tie a length of string around the neck of the duck and, holding the string, immerse the whole duck in the boiling water for 1 minute. Remove from the pot and hang in an airy place to dry overnight.
3 Combine the lemon juice, water, soy sauce, honey and rice wine in a saucepan. Stir over medium heat until the mixture is boiling. Remove from heat and spoon over the duck several times to ensure it is well coated. Place a tray under the duck and allow it to hang in an airy place for about 5 hours or until the skin is dry.
4 Preheat the oven to 450°F (230℃).
5 Remove the string from the duck, and place the duck on a roasting rack in a pan breast side up.
6 Roast in the oven for 15 minutes, then reduce heat to 350°F (180℃) and continue to roast for 60 to 70 minutes, until the skin is crispy and deep gold in color.
7 While the duck is cooking, prepare the scallions. Cut off the bottom 2 inches (5cm), which is the only part used here.

8 Use a very sharp knife to make four 1 inch (2.5cm) cuts starting from the greener end of each scallion. Place the scallions in a bowl of iced water for about 30 minutes, or until they take on a brush shape.
9 When the duck is cooked, allow it to stand for 10 minutes before cutting the skin and meat into bite-sized pieces and arranging them on a warmed platter.
10 The diners should prepare their own pancakes. Place a hot Chinese Pancake on smear it with hoisin sauce using a scallion brush, and top it with some skin, meat and the scallion brush. It should then be rolled up and eaten with fingers or chopstick.
11 The remaining meat from the duck is often served as a separate course.

CHINESE PANCAKES

MAKES 18

Ingredient

2 ¼ cups (9oz / 280g) all-purpose (plain) flour
1 ¾ cup (6~8 fl oz / 180~250mL) boiling water
sesame oil

Method

1 Place the flour in a bowl and stir in the boiling water. Knead until the dough is smooth.
2 Place the dough in a clean bowl, cover with a damp cloth and allow to stand for at least 30 minutes.
3 Knead again for about 5 minutes, then divide into 18 balls. Dip one side of one ball into a little sesame oil. Press the oiled ball together with an unoiled dough ball, oiled side toward the center, and roll out to form a 6 inches (15cm) circle. Repeat the process with the remaining dough balls.
4 Fry the pancakes in a lightly oiled pan over low heat turn and lightly cook the other side. Both Sides should be only very lightly browned.
5 Peel the pancakes apart and keep hot until ready to serve.

HOISIN SAUCE Hoisin sauce is a sweet yet spicy red-brown sauce that is essential in Chinese cooking. It was developed in China to add sweetness and bite to poultry dishes, and It is now an indispensable part of the Peking Duck banquet, along with the pancakes and scallions. Made from soy beans, garlic and spices, it is also used for marinating meat, in stir-fries and braised dishes, and as a dipping sauce. Hoisin sauce is sold in bottles and cans and will keep for up to six months in the refrigerator.

Wine Notes

Pinot Noir is an excellent match for this classic Chinese dish.

FRANCE : One can't go past Burgundy, the home of Pinot Noir. Try the always reasonably priced Bourgogne Rouge, or a top Volnay.

USA : Choose one of the very fine Pinots which are now coming from Oregon.

AUSTRALIA : Try the elegant, well-flavored Pinot Noir from the Yarra Valley in Victoria.

ITALY : Pinot Nero from the Alto-Adige would be one of the best choices, though good examples can be found throughout the north.

HAR GNEN DOUFU

Almost Junket with Lychees and Oranges

Fruit has been served at Chinese banquets throughout the centuries. Later junkets or jellies made with agar-agar as the setting agent became popular as an accompaniment to fruit. This classic south China dessert is made with regional fruits. Its delicious almond flavor used to be obtained by crushing whole almonds and soaking them in water, but it is easier for modern cooks to use almond extract.

SERVES 6

This is a delicious, light and refreshing dessert. It can be made up to several days in advance. Use canned lychees if fresh ones are not available. Try this recipe with other fruits-rambutan is often used. An equal quantity of gelatin may be substituted for the agar-agar.

Ingredient

1 tablespoon agar-agar
1 ¼ cups (10 fl oz / 310mL) milk
2 oranges, segmented
more or less to taste 3 tablespoons sugar
1 ¼ cups (10 fl oz / 310mL) water
1 ½ cups peeled lychees or rambutans
approximately 2 teaspoons almond extract (almond essence)

SYRUP
1 ¾ cups (14 fl oz / 430mL) water
½ cup (4oz / 125g) sugar

Method

1 Place half the water in a small bowl and sprinkle the agar-agar over it. Allow it to soften.
2 Place the softened agar-agar, remaining water, milk, almond extract and sugar in a medium-sized saucepan. Stir over moderate heat until the agar-agar and sugar have dissolved.
3 Pour into a 7 ½×12 inches (19×30cm) dish and chill for at least 4 hours, or until the junket has set. Alternatively, the mixture can be poured into individual decorative jelly molds. Chill until set, as above, then dip the molds in hot water for a few seconds before turning out to serve.
4 Cut the junket into small diamond shapes if not using jelly molds.
5 To make the syrup, combine the water and sugar in a saucepan and stir over high heat until the sugar has dissolved. Remove from heat and allow to cool. Refrigerate until cold.
6 Carefully place the junket diamonds in serving bowls and arrange the lychees and orange segments around them. Pour on the chilled syrup and serve garnished as desired.

Wine Notes

This sweet but delicate dish calls for a wine of similar qualities.

FRANCE : The attractive sweet wines of Monbazillac or Loupiac would be a good choice.

USA : Try a late-harvest (Johannisberg) Riesling from a coolish area such as Sonoma or Washington State.

AUSTRALIA : Choose from the botrytis-affected, late-picked Rhine Rieslings such as those from tollana or Henschke in the Eden Valley and from Hardy's or Andrew Garrett form Padthaway.

GERMANY : Try an Auslese or Spatlese from the Rheingau or the Mosel; Piesport and Bernkastel are names to look for.

PA SSI PING K'uo

Toffee Apple

This impressive Pekinese dish has achieved deserved popularity in the West. In some restaurants cooked pieces of apple are brought to the table already coated with the melted candied syrup, and in front of the diner the fruit is plunged quickly into iced water. Pieces of banana are also delicious cooked in this way. The contrast in texture between the crunchy coating and warm fruit inside is a delight.

SERVES 4

The iced water heats very quickly, so keep a few bowls of it within easy reach.

Ingredient

3 medium cooking apples, peeled and cored
1 egg, lightly beaten
2 cups (16 fl oz / 500mL) peanut oil
¼ cup (2 fl oz / 60mL) water
½ cup (20oz / 60g), all-purpose (plain) flour
1 teaspoon sesame oil
2 cups (1 lb / 500g) sugar
2 tablespoons black sesame seeds

Method

1 Cut the apple in quarters and then in half again. Mix together the flour, egg and sesame oil to create a smooth batter. Stir the apple pieces into the batter.
2 Heat the peanut oil in a wok or medium-sized saucepan. Carefully drop the coated apple pieces one by one into the oil to insure they don't stick. Cook the apple pieces in batches for about 3 minutes, or until golden brown. Drain on paper towels.
3 Place the sugar, water, sesame seeds and a tablespoon of the peanut oil used to cook the apple pieces in a wok. Heat the mixture until it boils, then boil steadily for 10 minutes, or until light golden-brown in color.
4 Stir a few of the apple pieces into the caramel, then remove one by one and dip into a bowl filled with cold water and a few ice cubes. Repeat this process until all the apple pieces are coated with caramel.
5 Sprinkle the sesame seeds over and serve at once on a lightly greased serving dish.

Wine Notes

A fully sweet, but not necessarily too complex dessert wine would be a good choice for this dish.

FRANCE : Try one of the sweet Muscats from the south, such as Muscat de Beaumes-de-Venise.

USA : Choose a Californian Muscat or Frontignac dessert wine from Quady's or Sutter Home.

AUSTRALIA : Try a late-picked botrytis-aggected Semillon from the Griffith area.

GREECE : Look for the Muscat of Samos.

FRANCE

World Cuisine

FRANCE has long been renowned for its fine food—be it the rarefied artistry of haute cuisine or the more robust flavors of cuisine bourgeoise. So, while debate rages as to whether the French have lost their identity in a fast-changing Europe, when it comes to their food, the answer is still a resounding no. Even on a wet Tuesday in March, good restaurants in outlying provinces are well patronized at lunchtime by a true cross-section of customers: everyone from a quartet of old ladies out for a midweek treat to local businessmen. Diners are still expected to order three courses in the proper fashion and it causes a stir if you ask the waiter for one dish only.

Starting with La Varenne in the seventeenth century, each generation of French chefs has produced outstanding figures who have left behind definitive cookbooks of their era and intense training techniques that only need to be fine-tuned as tastes change. The great turning point for French cuisine came with the Revolution. The lack of aristocratic employers prompted many great chefs to take their skills to other countries, spreading French ways and tastes to a wider market. Many others started up new eating establishments of their own, open to the public, that rapidly gained fame under the name "restaurant."

Even in modem France where hyper-markets—vast supermarkets—crowd the edges of any town of middling size, the French stick slavishly to their decades-old directive of "Suivez les marchés"—follow the markets. France remains a wonderfully seasonal country in spite of high tech refrigeration, storage and transportation. If it is asparagus time, you can bet that the big white or thin green spears of this vegetable will grace the menus of any restaurant with pretentions. The farmers' markets that proliferate throughout France aren't just there to look picturesque—home cooks not only plan their menus from the goods on display, they expect to find only the best, piled high on stalls or specially equipped trailers.

Out on the edge of metropolitan Paris is Rungis—the most fabulous food market in all Europe. Huge hangars fill the site which is not open to the general public but is meant for the buyers and chefs of good shops, restaurants and department stores. But this is the place for an overview of the way the French still eat today. Trucks rev up constantly and the noise levels reach a crescendo but spread before you are the freshest lobsters from Brittany, Belon oysters' corn-fed chickens from Bresse, geese from Alsace, a fair representation of the 365 or so cheeses of france. Only the fruits and vegetables of France. Only the fruits and vegetables are constantly kept under wraps. But the most wonderful feeling of all is that the dealers accord as much respect to small restaurateurs from the barely fashionable arrondissements as they barely fashionable arrondissements as they do to the foodhall buyers from the big department stores like Le Printemps and Galeries Lafayette.

But for the visitor who doesn't want to brave the din or the 5 am start, the next best pilgrimage is to the Fauchon and Hediard food shops on the Place de la Madeleine in Paris. The windows contain unbelievable platters of delicate vegetable mousse, foie gras pâtés, terrines, filled vol-au-vents, highly glazed ducks and tiny quail. Inside, the air is filled with the competing smells of import pineapples and guavas, fresh, salsify, okra and mignonette lettuces, imported teas and the distinctive odors of different cheeses—Reblochon, Munster and Pyrenèes.

Provincialism, in the best meaning of the word, is one of the great delights of traveling in France, Frequent visitors know the exact spot where cooking with better gives way to oil on the journey south to Provence, and where the finest garlic, the pink ail Lautrec of the south, remains as glorious it ever was.

Brittany, home of the crepe, still boasts as many creperies as it does bars, even if the waitress is wearing a UCLA sweatshirt. Touraine, Anjou and Maine feel almost like an extended fruit and vegetable garden, bursting with the garlic, strawberries, Golden Delicious and Reinette apples that feature strongly in the markets and hometown restaurants.

Normandy is one of the acclaimed food areas of France, a fact made all the more attractive by the knowledge that most of the farming is still done on a small, more personal scale. Cepes and morels crowd the vegetable stores and stalls during their brief spring season. The Vallée d'Auge yields up exceptional Calvados (the apple brandy of Normandy), Camembert and Pont-L'Eveque cheeses and cream—a happenstance best characterized by the area's most singular dish. Poulet Vallee d' Auge, is a palate-provoking blend of chicken, Calvados and cream (and frequently apples) that features in every tiny inn and hotel in Normandy.

When it comes to food, Burgundy is the true darling of an already heavily blessed country. The big fat Charolais cattle provide the best beef in France, the Morvan produces the best ham, Dijon is a synonym for mustard. Huge snails roam the many vineyards, in wait it seems for butter, garlic and parsley. But the reputation of Burgundy does not depend solely on ingredients. With amazing regularity, the province breeds the finest chefs. Burgundy has more Michelin-starred restaurants than any other French province. Coq au vin and boeuf bourguignon may have become the most over-cooked of dishes but on their home turf they are still two of the finest dishes ever to combine poultry or meat with wine.

Even those who have never been to Provence share a nostalgia for its lavender fields, orange groves. poplars and freeze-frame artists' canvases. Provençal markets are the envy of anyone who lives north of the Rhone river-long strings of garlic, big juicy olives, spiky scorpion fish, huge sardines and the large, oblong-grained rice of the Camargue. In Paris, everyone anticipates the arrival of the peaches and Cavaillon cantaloupe melons of Provence, sure indicators of high summer.

To the Romans. Provence was "the Province" and an Italian influence still prevails in definitive dishes like soupe au pistou with its profuse use of basil, and bouillabaisse, the fish stew directly related to the burrida and ciuppin of northern Italy. Orange flower water adds a musky je ne sais quoi to many Provençal desserts. Highly seasoned fish pastes are used to add zest to bland haricot and chickpea salads. But to truly believe oneself to be Provençal for even a moment is to sit in the main square of Aries, sipping the anise-flavored aperitif of southern France—pastis.

The modern boundaries of France were not set until the end of the nineteenth century and within these borders you have an almost overwhelming richness of folklore and culinary traditions that are being venerated in a rapidly homogenizing Europe. Even when the information super-high-ways make us as familiar with the rest of the human race as we are with ourselves, the French will still be showcasing poached fillets of sole in champagne, tarte tatin (that incomparable upside-down apple tart) and the splendid choucroute garni, the fresh or pickled cabbage and sausage extravaganza of Alsace.

SOUPE AU PISTOU

Soup with Pesto

This soup from the south of France captures all the flavors of summer in a generous bowl. The ingredients are all common to the region and are enhanced by the addition of the fragrant and flavorsome pistou. This is similar to the delicious pesta of Italy. Pistou is an excellent way of using the last of the season's basil and it may be stored throughout winter to add interest to cold-weather dishes.

SERVES 6

One of the very good commercially prepared pestos may be used for convenience. To prevent it drying out during storage, pour a little olive oil onto the surface of the pesto and store it in the refrigerator.

Ingredient

- 1 cup (6oz / 185g) mixed dried haricot and red kidney beans
- 2 large tomatoes, peeled and chopped
- salt and pepper, to taste
- 1 leek, sliced
- 1 cup (8oz / 250g) green beans, cut into 1 inch (2.5cm) lengths
- 2 tablespoons virgin olive oil
- 2 onions, chopped
- 5 cups (40 fl oz / 1.25L) water
- 2 potatoes, peeled and diced
- 2oz (60g) vermicelli, broken into small lengths
- 1 zucchini (courgette), sliced or coarsely diced
- ½ cup (2oz / 60g) freshly grated Parmesan cheese

PISTOU

- 3 garlic cloves, chopped
- 2~3 tablespoons extra-virgin olive oil
- ½ cup basil leaves
- 1~2 tablespoons freshly grated Parmesan cheese

Method

1 Soak the beans overnight in cold water. Drain the next day, rinse and drain again.

2 Heat the oil in a large saucepan, add the onions and saute until softened. Add the tomatoes and cook for a few minutes. Add the water and season with salt and pepper. When the water boils, add the drained beans, potatoes and leek. Simmer for about 20 minutes, then add the pasta, green beans and zucchini and cook until the pasta is tender.

3 While the soup cooks, combine the garlic and basil leaves in a mortar and grind together. Add the olive oil a drop at a time, rather like when making mayonnaise. Stir in the 1~2 tablespoons of Parmesan cheese.

4 Stir the Pistou into the hot soup, ladle into heated bowls at once, or spoon into a warmed tureen.

5 Pass around the extra Parmesan cheese separately.

DRIED RED KIDNEY BEANS The red kidney bean is the mature seed of Phaseolus vulgaris, shaped and colored as its name suggests. It is allowed to develop on the plant and then harvested. The bean's high nutritional value lies in its protein content and its good balance of amino acids. It is also an excellent source of minerals and vitamins. The kidney bean is second in importance in the bean industry to the soy bean. It originated in America, where it was grown by the Aztec Indians, and was brought to Europe in the sixteenth century. Today it is used extensively in Mexican cuisine and in the American southwest. In France the kidney bean features in soups and in stews with red wine and bacon. Two smaller varieties of these beans are pinto beans, which are pink with beige spots, and red beans (sometimes called chili beans), which are famous as an ingredient of chili can carne. All the varieties can be used Interchangeably. They are suitable for soups and stews, and are delicious in salads. They must be soaked before cooking, preferably overnight. To benefit from their high mineral content, particularly iron, cook the beans in the water in which they were soaked. The beans need to be soaked in a lot of water because the dried beans will absorb twice their weight in liquid. The beans must be fully cooked to get rid of a natural toxin. Dried or canned kidney beans are readily available. Dried beans will keep in an airlight container for up to a year.

Wine Notes

A "racy" variety such as Semillon or Sauvignon Blanc would form a good combination with this dish.

FRANCE : A Languedoc Sauvignon Blanc would be an interesting choice. Cassis (not the liqueur) is the best, liveliest Provençal white, but not widely seen.

USA : Choose any oj the Californian Sauvignon Blancs, these days often made with a proportion of Semillon. Avoid a heavy fume style.

AUSTRALIA : Try a Sauvignon Blanc, Semillon, or blend of the two, from Margaret River in Western Australia where these varieties have a wonderfully zippy character.

NEW ZEALAND : Select a Marlborough Sauvignon Blanc, lively and pungent, from the South Island.

OEUFS A LA TAPENADE

Eggs with Tapenade

A puree originating in Provence, tapenade is made from capers, olives and anchovies, and in many cases tuna fish. These flavours are brought out by incorporating olive oil and cognac (or brandy). It is served with raw vegetables as an hors d'oeuvre, or as a condiment to accompany meat and fish. The word tapenade is derived from tapeno, which is the local Provençal dialect for caper, an essential ingredient in the mixture.

SERVES 6

Serve as a light first course or as part of an hors d' oeuvre selection. The filling is delicious spread on thin toast triangles.

Ingredient

6 hard-cooked (hard-boiled) eggs, shelled
6 anchovy fillets, soaked in a little milk
1 tablespoon capers, rinsed and dried approximately $\frac{1}{3}$ cup (3 fl oz / 90mL) olive oil
2 teaspoons brandy, optional freshly ground black pepper, to taste lettuce leaves thyme sprigs, for garnish
10 black olives, pitted
2 tablespoons canned tuna, well drained
1~2 teaspoons lemon juice
sliced black olives, for garnish

Method

1 Cut the eggs in half lengthwise. Carefully remove the yolks and set aside.
2 Using a food processor or mortar and pestle, blend the olives, anchovies, tuna and capers to a coarse paste. Beat in the oil, a little at a time, until the mixture is thick and creamy. Mash the egg yolks and blend in. Add lemon juice to taste, brandy, if using, and pepper.
3 Spoon the mixture into the hollows of the egg whites. Arrange on a platter lined with the lettuce leaves. Garnish with the thyme and the black olives.

Wine Notes

In Provence, appetizers are usually accompanied by Pastis, the strong aperitif liqueur, but a sparkling wine would be an appropriate alternative.

FRANCE : Try a slightly pungent vin mousseux from alsace or the Loire Valley.

USA : Choose a Californian sparkling wine from a producer such as Maison Deutz, Iron Horse or Schramsberg.

AUSTRALIA : Try one of the crisp, cool climate méthode champenoise wines from southern Victoria or Tasmania.

ITALY : Select one of the numerous excellent brut style of sparkling wines from Piedmont. A good example is Fontanafredda Contessa Rosa.

QUICHE LORRAINE

This most famous quiche of all is now a classic dish. The recipe comes from Lorraine, the region in northeastern France where pastry cooks have long been noted for their style and inventiveness. There is much controversy regarding the "correct" traditional filling. Originally cheese was not an ingredient. Today Gruyère, or a similar cheese, is often included. In other areas of France, vegetables, seafood or ham, together with cheese, may be added to the basic mix of eggs and cream.

SERVES 4

To ensure that the base of the pastry cooks through, "blind bake" it first. Prick the pastry base well with a fork. Line with wax(greaseproof) paper and fill with dried beans. Bake until the crust is lightly colored and the base is partly cooked, about 10 minutes. Remove the lining and beans and set the crust aside to cool before filling.

Ingredient

SHORTCRUST PASTRY

2 cups (8oz / 250g) all-purpose (plain) flour

½ cup (4oz / 125g) butter chilled water

FILLING

4oz (125g) bacon, diced

3 eggs

1 ¼ cups (10 fl oz / 310mL) light (pouring) cream

⅓ teaspoon salt

¼ teaspoon ground nutmeg

4oz (125g) ham, diced

1 egg yolk

⅔ cup (5 fl oz / 160mL) milk

⅓ teaspoon freshly ground black pepper

Method

1 Rub the butter into the flour with your fingertips and add sufficient chilled water to bind.
2 Roll out the pastry thinly and transfer to a 9 inches (23cm) pie plate or flan pan.
3 Preheat the oven to 350°F (180℃).
4 Fry the bacon lightly for about 5 minutes. Cool for 5 minutes, then spread over the pastry. Add the chopped ham.
5 In a bowl, beat together the eggs, extra egg yolk, cream and milk, then add the salt, pepper and nutmeg.
6 Pour the egg and cream mixture over the bacon and ham.
7 Bake the quiche on a low shelf in the oven for about 45 minutes, or until puffed and golden brown.
8 Serve warm or cold.

Wine Notes

A dry white with the emphasis on fruit rather than oak would best suit this dish.

FRANCE : Select an Alsatian Riesling from Lorraine.

USA : Choose a Johannisberg Riesling from the Pacific Northwest or California—a more unusual variety like Viognier from California would also be interesting.

AUSTRALIA : Try a marsanne. Chateau Tahbilk, Mitchelton and Yeringberg, all in Victoria, are the leading producers.

GERMANY : Choose a Spatlese Riesling in the trocken style from the Middle Mosel or Rheingau.

COQUILLES SAINT-JACQUES AU SUD

Scallops with Garlic Butter

Saint Jacques is the patron saint of shellfishermen, hence the French name for scallop: coquille Saint-Jacques. Since medieval times the scallop has enjoyed a deserved reputation for firm flesh with a rich sea flavor. Raw scallops can be marinated and served in a salad, but scallops are more often cooked and are sometimes presented with a sauce. This treatment of scallops with garlic butter comes originally from the south or France.

SERVES 4

Coquilles Saint-Jacques are often served in their shells. Warm the shells in the oven if you wish to serve them this way. It is a good idea to fasten the shells to the serving plate with a good dab of mashed potato—it makes it much easier for the diner!

Ingredient

24 scallops with coral attached
⅓ teaspoon freshly ground black pepper
2 tablespoons (1oz / 30g)
4 lemon wedges
⅓ teaspoon salt
2~3 tablespoons all-purpose (plain) flour
3 tablespoons light olive oil
2 tablespoons finely chopped parsley

GARLIC BUTTER
½ cup (4oz / 125g) butter
1 garlic clove, finely chopped

Method

1 Rinse the scallops, then pat dry with paper towels. Season lightly with the salt and pepper. Toss the scallops in the flour-they only need a very light coating.
2 Melt the butter with the oil in a medium pan over moderate heat. Sauté the scallops in two batches, shaking the pan and stirring the scallops until they are golden. Remove with a slotted spoon and keep warm on a lightly heated dish.
3 To make the garlic butter, heat the butter in a small saucepan, pour off the clear "oil" and discard the residue left behind.
4 Heat the clarified butter in a small pan until it sizzles but does not brown. Add the garlic and cook over moderate heat for one minute, stirring constantly. Pour over the scallops, sprinkle over the chopped parsley and serve with the lemon wedges.

SCALLOPS The scallop is a bivalve mollusk. When buying scallops in the shell, tap the shell; it should then close. If it does not, discard the scallop. They may also be bought shucked and cleaned. Frozen, canned or vacuum-packed scallops are also available but fresh are to be preferred. The fresh shelled meat will keep for up to three days in a refrigerator, but live scallops should be cooked the day they are purchased. Broil (grill) or sautè scallops for a few minutes only, as the flesh toughens easily.

Wine Notes

A crisp, flinty dry white is the perfect accompaniment for this dish.

FRANCE : A Chablis of good quality would be delicious and Muscadet-sut-lie is another delightful shellfish wine.

USA: Select a Saubignon Blanc-Semillon blend from one of California's sooler areas.

AUSTRALIA : Choose a steely, slightly acid Rhine Riesling from Eden Valley.

NEW ZEALAND : Try a Marlborough Sauvignon Blanc—the crisp, herbaceous flavor will work well with this dish.

BOUILLABAISSE

Arguments rage as to whether a true bouillabaisse can be made anywhere outside the Mediterranean region, as two of the traditional fish, red gurnard and scorpion fish, are hard to come by beyond Mediterranean waters. Even in Marseilles, where this hearty soup originated as a way to use up fish that were too small or bony to sell at the market, there is disagreement. So if you have a French guest, make this dish as authentically as possible, then, as a precaution, call it "Fishermen's soup" instead of Bouillabaisse.

SERVES 8

The fish can be strained from the soup and served separately, accompanied by the soup in a tureen. The rouille (garlic spread) presented here is made using an abbreviated method, but it is still tasty.

Ingredient

4 lb (2kg) fresh fish, such as red snapper, sea perch, halibut, whiting, John Dory, stargazer (or red guruard and scorpion fish, if available)
1 strip orange peel
4 tablespoons chopped parsley
½ teaspoon freshly ground black pepper
1 baguette (French bread stick)
⅓ cup (3 fl oz / 90mL) virgin olive oil
3 young leeks, white part only, cut into julienne strips
1 lobster or crayfish, cut into pieces
5 cups (40 fl oz / 1.25L) hot fish stock
4 garlic cloves, finely chopped
1 tablespoon finely chopped fresh fennel
2 crumbled bay leaves
2 tablespoons tomato paste
1 tablespoon salt
½ teaspoon saffron threads, soaked in 3 tablespoons water
1 large white onion, finely chopped
4 ripe tomatoes, seeded and chopped
12oz (375g) mussels or clams, in shell
1 crab, cut into pieces

ROUILLE
3 garlic cloves, finely chopped or crushed
1 cup (8 fl oz / 250mL) mayonnaise
freshly ground black pepper, to taste
⅓ teaspoon finely chopped fresh red chill or ⅓ teaspoon chili powder
⅓ teaspoon saffron threads, soaked in 1 tablespoon water, optional

Method

1 Preheat the oven to 300°F (150℃).
2 Clean and scale the fish and trim off the fins. Cut into 1 inch (2.5cm) pieces.
3 Mix together the garlic, fennel, bay leaves, orange peel, tomato paste, parsley, salt, pepper and strained liquid from the saffron. Set aside this seasoning mixture.
4 Cut the bread stick into slices and bake for 30 minutes, or until crisp.
5 While the bread is drying in the oven, heat the oil in a large saucepan, add the seasoning mixture and the onion, leeks and tomatoes. Cook until the vegetables become soft.

6 Add the prepared seafood. Pour in the hot fish stock and cook over high heat for 15 to 20 minutes. Adjust seasoning.

7 To make the rouille, crush the garlic in a bowl or mortar, work in the chili or chili powder, then gradually stir in the mayonnaise and pepper and the saffron liquid, if desired.

8 Pour the soup into a warmed tureen.

9 Spread the rouille on the warm bread slices and serve with the soup.

LEEKS A member of the onion family, the leek (Allium porrum) originated in the eastern Mediterranean more than 3000 years ago. It was taken to Britain by the Ancient Romans. It later became the national emblem of Wales, following a victory by King Cadwallader against the Saxons (his troops each wore a leek in battle as a way of identifying each other). Widely used in both French and British cookery, leeks are cultivated for their pale, bulbous stalks. They are prepared and served in much the same way as asparagus: the base and leaves are trimmed, then the leeks are boiled, steamed, braised or microwaved; they may then be served in a cream or hollandaise sauce. Leeks offer a tangy flavor and thickening texture to savory pies, casseroles and soups, particularly when they are teamed with potatoes. Rich in vitamin C and dietary fiber, leeks should only be bought when they are firm and fresh. Because of the way leeks are grown—in trenches with earth covering their stem to foster their white color—dirt gets in between the leaves, so the vegetable must be very throughly washed before use.

Wine Notes

A big, flavorsome dry white is most appropriate with this dish.

FRANCE : Choose a good white Burgundy. Meursault is a reliable appellation and is often good value.

USA : Try a Chardonnay from one of the Californian districts noted for richness of flavor, such as Alexander Valley or Edna Valley.

AUSTRALIA : Select an aged Hunter Semillon from Lindemans, Tyrells or Rothbury.

NEW ZEALAND : A full-bodied Chardonnay from Hawkes Bay would be a good choice. Cooper Creek Swamp Road and Delegats Proprieters Reserve are ideal styles.

COQ AU VIN

Chicken in Red Wine

Throughout France, you will find a version of this dish. It was originally devised to cook the farmyard cock that had outlived its usefulness. Being old and tough, the bird would have required marinating and slow braising. The gravy was originally thickened with the reserved blood of the chicken, giving a great richness and a depth of color. Flour, far more acceptable to modern cooks, is now used as the thickener, yet today' s version is still delicious.

SERVER 6

If preferred, you can sauté the mushrooms in a little butter, then add to the pot for only the last 5 minutes (instead of 10) of cooking.

Ingredient

1 roasting chicken, about 3 lb (1.5kg)
4oz (125g) bacon or speck, diced
12 small peeled French shallots or baby white onions
1 carrot, sliced
1 tablespoon brandy
½ teaspoon fresh thyme or ⅓ teaspoon dried thyme
1 bay leaf
¼ teaspoon freshly ground black pepper
8oz (250g) button mushrooms
3 tablespoons olive oil, or equal quantities of mixed butter and oil
1 large onion, peeled and chopped
1 garlic clove, finely chopped
3 teaspoons chopped fresh marjoram or ⅓ teaspoon dried marjoram
1 teaspoon salt
2 cups (16 fl oz / 500mL) dry red wine
thyme sprigs, for garnish

Method

1. Cut the chicken into serving portions, removing any excess fat.
2. Heat the oil or combined oil and butter in a heavy saucepan, add the bacon and fry for about 3 minutes. Push to one side of the pan, add the French shallots, onion, carrot and garlic and sauté for 3 to 5 minutes.
3. Remove the vegetables from the pan with a slotted spoon and set aside.
4. Add the chicken pieces to the pan and brown well. Heat the brandy gently in a small pan, ignite with a match and pour over the chicken pieces while still alight.
5. Add the flour, marjoram, thyme, bay leaf, salt and pepper to the pan and mix in well. Gradually add the red wine, stirring constantly. Return the vegetables to the pan.
6. Cover the saucepan and simmer over low heat for about 1 hour, or until the chicken is tender. Add the mushrooms during the last 10 minutes of cooking.
7. Skim off any excess fat, remove the bay leaf and adjust seasoning.
8. Arrange the chicken pieces on a serving plate, spoon over the sauce and garnish with the thyme.

SHALLOTS A close relative of the onion, the shallot has a flavor somewhere between onion and garlic. The botanical name, Allium ascalonium, is derived from the name of the ancient port of Ascalon (Ashqelon in the modern State of Israel). Some sources credit the Crusaders with having brought the shallot to Europe after vanquishing Saladin at the battle of Ascalon in 1192; however, according to other sources, shallots are thought to have formed part of the herb garden of St Gall in Switzerland in the ninth century, and Charlemagne is supposed to have had shallots planted in his gardens in the eighth century. Small and brown with a tough skin, shallots grow in a bulb cluster similar to garlic. Shallots are a traditional ingredient in French cuisine, particularly in Bordeaux, but they are also widely used in Chinese, Vietnamese and Indian cooking. Excellent in salads and fish, chicken or lamb dishes, shallots are also widely used to flavor sauces such as béarnaise, red wine sauces and white sauces. They are particularly good for these as they emulsify more easily than onions. Shallots should be stored and prepared in the same way onions are. When buying shallots, make sure they are firm to touch. Once they have been cut, use them quickly. Do not store them in the refrigerator as the taste will be transferred to other foodstuffs. Keep them in a well-ventilated area.

Wine Notes

Break the old "white wme with white meat" maxim and serve Pinot Noir with this dish.

FRANCE : Choose a lighter style of red Burgundy from the Cote-de-Beaune, try a Savigny-les-Beaune or Pernand-Vergelesse.

USA : Select a Pinot Noir from one of the cooler areas, such as Oregon or the southern reaches of the Russian River.

AUSTRALIA : Choose an elegant Pinot Noir from the Yarra Valley or the Marnington Peninsula.

SOUTH AFRICA : Trv a Pinot Noir from Hamilton-Russell, Meerlust or Rustenberg.

CASSOULET

Dried Bean Casserole

Goose confit, a very rich preserve of goose that is cooked and stored in goose fat, has long played a role in the households of the Languedoc region of France. Before refrigeration, it could be kept in a cool larder for up to a year. Both the meat and fat were used to add richness and flavor to many winter dishes. The name of this recipe comes from "cassole," the glazed earthenware pot in which the dish is traditionally cooked.

SERVES 6

If It is not possible to obtain duck or goose confit, substitute a roast duck leg and wing and 4~5 tablespoons of goose fat. The flavor will not be quite the same, but the cassoulet will still be excellent. Goose fat is available in cans from specialty delicatessens.

Ingredient

3 ¾ cups (1 ½ lb / 750g) dried haricot beans
3 onions, sliced
4 garlic cloves, chopped
salt and pepper, to taste
1 leg and 1 wing of goose or duck confit
3~4 tablespoons goose fat or olive oil
8oz (250g) bacon, cut into cubes
2 large tomatoes, peeled and sliced
bouquet garni
5 cups (40 fl oz / l.25L) veal or chicken stock
1 lb (500g) garlic sausage, thickly sliced
4 tablespoons white bread crumbs

Method

1 Soak the beans overnight. The next day drain and rinse and cover with cold water. Simmer for 2 ½ hours, adding additional hot water as necessary.
2 Cook the bacon in a heavy pot until the fat runs, then add the onions, tomatoes, garlic, bouquet garni and salt and pepper.
3 Pour the stock into the pot and simmer for 30 minutes. Strain the stock.
4 Preheat the oven to 300°F (150℃).
5 Rub the base of a heavy casserole with a cut piece of garlic. Place the goose confit and the sausage in the dish with the goose fat. Pile the drained beans on top and pour in the stock. Heat slowly to boiling, lower heat and spread the bread crumbs evenly on the surface. Bake for 1 hour.
6 Serve at the table directly from the casserole. Cassoulet needs only a salad and red wine as accompaniments.

BACON In the United States the term "bacon" is used for the side of a pig after the spare ribs have been removed, and the meat has been cured with salt, and then smoked. However, different countries have varying ways of treating bacon and different cuts are available. Bacon is readily available fresh from supermarkets and butcher. It can also be purchased vacuum-packed, or frozen, but these forms can be less tasty.

Wine Notes

Red wine is the prescribed accompaniment but avoid heavy or tannic styles.

FRANCE : Try a wine from the Midi: Fitou, made from Grenache and Carignan, is very good, as are some of the Cotes-du-Roussillon Rouge.

USA : Choose a Rhone varietal Californian re featuring Syrah and/or Grenache and/or Mourvedre from Mendocino or the Monterey district.

AUSTRALIA : Try a blend of Shiraz and Grenache from the Barossa Valley.

SPAIN : Try a red from Catalonia, such as the Torres Coronas.

POULET VALLEE D'AUGE

Chicken from the Auge Valley

This classic from the Auge Valley in the heart of Normandy appears in cookbooks with many variations. Several versions include apples, though, interestingly, this chicken dish was originally made without them. Mushrooms also are an ingredient that is not always used. The region of Normandy is famous for its rich dairy products, its bountiful apple harvest and, of course, its famous apple brandy called Calvados.

SERVES 6

For variation, sauté 1 peeled and sliced cooking apple in butter until tender, then add the slices to the pan with the cream sauce and heat through

Ingredient

6~8 chicken pieces
¼ cup (2oz / 60g) butter
1 onion, chopped
1 sprig thyme
4 tablespoons heavy thick cream
salt and pepper, to taste
6oz (185g) small mushrooms, finely sliced
1 small bay leaf
3 tablespoons Calvados
fresh herbs, for garnish

Method

1. Season the chicken with salt and plenty of pepper. Melt the butter in a large pan over moderate heat and when hot, add the chicken and brown on all sides.
2. Add the mushrooms, onion, bay leaf and thyme.
3. Cover the pan and cook for 25 to 30 minutes or until the chicken is cooked through. Some cooks prefer to use chicken fillets—cook these for 15 minutes only.
4. Heat the Calvados in a spirit warmer or small saucepan, set it afire and pour over the chicken. Baste the chicken with the juices in the pan.
5. Remove the chicken pieces from the pan and place in a prewarmed serving dish. Keep warm without letting it overcook.
6. Remove the bay leaf and thyme, add the cream to the pan and simmer for 2 to 3 minutes. Adjust seasoning if necessary.
7. Pour the creamy sauce over the chicken pieces, garnish with your choice of fresh herbs and serve at once.

Wine Notes

A Riesling will best complement this chicken dish.

FRANCE : Alsace is the great Riesling district of France, with its dry, subtle but powerful style.

USA : This variety is known as Johannisberg Riesling in the USA. Try one from Washington State or the Monterey-Santa Barbara area.

AUSTRALIA : Choose a Riesling form Clare-Watervale, Eden Valley (both in South Australia) or Mt Barker (Western Australia).

GERMANY : Look for a Kabinett or Spätlese Trocken from the Rheingau.

CHOUCROUTE GARNIE

White Cabbage with Wine

This robust dish, a combination of cabbage (either fresh or pickled) and smoked meats and sausages, is a prime example of the German influence on the cooking of Its neighbor, the French region of Alsace. A peasant-style dish with no single recipe, choucroute Garnie ál'Alsacienne, to give it its full title, ushers in the winter, with many towns in Alsace holding choueroute festivals in September and October.

SERVES 8

Precede of follow this dish with the lightest of courses as it is rather heavy. Although the duck legs are not essential, they add flavor to the dish; smoked chicken legs and breast may be used if desired. Many versions of this recipe substitute sauerkraut for the fresh cabbage; fresh cabbage is used in one of Escoffier's famous recipes.

Ingredient

- 1 whole white (green) cabbage
- ⅓ teaspoon freshly ground black pepper
- 1 small ham hock, about 1 lb (500g)
- 2 onions, each studded with 2 cloves
- 1 tablespoon juniper berries (tied in muslin)
- ½ teaspoon salt
- 1 lb (500g) pork belly
- 2 legs smoked duck, if available
- bouquet garni
- chicken or veal stock
- 1 strasbourg sausage or smoked pork or smoked pork and beef sausage

Method

1. Discard the coarse outer leaves and stalk from the cabbage. Place the cabbage in a large saucepan and add the salt and pepper.
2. Blanch the pork by cooking it in boiling water for 3 minutes. Drain well and add to the saucepan with the cabbage, ham hock, smoked duck, onions, bouquet garni and juniper berries.
3. Add the wine and sufficient stock to just cover the cabbage. Cover and simmer for 1 hour. Remove the pork and set aside. Continue to simmer for another 1 to 1 ½ hours, or until the cabbage is very tender. (Pierce with a satay stick to test.) Return the pork to the pan. Add the sausage and poach until cooked, about 10 minutes.
4. When me sausage is cooked, remove and discard the bouquet garni, onion and jumper berries. Remove the pork, ham hock, duck legs and sausage and slice thinly.
5. Drain the cabbage well, place on a serving plate and cut into wedges. Arrange the meat slices around the cabbage.

Wine Notes

An Alsace-style white is the perfect choice.

FRANCE : In Alsace a spicy Gewurztraminer would be served.

USA : Choose from The fine, bone dry examples of Californian Gewurztraminer from Firestone, Navarro or Lazy Creek Vineyards.

AUSTRALIA : Choose a Riesling form central or western Victoria; from Bests or mt Langi Ghiran.

GERMANY : Choose a Riesling from around Nierstein.

GIGOT ROTI A LA BRETONNE

Leg of Lamb with White Haricot Beans

In France the roast leg is the family meal traditionally used for celebrations, and every region has its own version. This recipe comes from Brittany (haricot beans are a characteristic ingredient of this area). Originally mutton was used instead of lamb-in fact, mutton was highly valued in ancient times, but its place was taken by pork and then by poultry in the Middle Ages. It became popular again about the time of Louis XIV.

SERVES 6

Allow 25 minutes per pound for well-done meat and 15 minutes per pound for rare meat The lamb, cooked for the time suggested in this recipe, will be slightly pink at the bone. Calvados, the apple brandy which is made in Brittany as well as in Normandy, can be added just before serving.

Ingredient

1 leg of lamb, about 5 lb (2.5kg)
spring of thyme
4 bay leaves
4 cloves
1 onion
salt and pepper, to taste
6 small onions, sliced
1 teaspoon sugar
2 tablespoon Calvados, optional
2 garlic cloves, slivered
spring of marjoram
2 ½ cups (1 lb / 500g) dried white haricot beans, soaked in cold water overnight
bouquet garni
2 tablespoon (1oz / 30g) butter
2 tablespoons rich veal, lamb or chicken stock
2 tablespoons light (pouring) cream, optional

Method

1 Preheat the oven to 400°F (200℃).
2 Trim the lamb of any excess fat. Make a few slits in the meat and insert the garlic slivers. Place the lamb in a heavy baking dish and arrange the herb sprigs and bay leaves on top. Bake in the oven, allowing 20 minutes per pound. Baste occasionally.
3 While the meat is cooking, place the drained and rinsed beans in a large saucepan with the bouquet garni. Press the cloves into the onion and add the onion to the saucepan. Then add the salt and pepper, and enough water to cover the beans.
4 Heat to boiling, then reduce heat and cover. Simmer gently for about 1 ¼ hours, or until the beans are tender.
5 Melt the butter in a heavy pan and gently fry the sliced onions until soft, but not brown. Add the stock, heat to boiling, then simmer for 5 minutes. Remove from heat and add the sugar and the cream, if using.

6 Drain the beans and place on a serving platter, then pur the onion sauce over them. Remove the meat from the oven and add to the platter.

7 To serve the lamb, slice thickly and, if desired, pour the Calvados over the slices.

HARICOT BEANS Haricot beans (Phaseolus bulgaris) include a number of types, but the small white flageolet bean is the one most people associate with the name. Haricot beans are native to Central and South America and were known to the Aztecs (the name comes from the Aztec word ayacotl). From there they were introduced to Europe about 500 years ago, and other varieties were produced, with flageolets first grown in 1872 Another popular hancot is the red kidney bean, which is used extensively in American and Mexican cookery. Haricot beans are prized for their nutritional value, and their fairly bland flavor makes them a good partner for other tastier ingredients. They are used In soups, salads, stews and casseroles Available in cans or dried, the dried beans need lengthy soaking to soften them before cooking. The soaking water should be discarded. If there is no time to soak the beans, a quicker technique is to cover them with cold water, heat to boiling and simmer for 2 to 3 minutes and then stand for 1 hour, tightly covered.

Wine Notes

A Cabernet Sauvignon or Cabernet-Merlot blend would be an excellent partner for this dish.

FRANCE : Select a red from Bordeaux: a classed growth or a good cru bourgeois—the St Estéphe commune has many good examples of the latter.

USA : Try a Napa valley or Sonoma Cabernet, particularly one with some bottle age.

AUSTRALIA : Choose a Coonawarra Cabernet Sauvignon or Cabernet Merlot.

ITALY : Tuscany and Umbria produce outstanding Cabernet-style wines, ofter classified as vino da tavola—try the Lungarotti and Antinori labels.

NAVARIN PRINTANIER

Lamb Stew

A navarin is a stew in which mutton (nowadays lamb), potatoes and turnip are the principal ingredients. The origin of the name is not certain; perhaps navarin comes from the French for turnip: navet. This recipe also includes the young vegetables of spring; this is also reflected in its name. Breast or shoulder of lamb or mutton was used in the original dish, but modern cooks prefer to use a well-trimmed leg of lamb.

SERVES 8

Traditionally the vegetables are turned into the oval shape we see in the classic French dishes, but these days the demands of time and convenience dictate that it is more practical to dice the vegetables or to cut them into thick matchsticks.

Ingredient

2 tablespoons oil
2 cups (16 fl oz / 500mL) light lamb, veal or chicken stock
6 small new potatoes, peeled and turned, cut info thick matchsticks or diced, cut into thick matc-hsticks or diced
½ teaspoon salt
1 cup (8oz / 250g) green beans, cut into 1 inch (2.5cm) pieces
2 lb (1kg) leg of lamb, trimmed of fat and cut into large cubes
2 tablespoons tomato paste
6 small carrots, prepared as above
16 small pickling onions
3 small white turnips, prepared as above
⅓ teaspoon freshly ground black pepper
1 cup (4oz / 125g) green peas
½ cup finely chopped parsley

Method

1 Heat the oil in a heavy pan, then brown the meat on all sides. Transfer it to a large heavy-based saucepan. Pour off the fat in the pan and discard, then add the stock, stirring in the tomato paste. Heat to boiling, then add to the saucepan with the meat. Cover and Simmer gently at constant heat for about 1 hour.
2 Add the potatoes, carrots, onions, turnips and salt and pepper, cover the pot and simmer for an additional hour.
3 Prepare a saucepan of boiling water, add the beans and peas and remove after 1 minute, then refresh in cold water. Drain and set aside.
4 When the lamb and root vegetables are cooked, skim off as much fat as possible and gently stir in the beans and peas.
5 Reheat gently until warmed through and serve at once, sprinkled with the finely chopped parsley.

TURNIPS Turnip (Brassica rapa) is a cool-season root vegetable. Turnips can be grated and eaten raw in salads, boiled, roasted, or added to soups and casseroles. They should be peeled just before cooking, otherwise they will discolor. The leaves (greens) can be used in salads, or cooked the same way spinach is cooked. The root will keep for some weeks, but the greens should be used within a couple of day.

Wine Notes

A flavorsome, soft red without too much tannin astringency would enhance this dish.

FRANCE : Try a Pomerol or Saint-Emillion. These are the softest, most supple styles of quality Bordeaux.

USA : Look for a Merlot from Sonoria County or Washington State.

AUSTRALIA : Choose a Cabernet-Merlot blend from the Yarra valley.

NEW ZEALAND : The Merlot grape does particularly well in New Zealand. Try a Cabernet -Merlot blend from the Te Mata Estate.

BOEUF EN DAUBE

Braised Beef

The recipe for this dish varies from region to region. In a popular version from the Pyrenees in southwest France, the meat is diced after being marinated, while in other parts, it is cooked in one piece until it is almost falling apart. Here the meat is cut into thick portions before cooking. In pat years, a daube was cooked in a daubiére that was buried in hot coals. The olives in the recipe that follows reveal its Provençal origins.

SERVES 8

The pig's feet (trotters) are optional, but they have a gelatinous quality that gives the sauce a beautiful texture.

Ingredient

3 lb (1.5kg) piece good-quality lean beef
2 onions, sliced
1 bouquet garni
½ cups (12 fl oz / 375mL) red wine
I tablespoon brandy
2 pig's feet (trotters), optional
16 black olives
2 carrots, sliced
2 tomatoes, peeled and chopped
2 garlic cloves
3 tablespoons olive oil
4 thick bacon slices (rashers). rind removed
beef stock, If required

Method

1 Cut any fat from the meat and trim into a neat shape. Combine the vegetables, bouquet garni, garlic. peppercorns. wine, oil and brandy in a large bowl then add the meat. Cover and marinate for at least 8 hours. turning the meat occasionally.
2 When ready, cut the meat into 2 or 3 thick slices. Place 2 of the bacon slices on the base of a lightly oiled heavy saucepan. Place the meat on top, arrange the vegetables around the sides, then pour on the liquid from the marinade.
3 Add the remaining 2 slices of bacon, cut into pieces, and add the pig's feet if using.
4 Cover the saucepan and cook over the lowest possible heat for at least 3 hours—the meat should be meltingly tender. Occasionally check to ensure the liquid is not evaporating. If it is. add a little hot beef stock. Remove the pig's feet and discard. Skim as much fat as possible from the surface of the liquid.
5 Remove the meat and vegetables and keep warm. Add the olives and reduce the liquid by about one-third over moderate heat. Cut the meat into serving portions and spoon over some of the sauce and a few olives. Serve with noodles and beans.

BOUQUET GARNI A bouquet garni is a small bundle of herbs and/or spices tied together with thread or wrapped in cheesecloth. Bouquet garni is used to provide flavor to slow-cooking dishes such as stews without the herbs dispersing throughout the liquid; it also eliminates chopping. Originating in France, the classic bouquet garni combination is parsley, bay leaves and thyme, but almost any herbs, spices or even vegetables can be used

Wine Notes

A strong, robust red seems obligatory here.

FRANCE : Choose Bandol, made from the Mourvédre grape and probably the best red of Provence. The more commonlv seen Côtes-du-Rhône is an alternative.

USA : One of the Californian wines featuring Syrah, Mourvédre and Grenache will provide the necessarv spiciness and body.

AUSTRALIA : Select a Shiraz from the Hunter Valley or McLaren Vale.

ITALY : Try Montepulclano d'Abruzzo, the rustic, comfortable red of southern Italy.

OEUFS A LA NEIGE

Snow Eggs

Créme anglaise. the base for the classic French dessert Oeufs á la Neige. has been used extensively in French dessert-making since the nineteenth century. Unlike the English custard which is made with whole egg and from which it originated. créme anglaise uses egg yolks. The egg whites left over from making the custard are used to make individual "egg"- sized portions of meringue to be served on the créme anglaise.

SERVES 6

If a vanilla pod is not available, add 1 teaspoon vanilla extract (vanilla essence) to the créme anglaise just before it is aerated.

Ingredient

MERINGUE

3 egg whites

¼ cup (2oz / 60g) sugar

CREME ANGLAISE

2 cups (16 fl oz / 50 mL) milk

4 egg yolks, lightly beaten

½ vanilla pod (vanilla bean)

¼ cup (2oz / 60g) suger

SPUN SUGAR

½ cup (4oz / 125g) sugar

1 tablespoon water

Method

1 To prepare the meringue, whip the egg whites stiffly, then gradually beat in th sugar.

2 Bring the milk to the boil in a heavy-based saucepan and reduce to a simmer. Drop tablespoonfuls of the meringue mixture into the simmering milk and poach gently for about 4 minutes, turning once to ensure the egg whites cook.

3 Lift out gently with a slotted spoon and set aside on a plate.

4 Retain the milk to make the créme anglaise.

5 To make the créme anglaise, scald the milk in the top of a double boiler. Add the vanilla pod. Beat the egg yolks and sugar. and gradually stir into the milk.

6 Over simmering water, stir constantly until the custard begins to thicken.

7 Remove from heat. and remove the vanilla pod. Cool slightly. Add the vanilla extract if using.

8 Beat vigorously for 1 minute to aerate the custard. Pour into a serving bowl and chill.

9 When the custard is cold, gently slip the meringues on top.

10 Just before serving, prepare the spun sugar. Combine the sugar and water in a small saucepan and bring to a simmer. Do not stir.

11 Remove from heat when the caramel is a light golden-brown color, after about 5 minutes.

12 Using two forks, lift a small quantity of the toffee from the pan. Pull 1 fork away from the other to from fine toffee threads, using a swirling movement of the hand to shape the threads.

13 Place the spun sugar over the top of the meringues and serve at once.

VANILLA Vanilla comes from the golden-flowered orchid plant (Vanilla planifolia), a perennial climber native to Mexico and central America. The flower only lasts for a day and in commercial production it has to be hand-pollinated for the pod to develop Its long seed pods are picked when immature, at this stage they are odorless. The distinctive aromatic flavor is produced by vanillin, a white crystalline coating that appears during the curing and drying process. For centuries by the Aztecs used vanilla to flavor xocoatl. the chocolate drink Today the main sources of vanilla are Mexico. Malagasy, the Comoros. Uganda and French Polynesia. Vanilla was brought to Europe from Mexico by Spanish explorers in the sixteenth century. It is still widely used today as a flavoring in cakes, pastries. desserts and beverages such as mulled wine and sangía. By far the most popular usage, however. is for enhancing the flavor of milk and milk dishes. including custards, Ice cream and cream. Most recipes call for vanilla in the from of extract or pods (beans). An artificial vanilla flavored liquid called vanillin is available, but discerning cooks consider it inferior to real vanilla extract and do not use it. Vanilla pods are expensive but can be rinsed and dried after cooking and reused. A pod placed in a jar of sugar imparts a beautiful fragrance.

Wine Notes

This is delicious with a French Sauternes or equivalent.

FRANCE : Try a Sauternes or Barsac. They are rich and sweet but not heavy. Coutet from Barsac is excellent, although almost any first or second growths from a good year would be perfect.

USA : Try a late-harvest Riesling or Semillon. A Santino Late Harvest Dry Berrv Rlesling from Sonoma County has a concentrated caramel flavor of its own.

AUSTRALIA : Select a botrytis-affected late-picked Semillon or Rhine Riesling. A Semillon from the Griffith area would be ideal.

GERAMANY : Choose a wine towards the very sweet end of the German Rieslings, such as an Auslese, or even a Beerenauslese, preferably from the Rheingau or Mosel.

TARTE TATIN

Upside Down Apple Tart

This recipe sometimes appears in French cookbooks as Tarte des Demoiselles Tatin. The recipe was developed by two sisters who ran the Tatin hotel in Lamotte-Beuvron in central France at the start of the century. The dessert was originally cooked in a covered pan over hot coals which caramelized the sugar and butter in the base and gave the apple slices a golden glow when the tart was turned over for serving.

SERVES 8

In Parisian Pâtisseries, the tarts are often very dark indeed, with blackened edges on the apple slices. If you prefer this darker caramel effect, place the finished tart under a hot broiler for a minute or two until the desired color is achieved, but watch carefully. Some cooks like to soften the apple slices in the melted butter before placing them in the base of the pie plate.

Ingredient

PASTRY

1 ¾ cups (8oz / 250g) all-purpose (plain) flour
⅔ cup (5oz / 155g) unsalted buffer, at room temperature
1 tablespoon superfine (caster) sugar
1 medium egg
1 tablespoon chilled water

FIllING

⅓ cup (3oz / 90g) butter
3 lb (1.5kg) Golden Delicious apples peeled, cored and sliced
⅓ cup (3oz / 90g) sugar

Method

1 To make the pastry, sift the flour onto a pastry board, make a well in the center and place the sugar, butter and egg in the well. Mix together to make a paste, gradually adding the flour from the edges and using only your fingertips to mix the dough. Only add the water if the dough is dry and stiff. Shape into a ball, wrap in plastic wrap and place in the refrigerator for about 1 hour, or until the pastry is firm.
2 Preheat the oven to 400°F (200℃).
3 Butter a 10 inches (25cm) tart pan with I tablespoon (½ oz / 15g) butter and sprinkle 1 tablespoon of the sugar over it.
4 Arrange a layer of apple slices in the base of the pan. Make a second layer on top, then add the remaining slices to fill any gaps.
5 Dot the remaining butter over the apples, then sprinkle on the rest of the sugar.

6 Roll the dough thinly and cut a circle to fit inside the tin. Prick gently with a fork and carefully lay it over the apples.
7 Bake for 30 minutes in the oven. Remove from the oven, place a serving plate over the top of the tart and invert-the tart should drop out onto the plate, with the apple side up.
8 Serve with cream.

APPLES The apple (the fruit of the genus Malus) is the world's most popular fruit. The apple has been known since prehistoric times, and was certainly cultivated by the Ancient Egyptians and the Chinese. The Ancient Romans took seedlings to Britain where they flourished. The Pilgrim fathers took trees and scion stock for grafting (because the apple does not grow true from seed) to North America. The United Sates is now one of the largest producers of apples in the world. There are in the region of 7000 varieties of apples grown worldwide, but unfortunately only a tiny percentage are marketed, and their number is diminishing. The most popular varieties are the Golden Delicious, Red Delicious and Granny Smith. The apple is most commonly eaten as a fresh fruit, but it is also used in juices and ciders and in many different ways in the kitchen, from the Simple baked apple, to pies and tarts, elaborate Austrian strudels, jellies and conserves. It is also used in many savory dishes as a complement to the richer meats such as pork and goose. Chopped fresh apple is the mainstay of many salads, particularly the famous Waldorf Salad. Apples are readily available fresh all year round; however, dessert apples are at their best from fall through to spring.

Wine Notes

A sweet wine is needed to accompany this dish-ideally a style with real richness and concentration.

FRANCE : Choose an aged Sauternes, preferably one that is deep golden in color and thus deeper and more interesting in flavor.

USA : Select a dessert-style Muscat from California. Try Quady's outstanding wines.

AUSTRALIA : Try a batrytis-Semillon from the Riverina distric-dark in color, sweet, luscious and often slightly caramelized in character.

HUNGARY : Tokaji Aszú is absolutely delicious. It carries a sweetness rating, in the from of “putts” or “puttonos”, 5 “putts” is rich and treacle-like.

GREECE

World Cuisine

GREECE is a place with almost universal appeal The most vivid way to make your first entrance it to sail into the port of Piraeus, where the street scenery has remained unchanged fro decades except that new banks now tout for business along a waterfront once lined solely by low-lift sailors' bars. But few travelers give the port city more than a cursory glance before catching a cab to the noisy, traffic-infested center of Athens and the Acropolis, a visit that remains a mystical experience no matter how many times you make it, and an instant validation that you are in the heart. of Greece.

Other visitors put off until later their trip to the Parthenon and visit first the Temple of Poseidon at Sounion, on a two-hour round-trip. They go as much for the unsurpassed view as to fell the inspiration that prompted Lord Byron's famous poem. Still others head straight for the Plaka—the an-vil-shaped, historic heart of Athens, packed with ruins dating back 3000 years, pseudo-Byzantine churches, tavernas, and shops selling all types of goods, from furs to jewelry, T-shirts and pottery.

The best short tour for an insight into Greek life takes in the twelfth-century church of Agia Ekaterini, the monument of Lysicrates, Anafiotiki (a living model of a traditional Greek island village), the Tower of the winds and the permanently crowded food markets south of Omonia Square. Here whole carcasses of lambs are hung next to fat eggplants, okra and white haricot beans, and the buzz of buyers haggling for the best prices leaves as strong and impression as the hazy Mediterranean light.

Simplicity is the prime lure of Greek food and few vacation dreams are as compelling as enjoying a meal at a waterfront restaurant on one of the less crowded greek islands, hard by a harbor filled with fishing boats disgorging spiny lobster, squid and red mullet. The starters of choice would be an appetizer plate of mezethakia accompanied by a small glass of ouzo, the anise-flavored aperitif. The line-up of mezze, as each individual item is called, would include small squares of Feta cheese, vine-ripened tomatoes, picked peppers, olives, taramosalata (fish roe paste), dol-mathes (stuffed vine leaves) and keftethes (tiny meatballs).

The main even might be a whole fish, flash-broiled over a barbecue and flavored with fresh oregano, lemon and olive oil. In most cases, retsina, that most controversial yet most Greek of Willes, would be served. About 50 percent of the wine produced in Greece is resinated. Its detractors claim that retsina is reminiscent of turpentine, but anything that has been popular for thousands of years simply cannot be that bad. The reasons for the love-hate dichotomy are simple. Any drink with such a dominant, sappy palate is almost certain to produce opposing reactions. Retsina—white, red and rosé—is the lifeblood of Greek tavernas and the quality of an establishment's supplies can either make or break its reputation.

The olive is ubiquitous in Greece, and whether sprouting from silvery trees, eaten from snack bowls or used as olive oil it thoroughly dominates Greek food. The ancient Greeks used olive Oil as medicine, not just as a food—obvious when you consider the fruity thickness of Greek olive oil, which is far less liquid than the olive oils of Spain and Italy. The most famous of the Greek olives is the black juicy variety known as the kalamata.

The best known Greek cheese is Feta—salty, crumbly and made from goat's or sheep's milk. It turns up in small squares as an appetizer, with phyllo pastry in the small savory triangles known as tiropittakia, blended with spinach in spanakoppitta (cheese and spinach pie), and is used to add spice and texture to shrimp (prawn) and meat dishes. But perhaps its most famous role is in the salad that routinely features at eery meal and is known in English as "Greek Salad"—a mixture of tomatoes. cucumber. olives and Feta cheese.

Mizithra. an unsalted cottage cheese. is another traditional Greek cheese. very popular in Crete. Kefalotiri, a hard, sheep's or cow's milk cheese. has a distinctive tanginess that makes it the "Parmesan" of Greek cooking.

Phyllo pastry is made only of flour and water but that's where talk of the originary begins md ends. Even in Greece only a few people have the skill to make it by hand. The dough. ike the strudel dough of Austria needs to be worked and worked until it stretches into a sheet as fine as the thinnest paper. In Greece. as elsewhere. phyllo pastry is bought in packets and used to make sweet and savory pastries.

Lemons are mandatory in any Greek kitchen—flavoring and decorating fish, meat and chicken and the prime ingredient of the national sauce, avgolemono. The easiest and most common method of making avgolemono is a simple emulsion of eggs and lemon. but some recipes incorporate beaten egg whites to give a fluffy, soufflé-like appearance. Avgolemono provides extra body and flavor to fish and chicken soups, lamb and vegetable dishes, artichoke preparations and can also be spooned over dolmathes.

Long occupied by the Turks, Greece shares a Middle Eastern predilection for lamb. Taverna kitchens are filled with vast charcoal broilers (grills) which send the aromas of roasting or broiling lamb and wild oregano out onto she street Lamb is the minced meat layered with eggplant and bechamel sauce in moussaka, the most famous of Greek baked dishes. Easter lamb on a spit defines Easter celebrations and ami souvlakia (lamb kebabs) are the signature) offering at Greek restaurants all over the world. In Greece, lamb is never, ever served pink.

Surrounded as Greece is by the sea. and composed of thousands of islands, fish clearly plays and important part in the Greek diet. Like all Mediterranean peoples, the Greeks savor small fish—garfish, sardines, barbounia (small red mullet) are crisp-fried and eaten as appetizers or with a large green salad. Baking is the most popular way to cook thick-fleshed fish.

Sweetmeat and pastry shops are to be found all over Greece and modem Greek cakes are he descendants of confections known to the ancient Hellenes and the Egyptians—heavy with mts. honey. fruits. eggs, flour and flower essence syrups. Every pastry shop sports a few tables to serve up slices of baklava (a phyllo pastry packed with nuts and doused with syrup) md other rich confections. At home, a simple rice pudding flavored with lemon and vanilla is cherished as a dessert by children and adults alike.

The Greeks have a song that begins, "Retsina wine, with you I'll die, no earthly things with you can vie" that acts as the signature theme of the tavernas. One of the lasting memories of any visit to Greece is sipping a midnight cup of sweet, strong coffee and nibbling on one of the many honey pastries in a taverna where the only sound is a bouzouki playing. Time indeed to reflect on a Greek culinary heritage and a history of hospitality that each back over 2000 years and are little changed today.

MEZETHAKIA

Appetizers

In Greece dinner is usually served very late, between 10 and 11 pm but friends and family often gather earlier in the home or taverna, for savory snacks known as Mezethakia. Normally accompanied by fresh, crusty bread. They help to keep hunger at bay until the main meal is served. One of the classic Mezethakia, Dolmathes, has been popular since the time of the ancient Athenians, when fig leaves were often used to encase th filling.

TIROPITTAKIA

Cheese Triangles

MAKES ABOUT 48

Tiropittakia are best eaten on the day they are prepared as they become soggy when refrigerated. For convenience, the mixture may be cooked in a baking dish and cut into triangles after removing from the oven; follow the cooking instructions given for Spanakoppitta me Tyri.

Ingredient

FILLING
7oz (220g) Feta cheese
2 tablespoons chopped parsley
2 eggs, lightly beaten
freshly ground black pepper, to taste
¾ cup (6oz / 185g) butter, melted
1 cup (4oz / 125g) grated Kefalotiri or Parmesan cheese
¼ teaspoon nutmeg
12oz (375g) package phyllo pastry

Method

1 Preheat the oven to 350℉ (180℃)
2 Crumble the Feta into a bowl and mix with the remaining filling ingredients. Season well with the pepper.
3 Cut each sheet of pastry into 3 pieces, each measuring about 5×2 inches (13×30cm).
4 Brush 2 pieces of pastry with melted butter and place one on top of the other.
5 Place a heaping teaspoon of the cheese filling at the end of the pastry and fold the end over the filling to from a small triangle. Continue folding the pastry over the triangle shape until the pastry strip is used.
6 Repeat this process with the remaining pastry sheets and cheese filling.
7 Brush each of the triangles with a little melted butter and place on a greased baking sheet.
8 Bake in the oven for about 15 to 20 minutes, or until the pastry is crisp and golden. Serve hot.

DOLMATHES

Stuffed Vine Leaves

If extra liquid is needed during cooking, add very hot stock in order to avoid lowering the oven temperature and changing the cooking time.

Ingredient

FILLING

1 tablespoon oil
1 ½ lb (750g) ground (minced) lamb or beef
1 tomato, peeled and chopped
2 teaspoons chopped dill or fennel
8 oz (250g) fresh or preserved vine leaves
½ cup (4oz / 125g) butter, diced
1 large onion, finelv chopped or grated
⅓ cup (2oz / 60g) short grain rice
¼ cup chopped parsley
salt and pepper, to taste
2 cups (16 fl oz/ 500mL) beef stock
1 lemon, sliced. for garnish

Method

1 Place all the filling ingredients in a bowl. Use your hands to mix them together well.
2 If using fresh vine leaves. plunge them into boiling water for a minute to soften them, If canned leaves are being used, they should be rinsed well.
3 Place a heaping teaspoon of the meat mixture on each leaf and roll up to form a small package.
4 Line the base of a large saucepan with a few of the extra vine leaves to prevent the dolmathes from sticking while they are cooking.
5 Pack the dolmathes into the sauccpan. seam side down, layer upon layer.
6 Add the beef stock and butter. bring to a gentle simmer and cook for about 1 hour. A little more stock may need to be added if the dolmathes begin to dry out during cooking.
7 Serve hot or cold, garnished with the lemon slices.

TARAMOSLATA

Smoked Fish Roe Dip

Salted fish roe is available fresh from delicatessens or in cans from the supermarket. Buy a good brand, as the cheaper varieties can be oversalted. Traditionally, the egg yolk is used raw, but very finely mashed hard-cooked egg yolk may be substituted.

Ingredient

3 ½ oz (100g) tarama (salted fish one)
4 slices stale white bread, crusts removed
1 garlic clove, grated or minced
⅓ cup (3 fl oz / 90mL) virgin olive oil
1 egg yolk
¼ cup (2 fl oz / 60mL) water
3~4 tablespoons lemon juice
freshly ground white pepper, to taste

Method

1 Combine the fish roe and egg yolk in a bowl and beat until creamy.
2 Soak the bread in the water for a few minutes, then squeeze the bread until it is as dry as possible and add to the fish roe. Use a hand-held electric mixer to blend. then add the garlic and onion, beating until well mixed. Gradually add the lemon juice and oil and beat until light and fluffy. Season with plenty of white pepper.
3 Chill until required. Serve with crakers or bread.

OKTAPOTHE TOURSI

Pickled Octopus

SERVES 8

Octopus is highly regarded in Greek kitchens, both in homes and restaurants. It is caught in large numbers around the coastline and appears on the table in many guises. Often a small plate of octopus is served as a complimentary appetizer at the start of a meal in a Greek restaurant. Octopus should be pounded with a wooden mallet to tenderized it before It is cooked. This dish requires at least 12 hours of marination before serving.

Ingredient

1 × 2 lb (1kg) octopus
1 medium carrot, halved
6 peppercorns
1 garlic clove, sliced
½ cup (4 fl oz / 25mL) vinegar
2 lemons, cut Into wedges. for garnish, optional
2 small onions, halved
2 parsley stalks, cut into 2 inches (5cm) pieces
1 bay leaf
½ cup (4 fl oz / 25mL) olive oil
salt and pepper, to late
freshly ground black pepper, to taste

Method

1 To clean the octopus, remove the inkbag and skin. Cut out the eyes and beak and discard. and wash the octopus well.
2 Place the octopus, onions, carrot, parsley and peppercorns in a saucepan, cover and simmer gently in the octopus own juice until tender, about 50 minutes. Cool.
3 When cool, remove the octopus from the saucepan and cut into bite-sized pieces. Place in a bowl with the remaining ingredients and mix well Cover and refrigerate for at least 12 hours before serving.
4 Garnish with the lemon wedges, if desired Sprinkle with the black pepper.

VINE LEAVES Vine leaves used in cooking are the tender young leaves of the gape vine. They have been used In the cuisine of the eastern Mediterranean for centuries in much the same way they are today: as wrappings for delicious meat or rice stuffings. These are known in Greece as dolmathes, and in Turkey as dolmas. They young vine leaves are quickly blanched, and then with the vein side up they are used to wrap a mixture typical of the region. Larger vine leaves are also used to wrap fish or small game birds before baking or barbeacuing, to prevent them from drying out. Vine leaves are now available fresh in many regions that grow grapes, they can be found in specialty food stores during the growing season. They are also available packaged, preserved in brine. One opened, the vine leaves should be packed in an airtight container and stored in the refrigerator.

Wine Notes

A soft red with a fair amount of fruit would be good with these starters. However, a glass of ouzo or a neutral chilled spirit such as vodka would also be worth trying.

FRANCE : A Côtes-du-Rhône with some spicy flavors would be a good choice.

USA : Trv a medium-bodied Californian Zmfandel or Syrah.

AUSTRALIA : There are manv Shiraz blends from different districts to choose from; Andrew Garrett and Mt Hurtle Shiraz are good examples.

GREECE : Choose a Greek red such as Demestica, Goumenissa or Paros.

SOUPA AVGOLEMONO

Egg and Lemon Soup

While soups do not playa major part in greek cooking, Soupa Avgolemono's fame has spread beyond its homeland. In a way that is typical of traditional Greek cuisine, this dish uses very simple ingredients yet it has a distinctively Greek flavor. Part of that flavor comes from the lemons, a fruit that was brought to Greece by the soldiers of Alexander the Great In the fourth century.

SERVES 6

About ½ cup finely diced poached chicken may be added to the soup during the last 5 minutes of cooking time if you want a more substantial soup.

Ingredient

6 cups (48 fl oz / 1.5L) chicken stock
2 eggs
1 tablespoon chopped parsley
¼ cup (2oz / 60g) short grain rice
Juice of 1 lemon
salt and pepper, to taste

Method

1 Heat the stock to boiling, add the rice and continue to boil for about 20 minutes, or until the rice is cooked.
2 Beat the eggs until light and fluffy, then whisk in the lemon juice and ¼ cup (2 fl oz / 60mL) of the got stock.
3 Reduce the stock to a gentle simmer and pour in the egg mixture, stirring constantly. Cook over low heat for 2 minutes (do not let it boil) until the soup thickens a little.
4 Add the parsley, season to taste with salt and pepper and serve.

Wine Notes

A delicately flavored and unusual soup, this might be served with anv retsina or one of the grape varieties from the Rhône Valley.

FRANCE : Choose a White Hermitage or Condrieu. one of the most delicate whites from southern France.

USA : Try a Viognier or Marsanne from Preston Vineyards, Phelps or Ritchie Creek.

AUSTRALIA : A Marsanne from Goulbum Valley producer such as Chateau Tahbilk or Mitchelton would be excellent.

SALATA MELITZANES

Eggplant Salad

A Greek family meal is not complete without a salad, which is usually served as a separate course. This salad may also be served with barbecued or roast meat, and during Lent(when animal flesh is not eaten) with crusty bread as a main meal. This recipe features eggplant, a common ingredient in Greek cooking, and rigani(wild marjoram), herb that has been used by he Greeks since ancient times.

SERVES 6

Rigani is a Greek variety of oregano, and so oregano is the obvious substitute if rigani is not available Bunches of dried rigani are available from Greek or Middle Eastern food shops.

Ingredient

2 lb (1kg) eggplants (aubergines)
1 onion, finely chopped
1 red bell pepper(capsicum), thinly sliced
1 teaspoon dried rigani (wild marjoram) or oregano
2 tablespoons white wine vinegar salt and pepper, to taste
1 large garlic clove, finely chopped
2 firm ripe tomatoes, chopped
2 tablespoons chopped parsley
½ cup (4 fl oz / 125mL) vlrgin olive oil

Method

1 Preheat the oven to 400℉ (200℃)
2 Wash the eggplants, then dry with paper towel. Place on a baking sheet and bake for 30 a 40 minutes, until the skins are charred.
3 Allow to cool for 30 minutes.
4 Rub the skin off the eggplants with your fingers and discard. Squeeze the flesh to release any bitter juices, then chop roughly
5 Place the eggplant in a bowl with the onion, tomatoes, bell pepper, parsley and rigani.
6 Mix together the olive oil and vinegar and add to the other ingredients. Toss well to combine.
7 Refrigerate before serving.

Wine Notes

A full-flavored white would be a suitable accompaniment for this dish.

FRANCE : Select a simple white Burgundy style such as Montagny Rully or Saint-Veran.

USA : Choose a Fume Blanc from any of the main Californian wine districts.

AUSTRALIA : Try a Barossa or Margaret River Semillon.

NEW ZEALAND : Look for a Crisp, wooded Sauvignon Blanc from Gisborne or Hawkes Bay, on the north island.

SPANAKOPPITTA ME TYRI

Spinach and Cheese Pie

Although recipes abound for Greek meat, chicken, fish and vegetable pies, this one, made with spinach and cheese encased in flaky, phyllo pastry, is the most ell known outside of Greece. At one time it provided satisfying fare for peasants working in the field; today it is often cut into small portions and served as an appetizer. The Feta and Kefalotiri cheeses add their own distinctive flavor.

SERVES 8

If spinach is difficult to obtain, Swiss chard(silver beet) is an acceptable substitute.

Ingredient

FILLING

3 tablespoons olive oil
4 scallions (spring onions), chopped
1 cup (4oz / 125g) Feta cheese, crumbled
¼ cup (1oz / 30g) grated Kefalotiri or Parmesan cheese
2 teaspoons chopped dill or funnel
¼ teaspoon nutmeg
12oz (375g) package phyllo pastry
1 large onion, finely chopped
2 lb (1kg) spinach, well washed and drained
1 cup (8oz / 250g) cottage cheese
2 tablespoons chopped parsley
4 eggs, lightly beaten
salt and pepper, to taste
⅓ cup (3 fl oz / 90ml) olive oil

Method

1 Preheat the over to 350°F (180℃).
2 Heat the 3 tablespoons of oil in a large saucepan and saute the onion until soft Add the scallions and spinach, cover, and cook for 5 minutes, until the spinach has softened. Allow to cool slightly.
3 Stir in the Feta, cottage cheese. Kefalotiri, parsley dill, eggs, nutmeg. salt and pepper. and combine well.
4 Brush the pastry sheets with some of the extra olive oil Layer half the sheets in a greased 14×10 inches (35×25cm) baking. Spoon in the spinach and cheese mixture and top with the remaining pastry sheets.
5 Press the pastry edges to the sides of the baking dish to seal.
6 Brush the top with olive oil and bake in the oven for about 45 minutes, or until the pastry is crisp and golden.
7 Remove from the oven and let stand for 5 minutes before cutting.
8 This dish is delicious served hot or cold.

FETA CHEESE Cheese, like bread, was a traditional staple food for the Greeks, and was produced form the milk of the hardy sheep and goats that could thrive on the rocky mountainsides. Often cheese was the sole source of protein for the Villagers. Greek Feta was originally made by shepherds in the hills around Athens, and indeed rates a mention in the Odyssey. When Odysseus and his companions entered the cave of Polyphemus, the Cyclops, they were astonished by the racks of cheese (Feta, without a doubt) he had stored away. A soft, white, uncooked cheese, Feta is made by separation curdled milk, the curds are drained into the block molds that give it its characteristic shape. The large blocks are then stored in vrine, which contributes to the cheese's salty taste and ensures a rindless cheese. Although Greece still produces Feta cheese by centuries-old methods, it also makes, and successfully exports, a commercial factory-produced variety, which incorporates pasteurized cow's milk as well as sheep or goat's milk Bulgarian Feta, another commonly available variety, is very similar m taste and texture but is a little less salty. Feta is now made m many countries that have large dairy industries, including the United States, Australia and Denmark Sold either loose by weight or in prepacked cartons it should be kept in its brine (preferably In the refrigerator) to ensure freshness Feta is an excellent cheese for cooking and its used in spinach and cheese pies, ration dishes, and as a stuffing. It also has a deserved reputation as a complement to tomato, olive and cucumber salads, a combination which is often called Greek salad. Feta should always be well drained before use, to avoid mixing the brine the finished dish.

Wine Notes

A flavorsome white will suit this dish, or alternatively try a medium-bodied red wine.

FRANCE : Try a Bordeaux, either red or white with a touch of astringency.

USA : Choose a wine from the Napa-Sonoma area either a Fume Blanc or a Chardonnay.

AUSTRALIA : Look for a wood-aged Semillon or Sauvignon Blanc or Cabernet-Shiraz -Melrlot blend from the Hunter valley or McLaren Vale.

GREECE : Try Demestica, made by Achaia-Clauss, or perhaps the red retsina, often called Kokinelli, from Tsantali.

ARNI SOUVLAKIA

Skewered Lamb

The Greeks have a reverence for meat, as for many it was a rare luxury. Lamb is the meat traditionally associated with Greek cuisine, and, indeed, the lamb is very good, despite the often sparse pastures on which the animals graze. This dish is said to have been created by shepherds who used pointed sticks to hold chunks of meat over open fires. It is a close relation to the Turkish shish kebab.

SERVES 8

Use long, flat-bladed kebab skewers to hold the meat cubes firmly. Use plenty of pepper, and-if you like-add a generous sprinkling of thyme leaves to the marinade.

Wild thyme grows abundantly on the hill-sides of Greece, and its flavor works well in this dish.

Ingredient

- 1 large leg of lamb
- ¼ cup (2 fl oz / 60mL) lemon juice
- 1 tablespoon chopped rigani (wild marjoram) or oregano
- 2 lemons, cut into eighths
- 2 tablespoons chopped parsley
- ½ cup (4 fl oz / 125mL) olive oil
- ½ cup (4 fl oz / 125mL) dry white wine
- 4 garlic cloves, finely chopped
- 3 bay leaves, broken into pieces salt and pepper, to taste

Method

1 Cut all the meat from the bone and remove any fat. Cut the meat into 1 ½ inches (4cm) cubes.
2 Combine all the remaining ingredients except the lemon and parsley in a large bowl.
3 Add the meat and stir well so that it is coated with the marinade.
4 Allow to marinate In the refrigerator for about 24 hours, stirring occasionally.
5 Thread the meat onto skewers.
6 Cook under a hot broiler (griller) or on a barbecue, turning and basting frequently until cooked, about 15 minutes.
7 Serve with the lemon wedges and a sprinkle of chopped parsley.

BAY LEAVES The bay tree (Laurus nobilis) can grow to 50 feet (15 meters) given its preferred dry Mediterranean-type climate. Bay leaves are available fresh and dried. They should be used sparingly as they impart a strong savory flavor. They enhance marinades, pates and casseroles, particularly those made of lamb and beef. Whole bay leaves are often added to a dish while-it is cooking, and then removed before it is served.

Wine Notes

Look for a dry white with reasonable body and acidity; or a red such as a medium-weight Cabernet.

FRANCE : Try a Chardonnay or Sauvigonon Blanc from the Midi, or a Saint-veran or Rully.

USA : Choose a good Chardonnay or Fume Blanc from the Napa Valley.

AUSTRALIA : An oak-matured Barossa Valley Semillon would be a good style.

GREECE : Retsina, the popular resinated wine of Greece, would be an ideal choice. Choose one from Attica-Malamatina, Tsantali and Achaia-Clauss are all well-known producers.

PSARI LEMONATO

Lemon Fish

Greece consists of a multitude of islands and a mainland almost completely surrounded by water, so it is not surprising that seafood has always played an important part in the local cuisine and economy. Interestingly, vases from around 2000 years BC are decorated with illustrations of fish and fishermen. The Greeks eat more fish than meat and many recipes, like this one, cook the vegetables with the fish.

SERVES 4

It Is important to slash the fish deeply to ensure that the flavors permeate the flesh.

Ingredient

2 lb (1kg) whole fish, such as bream or sea bass
juice of 2 lemons salt and pepper, to taste
1~2 tablespoons capers
½ cup (4 fl oz / 125mL) olive oil
lemon slices, for garnish
3 potatoes, peeled and sliced
2 large tomatoes, sliced
3 teaspoons chopped rigani (wild marjoram) or oregano

Method

1 Preheat the oven to 350℉ (180℃).
2 Clean the fish and pat dry. Cut three diagonal slashes on both sides of the fish and sprinkle half the lemon juice over the fish and inside the cavity. Season the skin and cavity with salt and pepper.
3 Layer the potatoes and tomatoes into the bottom of a greased baking dish and pour over the remaining lemon juice.
4 Place the fish on top, sprinkle with the capers and rigani and drizzle a little olive oil over the top.
5 Cover with foil and bake for about 40 minutes. Remove the foil and cook for an additional 20 minutes, or until the potatoes are tender and the fish is cooked Garnish with the lemon slices and serve.

CAPERS Capers are the small, unopened buds of a prickly shrub (Capparis spinosa) that is native to the Mediterranean region. After harvestion they are picked. adding extra piquancy to their natural acidity. Capers were known to both the Ancient Greeks and Roman, and were used to flavor fish and lamb dishes. They are employed in the same way today and are also added to salad, use as a garnish, and in pizza toppings. Capers are sold in jars, either salted or picked in white wine vinegar. After being opened they should be stored in a container with a tight-fitting lid in the refrigerator, and used within six months

Wine Notes

A white Wine, preferablv a crisp style with some acidity, would be well suited to this dish.

FRANCE : Select a white Bordeaux, perhaps from the Graves district.

USA : Choose a Semillon or Sauvignono Blanc, or a blend of the two, from the Russian River district, Mendocino or the Lake Counties.

AUSTRALIA : Try a Margaret River Semillon, which has a "zesty" character.

ITALY : Look for a dry, citrus-flavored Verauzzo form around Trevlso and Friuli in the northeast or a Soave from the nearby Veneto.

KOTOPOULO RAPAMA ME HILPITTES

Chicken with Noodels

This is simple family fare from the Peloponnese peninsula, which is separated from the mainland only by the Corinth canal. Originally this dish would have been prepared with a farmyard fowl, a coarse homemade red wine, sun-ripened tomatoes, and noodles made on the kitchen table. Times change, but the good flavors remain. Greeks like chicken-and all their meat-cooked until it is falling off the bone.

SERVES 4

Any type of noodle can be used Choose a dry red wine of reasonable quality.

Ingredient

3 lb (1.5kg) chicken pieces salt and pepper,
to taste 2 tablespoons olive oil
13oz (410g) can tomatoes, chopped, juice reserved
1 bay leaf
1 onion, finely chopped
½ cup (4 fl oz / 125mL) red wine
2 teaspoons chopped oregano
11oz (350g) noodles
⅓ cup (1 ½ oz / 45g) grated Kefalotiri or Parmesan cheese

Method

1. Season the chicken pieces with the salt and pepper.
2. Heat the oil in a large saucepan and brown the chicken on all sides. Remove from the pan and set aside.
3. Add the onion to the pan and saute for 5 minutes, or until golden. Return the chicken to the pan and add the wine, tomatoes and their juice, oregano and bay leaf.
4. Gradually heat to a summer, cover the pan and cook gently for about 1 hour.
5. Cook the noodles in boiling salted water.
6. Remove the chicken from the sauce and keep warm.
7. Stir the Kefalotiri into the sauce.
8. To serve, arrange the drained noodles on a large platter and top with the chicken and the sauce.

KEFALOTIRI A hard, salty Greek cheese. Kefalotiri is traditionally made from ewe's milk. but today cow's milk is more commonly used after being salted, the cheese is matured for several months. Similar to Parmesan, Kefalotiri is mostly used for grating and for cooking. It is sold by Greek food stores and some specialty food stores. Kefalotiri should be stored in the refrigerator in an airtight container.

Wine Notes

A white wine with body but also a degree of acidity, would be a good choice.

FRANCE : Select a Chablis, for example, a Saint-Veran or a Pouilly-Fuisse.

USA : Try a crisp Fume Blanc(with slightly more "cut" than a Chardonnay) from the Russian River Valley district.

AUSTRALIA : Look for an unwooded Chardonnay from the Mornington Peninsula or Tasmania

GREECE : Try a Demestita white from the Peloponnese, or the white Makekonikos from northern Greece.

MELITZANES MOUSSAKA

Eggplant Moussaka

Greece was ruled by Turkey for four centuries, and the Middle Eastern influence on Greek cuisine is seen particularly clearly in this dish, which is also found in a similar form in the Balkans and Turkey. Some recipes substitute potatoes or summer squash(marrows) for the eggplant, but this is the version most often encountered in the cities and countryside of Greece Plump and richly purple, the eggplant plays a major role in Greek cooking.

SERVES 8

To save on fat, the eggplants in this recipe are broiled instead of fried in the traditional way In lots of oil. As this dish requires some fussing, it is a good idea to double the recipe and freeze half to serve on a later occasion.

Ingredient

2 lb (1kg) eggplants (aubergines)
3 tablespoons olive oil, salt

MEAT SAUCE
2 tablespoons olive oil
2 garlic cloves, finely chopped
1 ½ cups peeled and chopped tomatoes
½ cup (4 fl oz / 125mL) white wine
1 teaspoon sugar
1 large onion, chopped
2 lb (1kg) ground (mined) lamb or beef
2 tablespoons tomato paste
2 tablespoons chopped parsley
¼ teaspoon ground cinnamon salt and pepper, to taste

CREAM SAUCE
3 tablespoons butter
2 cups (16 fl oz / 500mL) milk
¼ cup (1oz / 30g) grated Kefalotiri or Parmesan cheese
1 egg, lightly beaten
4 tablespoons flour
½ teaspoon ground nutmeg salt and pepper, to taste

Method

1 Preheat the over to 350℉ (180℃).
2 Cut the eggplants into ¼ inch (0.5cm) slices. Sprinkle with a little salt and leaves for 1 hour.
3 Rinse, pat dry with paper towels, then brush each side with oil. Broil (grill) the eggplants on both sides until golden brown.
4 To make the meat sauce, heat the oil in a large pan and saute the onion and garlic for 10 minutes.
5 Add the meat and brown over high heat, stirring well.
6 Add the remaining meat sauce ingredients and stir well to combine. Allow to simmer, covered, for about 30 minutes.

7 To make the cream sauce melt the butter in a pan, stir m thc flour and cook for 2 minutes. Add the milk and stir constantly until the mixture boils. Allow to simmer for 1 to 2 minutes.

8 Remove from heat and stir in the nutmeg, salt, pepper and 2 tablespoons of the cheese.

9 Place one-third of the sliced eggplants over the base of a greased 13×9 inches (33×23cm) baking dish. Spread with half the meat sauce and top with another third of the eggplant slices. Spread with the remaining meat sauce, then top with the last third of the eggplant slices.

10 Mix the egg into the cream sauce and pout over the eggplant, spreading evenly over the entire surface. Sprinkle with the remaining cheese and bake in the oven for 1 hour.

11 Remove from the oven and allow to stand for 5 minutes before serving.

EGGPLANTS The eggplant (Solanum melongena), or aubergine as it is known in Europe. originated in India and was 15 used extensively by the Chinese as early as the seventh century BC. By AD 1400 it had made Its way to Europe and today plays a major role in the cuisines of the Mediterranean and the East. It is a distinctive egg-shaped vegetable with glossy purplish black skin (there are also less common white and orange varieties). Speed is of the essence when using this vegetable. for Its creamy flesh discolors quickly on contact with the air It also has a bitter juice that should be extracted by salting slices, leaving them for 15 to 30 minutes, then wiping off the juice and salt. Eggplants can be stuffed whole or sliced and fried or broiled(grilled). It is an important ingredient in the stewed vegetable dish called ratatouille, where Its unusual flavor complements tomato. zucchini, onion and garlic. It also harmonizes with lamb and beef. Greek, Turkish and Arabic cooking all incorporate pureed eggplant in a variety of recipes. In India, Bangladesh, Pakistan and Sri Lanka, eggplants often appear in chutneys or pickles. When purchasing eggplants make sure the skin is smooth, tight and glossy and the green stem end is fresh and firm. Fresh eggplant will keep for about two weeks without refrigeration.

Wine Notes

In Greece white wine is usually served with Moussaka, but red is also an option.

FRANCE : A spicy Rhône valley red such as Chateauneuf-du-Pape would be a good choice.

USA : Choose a Zinfandel, Syrah or Merlot, from any of California's wine-growing regions.

AUSTRALJA : Choose a youthful Shiraz. particularlv one from Ruthergten or McLaren Vale.

ITALY : The Merlot of the northeastern regions would be perfect.

KEFTETHES ME SALTSA DOMATA

Meatballs with Tomato Sauce

You will find meatballs served in every part of Greece. The meat with which they are made ranges from beef to lamb 10 goat (but lamb and young beef are the most popular). Cattle are difficult to raise on the rocky terrain of Greece, so beef is often Imported and it can be expensive. The sauces in which the meatballs are cooked can be varied: the tomato sauce in this recipe would traditionally have been homemade.

SERVES 4

In some areas of Greece 1 or 2 teaspoons of ground cumin are added to the meatball mixture. The sauce may be prepared well in advance and reheated when you are ready to add the meatballs.

Ingredient

1 lb (500g) ground (minced) beef or lamb
1 garlic clove, finely chopped
2 tablespoons lemon juice
1 ½ tablespoons very finely chopped fresh rosemary
⅓ teaspoon freshly ground black pepper
finely chopped parsley, for garnish, optional
1 small onion, grated
½ cup (2oz / 60g) soft white bread crumbs
2 tablespoons chopped parsley
⅓ teaspoon salt
2 teaspoon all-purpose (plan) flour 2~3 tablespoons olive oil

SAUCE
1 tablespoon virgin olive oil
1 garlic clove, finely chopped
½ cup (4 fl oz / 125mL) dry red wine
⅓ teaspoon salt
1 medium onion, finely chopped
4 large ripe tomatoes, peeled and chopped
½ teaspoon sugar
⅓ teaspoon freshly ground black pepper

Method

1 In a large bowl mix together the meat onion, garlic bread crumbs, lemon juice, parsley, rosemary, salt and pepper. Use our hands to mix very thoroughly. Form the mixture into walnut-sized balls, and roll lightly in the flour.
2 Heat the oil in a skillet and fry the meatballs in batches until golden brown, adding extra oil if necessary. Drain the meatballs on paper towels.
3 To make the sauce, heat the oil in a large saucepan and cook the onion for 4 minutes, stirring often. Add the remaining ingredients and simmer for 15 minutes.
4 Add the browned meatballs to the sauce and cook gently for an additional 5 minutes, or until the meatballs are well heated through.
5 Serve at once sprinkled with freshly chopped parsley, if desired This dish can be served with potatoes or rice.

ROSEMARY A beautiful herb, rosemary (Rosmarinus officinalis) has always been surrounded by legend and myth. One piece of folklore has it that if a girl takes rosemary mixed with thyme on St Agnes Eve she will be sent a vision of her lover-to-be. Rosemary is also a symbol of remembrance. A native of the Mediterranean region, it grows wild in that area. It is very hardy and thrives in harsh conditions. There are upright and horizontal varieties, both of which have dark green, narrow spiky leaves and pale lavender flowers. Rosemary has a strong and distinctive fragrance and is used in both savory and sweet dishes. It is traditionally associated with lamb and pork, and is often included in wine based marinades. Rosemary's flowers can be used as a garnish for salads and fruit salads, and are sometimes candied (crystallized), similar to violets. This herb yields a fragrant essential oil which is widely used in the perfume industry and in aromatherapy. Rosemary can be bought both fresh and dried, but the dried leaves and rather spiky and need to be finely chopped or crumbled before use. A few sprigs of fresh rosemary added to a jar of sugar impart a lovely fragrance.

Wine Notes

A medium-bodied red, not too heavy in tannin, could be served with this dish.

FRANCE : A Bourgogne Rouge (the most basic red Burgundy appellation) would be ideal.

USA : Choose a good commercial Californian Merlot. The Napa Valley and Sonoma regions are the best known.

AUSTRALIA : Select a lighter style Shiraz or a blend featuring Pinot Noir or Merlot.

GREECE : Try one of the popular non-resinated reds sluch as Makedonikos, which comes from the Macedonian region in the north.

ARNI LEMONATO ME PATATES

Roast Lemon Lamb with Potatoes

Before home ovens became common in Greece-and even today in many villages-cooks would take their meat to the village baker. After the bread was cooked, he would put the meat in the oven, basting it and adding and turning the vegetables as required. Potatoes are a comparatively recent addition to Greek Cuisine, showing up in the early 1800s. Today the island of Naxos, in the Cyclades, is considered to produce the country's best potatoes.

SERVES 6

It is important that the herbs be generously applied to the meat to ensure a flavorful dish. Cook the meat until very tender and almost falling from the bone. There should be no trace of pink.

Ingredient

4 lb (2kg) leg of lamb
1 tablespoon fresh rosemary leaves
¼ cup (2 fl oz / 60mL) olive oil
2 teaspoons chopped oregano
2 garlic cloves, sliced
2 lb (1kg) potatoes, peeled and quartered
juice of 1 lemon finely grated zest of 1 lemon
2 teaspoons fresh thyme leaves salt and pepper, to taste

Method

1 Preheat the oven to 425°F (220℃).
2 Using a small sharp knife, make small slits over the surface of the meat and insert the garlic and rosemary pieces into them.
3 Place the lamb in a large baking dish and arrange the potatoes around it.
4 Mix the remaining ingredients together and pour over the lamb and potatoes.
5 Bake in the oven for 20 minutes, then reduce heat to 375°F (190℃) and cook for another hour. Baste the meat occasionally and turn the potatoes halfway through the cooking time.
6 Turn the meat over and season with more salt and pepper. Return to the oven. increase heat to 425°F (220℃) and cook for another 20 minutes.
7 Serve the meat and potatoes on a large platter.

LEMONS All parts of the lemon(fruit of the tree, Citrus lemon) have their uses. The juice has a high pectin content and helps to set jams and jellies; it can replace vinegar in salad dressings. It is well known for Its use in drinks, such as lemonade and tea. Its acidit complements fish and meats like lamb, pork and chicken. The zest of the lemon is used flavorring and decoration; candled peel is used in sweets.

Wine Notes

Cabernet Sauvignon is a natural choice with lamb; preferably a young wine with a touch of astringency.

FRANCE : A Bordeaux is the obvious choice; perhaps a young chateau-bottled wine from Saint-Julien, Pauillac or the Haut-Médoc.

USA : A good Cabernet from Sonoma or the Napa Valley would be fine.

AUSTRALIA : Try one of the many fine Cabernet Sauvignons or Cabernet blends from the Coonawarra.

ITALY : Try one of the newer Tuscan reds (made by Antinori or Frescobal) with Cabernet Sauvignon blended with the traditional Sangiovese variety.

BAKLAVA

Everyday Greek desserts are simple, featuuring fruit, nuts, yoghurt and cheese. But on festive occasions the rich pastries associated with Greece are served. Baklava, a favorite, uses mixed nuts, honey and phyllo pastry to great advantage. Onginally the phyllo would have been laboriously made at home; today commercially made phyllo greatly simplifies a cook' s life. Greek desserts are usually served with thick, strong coffee; sugar can be added, but no milk or cream are offered with it.

MAKES 15 PIECES

As the fragile phyllo pastry dries out very quickly, it is a good idea to keep the pieces covered with a slightly dampened dish towel until you are ready to use them.

Ingredient

12oz (375g) package phyllo pastry
2 cups (8oz / 250g) finely chopped walnuts
¼ cup (2oz / 60g) superfine (caster) sugar
⅔ cup (5oz / 155g) unsalted butter, melted
1 cup (4oz / 125g) finely chopped almonds
2 teaspoons ground Cinnamon pinch ground cloves

SUGAR SYRUP
2 cups (16oz / 500g) sugar
2 tablespoons honey
1 cinnamon stick
1 thin strip lemon zest
2 cups (16 fl oz / 500mL) water
3 whole cloves
1 tablespoon lemon juice

Method

1 Preheat the oven to 325°F (165℃).
2 Butter the base and Sides of a 13×9 inches (33×23cm) baking dish. Trim the phyllo pastry sheets to 14×10 inches (35×25cm) pieces.
3 Place 10 sheets of phyllo, separately, into the pan, brushing each sheet with the melted butter.
4 Mix together the nuts, sugar, cinnamon and cloves and spread half this mixture over the pastry.
5 Layer another 3 sheets of pastry over the nut mixture, brushing each sheet with the melted butter.
6 Spread over the remaining nut mixture and top with the remaining pastry sheets, each brushed with melted butter.
7 Brush the top sheet with melted butter again and slice through the top layers with a very sharp knife to create diamond shapes, Sprinkle lightly with water to prevent the pastry from curling and lifting.
8 Bake in the oven for 1 hour. Cover the pastry with aluminum foil if it begins to brown too quickly.

9 Meanwhile, prepare the sugar syrup Place all the syrup ingredients in a saucepan and heat until the sugar has dissolved. Heat to boiling and boil for 10 minutes, stirring often.

10 Remove from heat and cool. Strain, and pour over the baklava when it is removed from he oven. Let the syrup soak in for 3 hours before cutting and serving.

Wine Notes

Serve a very sweet, fortified dessert wine with this distinctive Greek specialty.

FRANCE : Try one of the very good vins doux naturels from the Cobieres-Roussillon region.

USA : Select a Californian Central valley fortified wine, in the rich Madeira style.

AUSTRALIA : Choose a sweet, old liqueur Muscat from Rutherglen.

GREECE : Look for Mavrodaphne, as specialty of the Patros region, or Samos, made on the island of Samos, Greece's best known dessert wines.

TSOUREKI PASCHALINO

Easter Bread

Greek families gather together to celebrate Easter, and to break the Lenten fast. This bread is traditionally baked during Holy Week, the week immediately before Easter. Families share it at the midnight supper served after the Resurrection Service. The three strands of the bread in which the colored eggs nest represent the Holy Trinity; the red color of the eggs symbolizes the blood of Christ.

SERVES 8

This bread also tastes delicious when served with Mizithri(a soft goat's cheese similar to ricotta cheese) and honey.

Ingredient

- 1 cup (8 fl oz / 250mL) warm milk
- ⅓ cup (3oz / 90g) superfine (caster) sugar
- 1 teaspoon salt
- 1 teaspoon ground cinnamon
- ⅓ cup (3oz / 90g) butter, melted
- 4 Red Dyed Eggs (see recipe)
- 2 tablespoons sesame seeds
- 3 teaspoons active dry yeast
- 3 ½ cups (14oz / 435g) all-purpose (plain) flour
- 1 teaspoon allspice
- 1 teaspoon grated lemon zest
- 2 eggs, lightly beaten
- 1 egg for glazing, beaten

Method

1. Mix together the milk, yeast and 1 tablespoon of the sugar m a small bowl and set aside in a warm place for about 10 minutes, or until foamy.
2. Sift the flour, salt, spices and remaining sugar into a large bowl. Mix together the lemon zest, butter, 2 beaten eggs and yeast mixture and stir into the flour. Mix to form a soft dough. Turn the dough onto a floured board and knead for about 10 minutes, until smooth and elastic.
3. Place the dough in a greased bowl, cover, and leave in a warm place until the dough has doubled in size, about 1 hour.
4. Punch down and knead until smooth. Divide into 3 equal portions and roll each portion into a 24 inches (60cm) rounded "rope," about 1 inch (2.5cm) wide. Secure the dough strips together at one end and braid them. Pinch the ends of the rope together.
5. Arrange in a ring and place on a greased baking sheet.
6. Press the polished Red Dyed Eggs into the dough at even intervals, cover and allow to rise in a warm place for about 30 minutes.
7. Preheat the oven to 350°F (180℃).
8. Brush the dough with the beaten egg and sprinkle with the sesame seeds.
9. Bake for about 30 minutes, or until the bread is golden and sounds hollow when tapped on the base.

RED DYED EGGS

Sachets of Greed red egg dye are usually available in specialty food shops at Easter time. A few drops of dark red edible food coloring can be used as a substitute.

Ingredient

- ½ teaspoon Greed red egg dye
- ½ cup (4 fl oz / 125mL) warm wafer
- 1 cup (8 fl oz / 250mL) white vinegar
- 4 eggs, washed

Method

1. Place the egg dye, white vinegar and warm water in a small saucepan and stir to dissolve the dye. Add the eggs and cover with cold water. Heat to boiling and boil for 10 minutes.
2. Remove the eggs and allow to cool. Polish the eggs with a lightly oiled cloth before using.

Wine Notes

This dish call s for a sparkling wine with some sweetness.

FRANCE : Look for a sparkling Vouvray in the sweeter style.

USA : A number of Californian wineries produce ver good sparkling wines, hut steer away from the very dry examples.

AUSTRALIA : Choose from among the many popular sparkling wines labelled "non brut" Yellowglen Crémant and Seaview Grand Guvee are good example.

ITALY : Choose a good demi-ser Spumante from the Piedmont district.

INDONESIA

World Cuisine

INDONESIA

has more than 13000 islands—from Kalimantan (Borneo) to Java and Sumatra—and these islands are fill of magical moments. Watching the sun set over Borobodur, Java's awe-inspiring temple complex, can be a mystical experience. Switch the setting to Jimbaran Bay, one of Bali's least sullied stretches of coastline and you can understand why this lush land has been called: "Morning of the World." You may even be converted to the feeling of a "Grand Plan."

The Indonesians remain a spiritual and traditional people in spite of the modern onslaught of tourism and economic development. Every village has its temples and mosques, with many shops, hotels and even discos featuring shines or portraits of a religious leader. The crowning glory of this culture is a brilliant cuisine as glorious as the sum of its parts: Hindu, Buddhist, Muslim, Chinese and Dutch colonial.

Like all Asians, the Indonesians have a lexicon of rice-centered proverbs, the most famous of which is "It is not a meal unless there is rice." The rich Indonesian soil that produces lush vegetation, rainforests and flowers of staggering beauty is also a god-send for rice-growing, with large areas of Java and Ball producing two too three crops a year. Eating plain steamed rice is an everyday pleasure.

Indonesia is historically most famous as the spice Islands. a tag used today by the huge influx of cruise ships weaving around the country's shores. Far from creating a blindingly hot cuisine, the Indonesians believe in moderation whether trying to achieve pungency, mildness or perfect balance in a dish. Spices that are well known in almost every country—pepper, cilantro(coriander), cloves and cinnamon—are in regular use, but the individuality of Indonesia's culinary heritage comes from the combination of these with such flavorings as lim leaves and salam leaves. These and other spices are routinely teamed with chilies, coconut cream, candlenuts, palm sugar, laos (galangal) and lemon grass to produce the Indonesian trademark: deeply aromatic and fragrant food.

The Indonesians believe that food serves not only to satisfy hunger, but that many foods engender liveliness and well being. Soto—meat-based soups—and other vegetable soups are the core of every meal. Sotos are often served as a mam course, accompanied by plain rice or dumplings.

Vegetable-only dishes feature strongly in the Indonesian diet, a fact confirmed by a casual stroll through any village or city produce market. Indonesian cooks serve up finger-snapping fresh vegetables in a variety of styles, many incorporating coconut milk, chilies and spices. Popular leaf vegetables include amaranth (spinach). Chinese, swamp and flower cabbages and large leaf watercress. Bean sprouts, cucumber, corn, bamboo shoots, yougjackfruit eggplant(aubergine). chayote(choko) and snake beans all qualify as favorites. The famous gado-gado frequently incorporates local leaf plants such as daun lembayung(snake bean leaves), in addition to the familiar line-up of beans, spinach, tomatoes, cucumbers and so on just waiting for the superb accompanying peanut sauce.

Every Visitor to Indonesia quickly notices the ubiquitous presence of the word ikan on restaurant menus, that is, fish. Fish is the number one protein for most of Indonesia's population and even today many people catch their own dinner with a line hanging from the back verandah. Both freshwater and sea fish turn up in a astonishing array of recipes.

Tuna, badeng (a type of salmon trout) and silver bream are sold fresh each day at local markets. Red snapper, squid and small sardines are everyday treats, while shell-fish—crabs, sweet shrimp and lobsterl—represent meals for "big occasions." The meatier fish are often steamed or deep-fried before blending with coconut curry sauces.

While meat is not eaten daily in Indonesia, satay is one of the country's most popular dishes. Meat also features when entertaining lavishly in Selamatan festive feasts, the forerunner of the Dutch banquet-style meal, rijsttafel. Soy sauce and spices are used in seductive marinades for slow-cooking beef dishes. The constant craving for satay dishes makes a charcoal barbecue a staple in Indonesian homes. Bali, the only non-Muslim state of Indonesia, specializes in exquisite, almost Chinese-style pork dishes. Variety meats—tongue, liver and kidney—are also widely eaten throughout the country.

Chickens are almost members of the family in Indonesia but sentimentality doesn't exclude hem turning up on the table, cooked with coconut milk, with chilies and onions, or in curries or satays. For all Indonesian chicken recipes, free-range birds are best for their fuller flavor and firmer flesh.

Relishes, accompaniments and condiments fill out a true Indonesian meal. Nowadays, many of us eat krupuk, the Indonesian rice and prawn crackers, as snacks but they act in Indonesia is important side dishes (similar to bread in other cuisines). Vinegar, sugar and salt are combined with carrots, chilies, celery, beans, cauliflower and cucumber to produce relishes that match closely with rice, chicken or fish dishes.

Sambal ulek and sambal kecap are well known as bottled condiments in Western supermarkets and delicatessens, but Indonesian cooks make their own with a mortar and pestle, and then serve the chili paste direct from the same bowl in which it was ground for immediate freshness.

Tropical fruits tend to rule Indonesian dessert choices. All after-dinner fruits are eaten out of hand—ever-popular bananas in all their varieties, rambutans (similar to lychees), pineapples, mangoes and avocados. Durian, the spiky fruit with the cream cheese interior and the appalling smell, is bought extensively in its frequently expensive season.

Tropical fruits aren't the only dessert options in Indonesia. There are many prepared desserts: soft molds made of palm sugar, agar-agar, coconut cream, milk and eggs lead a repertoire including agar-agar serikaya—a double layer of jelly mold with brown sugar and coconut cream. Steamed bananas and coconut custard are another popular dessert.

No visitor to Indonesia should miss a puppet play, the graceful retelling of ancient Javanese myths. At the very least these intricate and skillful shows draw your attention to the Indonesian philosophy of the importance of a good meal. The grace, litheness and almost supernatural finger movements are similar to the Indonesian ideal of serving an authentic home-cooked meal in the best possible way—by the warmth of the hand.

SOTO AYAM

Spiced Chicken Soup

Soups in Indonesia are not served as a first course, in the Western way. They are eaten, with or without rice, as a meal in themselves, a special between-meals snack or as one of many dishes all served at once. Soto Ayam is popular all over Indonesia, and there are as many versions of it as there are cooks. The use of ginger in this suggests that it originated in Sumatra, where the spice was introduced by Arab traders centuries ago.

SERVES 8

In Indonesia the tough, stringy birds that roam the Villages would have to be simmered far longer than in this recipe, which is for the tender, fat fowls found in Western supermarkets. Remove their skin before cooking or the stock will be too fatty.

Ingredient

2 tablespoons oil
3 garlic cloves, crushed
½ teaspoon chili powder
1 tablespoon cruched candlenuts or macadamia nuts
8 cups (64 fl oz / 2L) water
1 onion, finely chopped
½ inch (1.25cm) piece ginger, finely chopped
1 teaspoon ground cilantro (coriander) seeds
2 lb (1kg) chicken pieces
salt and pepper, to taste

GARNISHES

2 hard-cooked (hard-boiled) eggs, sliced
3 ½ oz (100g) cooked fin noodles
4 scallions (spring onions), chopped

Method

1 Heat the oil in a large saucepan and stir-fry the onion, garlic and ginger for 3 minutes. Stir in the chill powder, cilantro seeds and crushed nuts and cook for 2 minutes.
2 Place the chicken pieces in the saucepan and coat well with the spic mixture. Cook for a few minutes, until the chicken is starting to brown.
3 Pour in the water and season with salt and pepper. Heat to boiling, then reduce the heat and simmer for 45 minutes or until the chicken is tender. Remove the chicken and allow the remaining stock to simmer for 15 minutes.
4 Take the meat from the chicken bones and cut into small pieces.
5 Distribute the chicken meat and garnishes between 8 small soup bowls and top with the chicken stock.
6 Serve hot.

Wine Notes

Wine can be diffiicult to combine with soups as it makes for a high fluid intake for one course. However, a soft fruity white would best suit the rather complex flavors of this dish.

FRANCE : Choose a dry Vouvray, with its gentle, rather honey-like flavor.

USA : Try a Chenin Blanc from the hilly regions of California's wine country.

AUSTRALIA : Like California, Australia produces some very attractive Chenin Blancs; or choose one of the popular "classic dry white" blends.

CHINA : Try Chinese rice wine (shao hsing).

NASI GORENG

Simple Fried Rice

Nasi Goreng is popular throughout Indonesia; most restaurants and cafes feature it on the menu. It was originally a breakfast dish, made with left-over boiled rice. Garnished with a moist fried egg and slices of tomato and cucumber, it is perfect for lunch or supper. This basic recipe is very adaptable, and often includes meat, seafood, vegetables and herbs, depending on the region. West of Jakarta, for example, chicken is a standard ingredient.

SERVES 2~4

The rice for this dish should always be boiled a few hours before it is to be used, and allowed to cool completely.

Ingredient

1 onion, chopped
½ teaspoons shrimp paste
2 fresh red chilies, thinly sliced, seeds discarded
1 tablespoon soy sauce
1 cup cooked shrimp (prawns), optional
1 egg per person
1 tomato, cut into wedges
1 garlic clove
2 tablespoons vegetable oil
4 cups cooked long grain rice
4oz (125g) cooked chicken, diced, optional
2 tablespoons peanut oil
½ cucumber, thinly sliced

Method

1 Blend the onion, garlic and shrimp paste.
2 Heat the oil in a large skillet and stir-fry the paste and chilies for about 1 minute. Stir in the rice and soy sauce and mix until the rice is well coated and heated through.
3 Add the chicken and shrimp, if desired. Check for flavor and add a little salt if necessary. If the rice is too dry a little extra vegetable oil may be added.
4 Heat the peanut oil and lightly fry the eggs. The yolks should still be soft.
5 Serve the rice hot with the fried eggs on top, and garnish with the cucumber slices and the tomato wedges.

Wine Notes

This dish features a combination of such diverse flavors! The "right" wine is anything but obvious. A light, "carbonic maceration" style of red (made by fermenting whole bunches of grapes) may be the answer.

FRANCE : Beaujolais is the archetypal young, fruity, lively yet light red.

USA : Zinfandel and Grenache in California yield some very interesting light wines to be drunk young.

AUSTRALIA : Choose a spicy Shiraz; with carbonic maceration, the wine can be light and soft.

SOUTH AFRICA : Pinotage is peculiar to South Africa; its style is soft and fruity.

SAYUR LODEH SAMA ABON DAGING

Vegetables in Coconut Milk with Crisp Shredded Beef

"Sayur" is a term for vegetable dishes cooked in a coconut milk stock.

Like the soups, they are often served with rice as part of a larger meal. The vegetables in this recipe, like many used in Indonesia, have Dutch names—indicating perhaps that they were introduced centuries ago in colonial times.

Abon Daging evolved because the toughness and strong flavor of Indonesian beef required robust spicing and long cooking times.

SAYUR LODEH

SERVES 4

This dish is supposed to have a soupy consistency. Other vegetables may be substituted if preferred.

Ingredient

1 tablespoon all
2 garlic cloves, crushed
1 tablespoon ground cilantro (coriander) seeds
1 teaspoon shrimp paste
2 salam leaves or 4 curry leaves
½ cup (4oz / 125g) green beans, cut into 1 inch (2.5 cm) pieces
1 chayote (choko), peeled and diced
3 ½ oz (100g) Chinese cabbage leaves, finely shredded
1 onion, sliced
2 flesh red chilies, finely chopped, seeds discarded
1 inch (2.5cm) piece ginger, finely chopped
1 ½ cups (12 fl oz / 375mL) coconut milk
2 small eggplants (aubergines), about 4oz (125g) each, sliced
1 small tomato, peeled and diced
salt, to taste

Method

1 Heat the oil in a large saucepan, add the onion garlic and saute for 3 minutes. Stir in the chilies, chilantro seeds, shrimp paste, ginger and salam leaves, and stir-fry for 2 minutes.
2 Stir in the coconut milk and heat to boiling. Add all the vegetables except the cabbage and simmer until the vegetables are almost cooked. about 10 minutes.
3 Stir in the cabbage, season with salt and allow to simmer for another 3 minutes.
4 Serve hot.

ABON DAGING

MAKES ABOUT 4 CUPS

Abon Daging is often used as a garnish or served as a side dish. If galangal is unavailable, substitute fresh young ginger.

Ingredient

1 lb (500g) top round (topside) beef
2 garlic cloves, crushed
1 cup (8 fl oz / 250mL) water
1 medium onion, grated

½ teaspoon galangal powder
½ teaspoon ground cumin
1 tablespoon tamarind water (see glossary) or 2 tablespoons lemon Juice
½ cup (4 fl oz / 125mL) vegetable oil
1 tablespoon ground cilantro (coriander)
salt and pepper, to taste
2 tablespoons brown sugar
½ cup (4 fl oz / 125mL) coconut cream

Method

1 Trim the fat from the meat and cut into large cubes. Place the meat and the water in a saucepan with a tight-fitting lid. Boil the meat for about 1 hour, or until it is very tender. It may be necessary to add a little water occasionally to prevent the meat from boiling dry.
2 Drain the meat well, then beat it flat with a meat mallet and shred it with a fork to produce single fibers.
3 Place the shredded meat and all the remaining ingredients except the oil in a large skillet and cook over medium heat, stirring occasionally until all the coconut cream is absorbed.
4 Stir in the oil and stir-fly the meat until it becomes golden brown and crisp. Remove from heat. Allow the meat to cool slightly, then place it between sheets of paper towel and press to absorb any excess oil. Allow it to cool completely.
5 Spoon into an airtight container and refrigerate until needed. Abon Daging will keep for 3 to 4 weeks in the refrigerator.

GALANGAL Known as kha in Thailand and laos in Indonesia, galangal (Alpinia galangal) is a close relative of the ginger plant. A semitropical plant, it is native to Southeast Asia and China and has been in use as a herb (and sometimes an aphrodisiac) for at least a thousand years. Smooth-skinned and deep buff in color, galangal resembles ginger but is more delicate and fragrant In flavor. It is used extensively in Southeast Asian and food stores. If fresh rhizomes are unavailable, dried galangal and preserved galangal are acceptable substitutes. Dried galangal is sold in slices that should be reconstituted in hot water, for 1 hour before using. It is also available in powder from.

Wine Notes

The aromatic nature of this dish calls for a white wine with similar qualities.

FRANCE : Choose white wines from the regions of Alsace and Vouvray.

USA : Try a traditionally fruity Johannisberg Riesling from the Napa Valley or one of the more flavorsome whites of the Pacific Northwest.

AUSTRALIA : Choose from the soft grapey Rhine Rieslings of the Barossa Valley or from the fine examples made in the Great Southern Region of Western Australia.

GERMANY : Select one of the white wines from around the villages of Neirstein and Oppenheim in the Rheinhessen.

GADO GADO

Salad with peanut sauce

Raw and cooked vegetables with a spicy peanut sauce offer a delightful combination of textures and flavors in this classic salad. It is popular throughout Indonesia. Gado Gado may be served hot in winter and at room temperature in summer. It can be eaten on its own as a light lunch, in combination with rice and other side dishes as a full meat, or as a salad dish at a rijsttafel.

SERVES 4~6

Prawn crackers, or krupuk, are large crispy slices made from dried prawns. They are usually available, ready to eat, in Asian grocery stores. Alternatively you may buy them uncooked, as small translucent disks, and prepare them at home.

Ingredient

PEANUT SAUCE

2 tablespoons vegetable oil
1~2 teaspoons chill powder
1 cup ground roasted peanuts or 1 cup peanut butter
1 tablespoon vinegar
1 onion, finely chopped
2 ½ cups (20 fl oz / 625mL) water
salt, to taste
1 teaspoon sugar

SALAD

6 uncooked prawn crackers
½ medium cucumber, sliced
6 lettuce leaves
2 potatoes, boiled, peeled and sliced
½ cup (4oz / 125g) green beans, cut into 2 inches (5cm) piece and blanched
vegetable oil, for deep-frying
3 ½ oz (100g) been sprouts
2 carrots, sliced lengthwise and blanched
2 cabbage leaves, blanched and sliced
2 tomatoes, cut into wedges
3 hard-cooked (hard-boiled) eggs, sliced

Method

1 To make the sauce, heat the oil in a saucepan, add the onion and saute until transparent. Add the chill powder and stir-fry for about 30 seconds.
2 Stir in the water and peanuts and gradually heat to boiling, stirring often. Allow to simmer for about 5 minutes, or until the mixture is smooth.
3 Season with the salt, vinegar and sugar.
4 Deep-fry the prawn crackers singly in the vegetable oil. If they sink to the bottom the oil is too cool-they should puff up as soon as they touch the oil. Remove quickly before they brown.
5 Drain the prawn crackers well on paper towel, then break into small pieces.
6 Arrange all the other salad ingredients on a large platter.
7 Pour the sauce over the vegetables and sprinkle with the prawn crackers.

PEANUTS Although generally thought of as a nut, the peanut is actually a legume. Also known as the ground nut or monkey nut, it grows underground on the roots of Arachis hypogaea, in a way that is similar to how potatoes grow. The outer shell of the peanut is actually the dried pod of the plant. The plant is native to Brazil and now thrives in many tropical countries, especially India and parts of China. Peanuts have been found in tombs almost 3000 years old. Raw or roasted, the nuts can be caten by themselves as a snack or they can he chopped and used in a variety of dishes, ranging from salad to ice cream. Peanuts are skinned, roasted and ground to make peanut butter and are also the basis of satay sauce. The nuts are rich in protein and high in monounsaturated oil. This oil is extracted and sold as peanut or groundnut oil, and is widely used in cooking and salad dressings. Peanuts are sold in many forms: in the shell; shelled, with or without their skins; and roasted, salted or unsalted. If they are to be kept lor a long time, they are best bought in the shell. Discard any moldy peanuts—they may be toxic.

Wine Notes

This dish is a challenge to any winemaster! A dry medium dry white or a very light fruity red would be the best options to pursue.

FRANCE : Try a beaujolais, or perhaps a Rose from he Loire Valley.

USA : Select a light, perhaps rose slyle of Grenache or Zinfandel.

AUSTRALIA : The zesty Colombard whites from South Australian regions such as Southern Vales would provide liveliness of flavor.

ITALY : Choose a “frizzante” style of white(style spritzig), such as a good Frascati.

BAHMI GORENG

Stir-fried Noodles

The noodles in this dish are an indicator of its Chinese origins, as are the chopsticks with which it is eaten. Indonesians traditionally ate most dishes with their fingers (right hand only!) although tables nowadays are commonly set with spoon and fork. Bahmi Goreng is served on its own as a snack or light meal. The preparation method stays the same, but the ingredients can vary greatly; it can include vegetables only, or a range of seafood.

BAHMI GORENG

SERVES 4~6

To shred the omelette, first cool, then roll up and cut into strips using a very sharp knife.

Ingredient

12oz (375g) dried egg noodles
3 tablespoons oil
3 garlic cloves, crushed
1 small chicken breast fillet, cut into strips
4oz (125g) shrimp (prawns), peeled, cleaned and halved
½ cup sugar peas (snow peas / mange-tout)
¼ cup Goreng Bawang (see recipe)
2 eggs; lightly beaten
3 onions, thinly sliced
4oz (125g) sirloin (rump) steak, cut into thin strips
2 tablespoons soy sauce
½ cup (4 fl oz / 125mL) chicken stock
½ cup bean sprouts

Method

1 Cook the noodles in a large saucepan half-filled with boiling salted water. Boil for about 5 minutes, or until the noodles are Just cooked. Rinse with cold water and drain well.
2 Pour the eggs into a heated non-stick pan and cook for about 3 minutes, or until the omelette is lightly set. Carefully slide from the pan.
3 Allow the omelette to cool, then cut it into thin strips.
4 Heat the oil in a large wok or skillet and stir-fry for about 5 minutes, or until the meat is cooked through and the shrimp are opaque.
5 Stir m the sugar peas and bean sprouts and continue cooking until they are well heated, but not overcooked.
6 Mix in the noodles and heat through, adding seasoning to taste.
7 Serve topped with the omelette strips and Goreng Bawang.

GORENG BAWANG

Crisp Fried Onion Flakes

Onions flakes are often served as a garnish to Indonesian dishes. For convenience it is a good idea to make a large quantity and store in a sealed container until needed. To ensure onion flakes retain their crispness, do not store until quite cold. If they do become a little "flabby," they can be recrisped by heating on an oven tray in a moderate oven (350°F / 180℃) for about 1.5 minutes, then draining on paper towels again.

Method

1 Slice desired amount of onions very thinly. One cup of sliced raw onions will make about ¾ cup of Goreng Bawang.
2 Heat enough oil in a pan to cover the onions. When hot, add the onions and fry, stirring frequently.
3 Reduce heat and slowly fry the onions until they are golden brown.
4 Drain well and place on paper towels to extract excess oil.
5 Sprinkle over Bahmi Goreng or cool and store until required.

EGG NOODLES China is thought to be the place of Asian egg noodles and wheat noodles. The egg noodles (made with wheat flour and egg) have only been around for a short time (about 400 years) compared to wheat noodles (made with wheat flour and water), which are believed to date black about 2000 years. Egg noodles feature in the cuisine of many Asian countries. They are a brighter yellow in color than wheat noodles, and are produced in a variety of thicknesses. Like wheat noodles, they can be cooked in boiling salted water and served soft; they can also be boiled, then fried in a little oil and served crisp. Egg noodles and wheat noodles are available fresh and dried; the fresh ones will keep for several days in the refrigerator

Wine Notes

A lightish to medium soft red would accommodate the unusual combination of chicken, beef and seafood in this dish.

FRANCE : Choose a red wine of Macon or a lightish vin de pays.

USA : Much Pinot Noir is produced in the US these days; try a good quality, medium-range example, rather than a "designer" model.

AUSTRALIA : Merlot and Malbec are usually soft and medium-bodied in Australia, when thev are not blended with other varieties. Select one from McLaren vale or the Riverland in South Australia.

ITALY : Dolcetto d'Alba, from the Piedmont region, is one of Italy's most appealing soft and fruity reds.

SATAY AYAM SAMA NASI GURIH

Chicken Satay with Fragrant Coconut Rice

It Is not known whether the Chinese or the Muslims first introduced Indonesia to the idea of cooking piece of meat on skewers. Whichever was the case, the Indonesians refined the concept, marinating the meat before cooking it and serving it with a spicy peanut sauce. Satays make a delicious complete meal when served with Nasih Gurih, a spice-laden rice dish popular over much of Indonesia.

SATAY AYAM

SERVES 4

To prevent wooden satay sticks from charring as the chicken cooks, soak them in cold water for several hours before using.

Ingredient

1 lb (500g) chicken breast fillets, skinned
1 teaspoon brown sugar
2 tablespoons lemon juice
Peanut Sauce (see Gado Gado)
3 tablespoons soy sauce
1 small onion, finely chopped
¼ teaspoon chili powder

Method

1 Cut the chicken into ¾ inch (2cm) cubes.
2 Combine the soy sauce, brown sugar, onion, lemon juice and chili powder. Add the chicken pieces, stir, and allow to marinate for a couple of hours.
3 Thread the chicken onto satay sticks, and place under a hot broiler (griller). Cook until golden brown, about 3 to 4 minutes each side. (Alternatively the satays can be cooked on a barbecue over coals, which is a more traditional technique.) Baste the satays with the marinade during cooking.
4 Serve the satays with the heated Peanut Sauce and the Nasi Gurih.

NASI GURIH

SERVES 4~6

Curry leaves are given first preference here, rather than salam leaves. However, if fresh salam leaves are available, do give them a try. They can sometimes be found in Asian supermarkets. Salam leaves are larger and softer than curry leaves.

Ingredient

2 ¾ cups(22 fl oz / 700mL) fresh or canned coconut milk
¼ teaspoon ground cloves
½ teaspoon cinnamon
2 curry leaves or 1 salam leaf
1 teaspoon salt
¼ teaspoon freshly ground black pepper
½ teaspoon nutmeg
1 teaspoon chopped lemon grass
2 cup (11oz / 340g) long grain rice

Method

1 Place all the ingredients except the rice in a large saucepan and heat to boiling, stirring constantly.
2 Add the rice and continue to stir until boiling, then reduce heat a little and cover with a tight-fitting lid. Simmer for 20 minutes.
3 Remove from heat, stir, replace the lid and allow to stand for 5 minutes. Remove the curry leaves and serve.

CURRY LEAVES The curry leaf comes from the curry leaf tree (Murraya koenigii), an evergreen that is native to India and Sri Lanka. The tree's leaves are small, dark green and glossy, with a strong pungent aroma.
Curry leaves are used In some prepared curry mixes. In Western countries they can sometimes be bought fresh or frozen, but are more likely to be found dried.
The dried leaves are sold in many Asian grocery stores. If using fresh curry leaves, tear them to release the volatile oils which give them their flavor. The flesh leaves can be stored in the refrigerator in plastic wrap. To prevent loss of flavor and aroma, store dried curry leaves in a tightly sealed container.

Wine Notes

A flavorsome, perhaps wood-aged, white would go nicely with this traditional satay.

FRANCE : The regions of Macon and Chalon provide many dry, full-bodies whites, such as Macon-Villages, Saint-Veren and Rully.

USA : The nutty flavors of Mapa Valley. Chardonnay, especially a cook-matured style, would provide the right note.

AUSTRALIA : Select a good bak-matured Semillon or Charonnay from the Hunter valley.

SPAIN : Spain produces many robust dry whites. One of the best types is the White Rioja.

PANGEK BUNGKUR

Fish in Banana Leaves, Padang Style

As one might expert from a country of over 3000 islands, fish features prominently in Indonesian cuisine. And not just in coastal areas; many inland villages have well-stocked ponds where fish is bred lor the table. At some restaurants diners may choose their fish as it swims in a pond, to be netted and cooked over a charcoal fire. This dish is often served as the centerpiece at formal meals in Padang, a seaport in western Indonesia.

SERVES 4

For generations banana leaves have been used for this type of cooking; however, in the same way that modern cooks use a food processor rather than a mortar and pestle, lightly oiled aluminum foil can be substituted for the leaves. If you prefer the traditional method, you will find banana leaves in most Asian supermarkets.

Ingredient

2 lb (1kg) whole bream or snapper, cleaned
2 large onions, roughly chopped
5 candlenuts or macadamia nuts
2 Inches (5cm) piece ginger
banana leaves
I stalk lemon grass, finely shredded
4 scallions (spring onions), cut in 2 inches (5cm) pieces
¼ teaspoon salt
2 garlic cloves
8 red chilies, halved. seeds discarded
¼ teaspoon turmeric
I tablespoon chopped basil
2 small tomatoes, sliced

Method

1 Preheat the oven to 350°F (180℃)
2 Dry the fish well with paper towels. Score the fish diagonally on both Sides and season with the salt.
3 Place the onions. garlic, nuts red chilies, ginger and turmeric into a food processor, and pulse to create a smooth paste. Rub this paste onto the outside of the fish and into the cavity.
4 Lay out enough banana leaves to envelop the whole fish and arrange half of the basil lemon grass, tomato slices and scallion pieces on the banana leaves.
5 Place the fish on top and arrange the remaining ingredients on the fish. Wrap the banana leaves around everything, securing with toothpicks.
6 Place in a shallow baking pan and bake for 35 minutes.
7 Place on a serving platter. Turn back the banana leaves before serving.

CANDLENUTS Known as kemiri in Indonesia and buah keras (hard shell) in Malaysia, candlenuts come from the clandleberry tree (Aleurites moluccana). This large tree, growing to 60 feet (18 meters), is native to eastern Asia and some of the Pacific Islands. Originally introduced to Hawaii by the Polynesians, it is now an important element of the vegetation there. In fact, in 1959 the candlenut was adopted as Hawaii's state tree. At one time the people of what is now known as Indonesia burned the kernels of these nuts, using them as a primitive type of clandle; hence the name. "candlenuts." They are also known as kekuni, kemiri or lumbang oil—is widely used as a drying agent and varnish, and plays an essential part in the paint and gum industries. In Indonesia today candlenuts are used to thicken and flavor curries. They are also a good energy source, and in some areas, particularly Java, Candlenuts are often sold at Asian nuts can be used necessary, as they are quite smilar in texture.

Candlenuts should be stored in a cool, dry place in a container with a tight-fitting lid. In these conditions they will keep for some months.

Wine Notes

A white wine, dry hut with sufficient "punch" of its own to match the Spicy, herby flavors, would he appropriate with this dish.

FRANCE : Choose from the drier whites of the Loire-Valley, particularly Sancerre or Pouilly Fume.

USA : Select a young Fume Blanc from the Napa or Sonoma areas of California.

AUSTRALIA : Many Australian regions produce excellent Sauvignon Blancs and Sauvignon -Semillon blends; Western Australian examples are particularly good.

ITALY : Try the spicy Pinot Grigio from the north of Italy.

GULAI KAMBING SAMA SAMBLAS

Lamb Curry with Samhals

In Indonesia, curries are made up m large quantities and used throughout the week with different accompaniments: boiled or fhed rice, noodles, cucumber salad, or a variety of sambals. This mild curry is a specialty of Sumatra, where the cuisine is generally spicier than In other parts of Indonesia; a dash of heat is supplied instead by the sambals—the very got condiments that are served as accompaniments 10 most Indonesian dishes.

GULAI KAMBING

SERVES 6

Gently spicy, this dish, like most crries, improves with reheating. Shoulder of lamb is a good choice of meat for this recipe.

Ingredient

1 tablespoon cilantro (coriander) seeds
1 teaspoon turmeric
¼ teaspoon nutmeg
3 tablespoons vegetable oil
2 garlic cloves, crushed
1 stalk lemon grass, cut into 3 inches (7.5cm) pieces
2 lb (1kg) lean lamb, diced
salt, to taste
1 teaspoon cumin seeds
1 tablespoon chili powder
2 inches (5cm) piece ginger, sliced
2 onions, sliced
1 cinnamon stick
3 cloves
2 tomatoes, peeled and chopped
3 cups (24 fl oz / 750mL) fresh or canned coconut milk

Method

1 Using a mortar and pestle or a food processor, grind together the cilantro seeds, cumin seeds, turmeric, chili, nutmeg and ginger to form a paste.
2 Heat the oil in a large saucepan and fly the onion and garlic until they start to brown. Add the paste, cinnamon stick, lemon grass and cloves and stir-fry for 3 minutes. Add the lamb and brown on all sides,
3 Stir in the tomatoes and cook over moderate heat until soft. Season with the salt.
4 Add the coconut milk and slowly heat to boiling, then reduce heat and allow to simmer until the meat is tender, about 40 to 45 minutes, stirring occasionally.
5 Remove the cinnamon stick. Serve with your choice of accompaniments.

SAMBAL KELAPA

Coconut Condiment

MAKES ⅓ CUP

Ingredient

1 tablespoon thinly sliced red bell pepper (capsicum)
½ garlic clove
pinch salt
¼ cup (1oz / 30g) grated fresh coconut (remove brown outer skin before grating)
1 small red chili, thinly sliced, seeds discarded
½ inch (1cm) piece salam leaf or 1 curry leaf
pinch sugar

Method

1 Place all ingredients except the coconut into a mortar and pestle and grind until a smooth paste is formed. (A food processor can be used if preferred.)
2 Mix in the grated fresh coconut and press lightly with the pestle to mix.
3 Spoon into a jar and seal well. Store in the refrigerator until needed. It will keep for several days.

SAMBAL IADA UDANG KERING

Dried Shrimp Sambal

MAKES 1 ¾ CUPS

Ingredient

⅔ cup dried shrimp(prawns)
2 onions, thinly sliced
2 tablespoons lemon juice
½ cup (4 fl oz / 125mL) peanut oil
4 oz (125g) red chilies
salt

Method

1 Soak the shrimp in hot water for 10 minutes or until tender, then drain well and grind (mince) or chop finely.
2 Heat the oil in a skillet and stir-fry the onions until golden brown.
3 Place the chilies in a food processor and pulse until well ground. Add the chilies to the onions and cook for 2 to 3 minutes. Add the lemon juice and the shrimp, season well with salt and allow to simmer for 10 minutes.
4 When the mixture is cool spoon it into a Jar, seal well and refrigerate until needed. It will keep for about 2 weeks. If it dries out stir in a little oil.

SAMBAL ULEK

Chili Paste

MAKES ½ CUP

Ingredient

- 8~10 red chiles (use dried if fresh chilies are not available)
- 1 teaspoon brown sugar
- 1 teaspoon chopped lemon grass
- 2 tablespoons peanut oil
- 1 small onion
- 2 garlic cloves
- 2 tablespoons water
- ½ teaspoon salt

Method

1 Place all the ingredients except the oil in a food processor and process to form a smooth paste.
2 Heat the oil in a small pan and stir in the paste. Allow to simmer for about 8 minutes.
3 When the mixture is cool, spoon it into a Jar and seal well. Store the sambal in the refrigerator until needed. It will keep for at least 1 month.

TURMERIC Turmeric(Curcuma domestica) is a leafy plant which has an aromatic golden or orange rhizome (knbby root) that is used in cooking. It belongs to the same family as ginger and is thought to have originated in southern Asia. The rhizome is dried and ground to create yellow turmeric powder, which is used to add both color and flavor to mustard, pickles, chutney and curries. Its distinctive flavor is found in many Indonesian dishes. Although sometimes called Indian saffron, it should not be used as a substitute for the very expensive true saffron as its flavor is quite different.

Wine Notes

Matching wine to curries is reallv a matter of personal preference. Try fruity, aromatic whites

FRANCE : The wines of Alsace (including Gewurztraminer, of course) are scented and attractive. A dry Muscat from this region would also be excellent.

USA : Choose a Gewurztraminer from the cooler wine districts, such as the Anderson Valley of Mendocino, Sonoma and the Edna Valley.

AUSTRALIA : Try the soft, fruity blends of Rhine Riesling and Traminer, especiallv those from the Barossa Valley.

GERMANY : Select a Kabinett or Halbtrocken style from the Rhine and Mosel Valleys.

AGAR-AGAR SERIKAYA

Agar-Agar Coconut Pudding

After the rich spread of a traditional Indonesian meal, dessert is usually restricted to fresh fruit. Not that this is a restriction; Indonesia abounds with a staggering variety of fruits. Sweets such as this are likely to be served with fruit on a special occasion. They can also be eaten as snacks with tea or coffee. This dessert is particularly attractive, separating as if sets into two layers: a transparent top layer and a creamy, opaque lower layer.

SERVES 6~8

The distinctive flavor and aroma of pandanus plays an important role in this dessert. Fresh pandanus leaf works best, but a dried leaf or pandanus extract can be substituted if necessary.

Ingredient

5 cups (40 fl oz / 1.25L) water
1 cup (5 ½ oz / 170g) brown sugar
1 small cinnamon stick
2 cups (16 fl oz / 500mL) coconut cream
¼ teaspoon salt
your choice of fresh fruit
1 tablespoon agar-agar powder
1 teaspoon aniseed
4 inches (10cm) piece pandanus leaf or ½ teaspoon pandanus extract
4 eggs, beaten

Method

1 Pour the water into a large saucepan and sprinkle over the agar-agar powder Stir in the brown sugar, aniseed, cinnamon stick and pandanus leaf and heat to boiling, stirring until the agar-agar has dissolved.
2 Add the coconut cream and salt and allow the mixture to boil.
3 Remove from the heat and allow to cool a little. Strain the mixure into the beaten eggs and whisk together. Pour into an 8 cups (65 fl oz / 2L) mold and refrigerate until set.
4 Unmold onto a serving platter and decorate with fresh fruits before serving.

Wine Notes

A dessert wine is clearly called for here, and many countries have wonderful sweet wines.

FRANCE : The almost Sautermes-like Monbazillac from near Bordeaux is amply rich and sweet.

USA : Try any of the attractive dessert wines being made from a number of different (and sometimes unusual) vaneties in many regions.

AUSTRALIA : One of the many botrytis-affected Rieslings and Semillons would be excellent. The Tuscios dessert Semillons from around Griffith are often outstanding.

PORTUGAL : Try the fragrant Moscato de Setúbal; it may not be easy to find, but it would be worth searching for.

NASI TUAI

Glutinous Rice with a Sweet Creamy Sauce

Rice for breakfast, lunch, dinner and even dessert—a staple food indeed. Rice is the basis of the Indonesian diet. Glutinous rice, also called sticky rice, is used for many Indonesian desserts. Fragrant with spices and sugar, these delicious "rice puddings" are a world away from bland nursery food. Nasi Tuai is rich with coconut flavors. Traditionally cooked in an iron pot, it is often served at the morning break during th harvest.

SERVES 6

Glutinous rice has fat grains that become sweet and sticky when boiled one of the few occasions when "gummy" rice is what the cook actually hope to achieve! Glutinous rice, white or black, is a major ingredient in many Asian recipes and is readily available in Asian grocery stores. If you cannot find it, substitute short-grain rice and cook it to the "gummy" stage, though the texture will be different.

Ingredient

RICE
2 cups (11oz / 340g) glutinous rice
pinch salt
2 ½ cups (20 fl oz / 625mL) water
1 cup (8 fl oz / 250mL) coconut cream

SAUCE
2oz (60g) brown sugar
1 cinnamon stick
2 cups (16 fl oz / 500mL) coconut milk
pinch salt

Method

1 Soak the rice in water overnight. then wash the rice under cold running water until the water runs clear.
2 Place the rice, water and salt in a large saucepan and heat to boiling. Cook until all the water has been absorbed, stirring frequently.
3 Stir in the coconut cream, then spoon the rice into a steamer. Steam for about 15 minutes, until the rice is very tender.
4 To make the sauce, combine all the ingredients in a saucepan and heat to boiling. Reduce the heat and allow to simmer for 3 minutes. Remove the cinnamon stick before serving.
5 Serve the glutinous rice in individual bowls, topped with the creamy sauce.

Wine Notes

Traditional fruit Juice beverages seem the most appropriate choice, but a light, sweet, perhaps fortified wine could be a satisfactory partner.

USA : Try one of the various light sweet wines from the Central Valley area in California. Some of these are based on Madeira and other traditional, European sweet wine style.

FRANCE : Try a Beaumes-de-Venise Muscat from the Rhone Valley in the south of France.

AUSTRALIA : Choose a light fortified Frontignac or one of the dessert-style Muscats.

SPAIN : Select a pale, golden cream-style sherry.

ITALY

World Cuisine

ITALY is everyone's second country. When most of us visit Rome for the first time a feeling of familiarity as much as wonder floods over us. Many of us have, since childhood, imagined a visit to the Basilica of St Peter's, the Capitol, the Forum and the Via Veneto without dense traffic or crowded narrow streets to sully the dream. Rome is best explored in parts in order to pick up on the many subtleties of Roman life as comfortably as possible while immersing in the city's daily rhythms where much of the beat is attuned to the knife and fork.

Roman cuisine is not for the diet conscious traveler: a full meal for one m Rome would be fine for two anywhere else. Restaurants run the gamut of prices from the wildly expensive to the prize collection of economical trattorias in rapidly gentrifying Trastevere, the true home of Roman food. The visitor finds a cross-section of Italian cooking m Rome, from pizza to polenta, but many dishes do have an authentic "Made in Rome" stamp, descnbed as "alla Romana" on the menu.

Herbs and spices are used sparingly in Roman cuisine. Mozzarella, the cheese best known in foreign kitchens as a pizza topping, stars in many dishes. Another well-known cheese of the area is ricotta alla romana, which is made from whey and looks like cottage or farmer's cheese.

The artichokes, celery, lettuces and beans that you find in Roman markets are exceptional, thanks to the rich volcanic soil of the surrounding Lazio countryside. The area also abounds in sheep, suckling kid and lamb, which Pecorino, an ewe's milk cheese perfect for finishing off any meal.

Florence is the capital of Tuscany, one of Italy's largest regions, and the tentacles of Florentine and Tuscan cooking spread through ten provinces from the foothills of the Appenninto to the flat Arno Valley. Thehilly land is smothered with olive trees that provide the region's famous green olive oil. Along with regular Italian ingredients, the markets of Tuscany are lavish with regional specialties such as prosciutto ham, soprasesseta (a hard, aged sausage eaten raw), eels, dried white beans and armfuls of the armfuls of the aromatic herbs used for such dishes as the acclaimed roast pork.

Tomatoes, richly married with garlic and herbs, are the basis of many Tuscan dishes, while fagioli bianchi, the white beans Catherine de Medici took with her ti France on her marriage, turn on in many dishes, including the famous minestrone.

To the north of Tuscany lies Emilia Romagna and its capital Bologna, a region as famous in Italy for its food as Burgundy is in France. Bologna's name is immortalized in bologna sausage and bolognese sauce is used for such famous pasta creations as spaghetti alla bolognese and lasagne. Chianti, the noblest wine of Tuscany, is a perfect partner for these hearty dishes.

The scenic coastline of northwest Italy is as much a pleasure for the stomach as for the eye. Seafood is paramount on the Ligurian coast: fisherman at Genoa and other coastal towns haul in copious quantities of red mullet, mackerel, shrimp, calamaretti(baby squid) and bianchetti(very tiny white fish). Fromthe hillsides overhanging the sea come the key ingredients of the staples used by Ligurian cooks: olive oil and pesto.

Pesto sauce, invented in Genoa. is a deeply penetrating blend of chopped basil leaves. grated Parmesan cheese, pine nuts and olive oil. Genoa is also famous for the invention of ravioli which is now popular everywhere in Italy and superb with a light dousing of basil-flavored tomato sauce. Focaccia is originally a Ligurian specialty, a flatbread utilizing the light olive oil of the region, sage and cheese.

Situated in the heart of Lombardy is Milan. the northwest's most opulent city. Its cuisinmatches its operatic, fashion and cultural virtues in the elegant and homely restaurants found throughout the city. The classic rice dish, risotto alia milanese, offers the golden elegance of saffron tinting at its best and the Milanese claim to have invented the first and finest minestrone. Ossobuco, the succulent tomato and veal casserole, is often served with gremolata, a harmony of lemon, parsley and garlic panettone has become a traditional Christmas cake throughout Italy—a large, slightly sweet bread, with flecks of candied fruits, citrus peels and raisins.

Naples, located in the heart of the rich farming country of Campania and well provided with local wines, cheese and sausages, has evolved a style of cooking more colorful and more highly seasoned than the creamy cooking of the north.

The interior of Campania combines with the ever-present sunshine produce some of Italy's prime grade fruit and vegetables. The tomato, particularly, grows lavishly here. Tomato sauce s the base for pizza, Naples' gift to the world, and here eggplant (aubergine) is often treated like lasagne and layered with a tomato sauce and Mozzarella and sprinkled with Parmesan cheese.

Naples has also produced many unique fish dishes, including a spicy meal-in-one of fish, garlic, chilies, tomatoes and parsley finished off with a topping of toasted bread.

Sicilian cooking has been influenced by every culture that invaded the island-Greek, Roman, Arab, Norman, German and French. Sicily sports almost tropical vegetables in Italian markets are recognized as the first sign of spring. Pasta with fish is a distinct Sicilian cooking theme. But it is in the dessert department that Sicily enjoys greatest fame. Richricotta desserts are famous far beyond the island's confines, and ice cream, ices and sherbets are credited to Sicily. Almond nougat and sugar marzipan also help to satisfy the sweet tooth.

Restaurants and trattorias crowed the walkways and canals of Venice offering up the many rich and varied specialties that make up the local cuisine. Nothing is more typical of Venice than the fish restaurants that dot each neighborhood the fish are cooked in traditional ways—deep-fried, or broiled on a white-hot charcoal fire.

Polenta, a dish of cooked cornmeal, sometimes baked with cheese, is a constant everywhere in Italy but it is a special treat in the corn-growing Veneto, the region that surrounds Venice. Extremely versatile, polenta blends superbly well with countless meat, gane and fish dishes. It can be eaten with or without sauce but "with" is definitely superior. The cooking of Venice, and of all Italy, is the legacy of the grandest of pasts. A past kept gloriously alive at the grassroots level by the superb farmers' markets that thrive not only in country areas but also in cities like Rome, Florence and Venice. These picturesque open-air food the surrounding countryside still provide the sort of scene that made one early English traveler describe Italy is the epicure's heaven.

ANTIPASTI

Appetizers

Antipasto is the first course of a formal Italian dinner normally served at home on Sundays or special occasions. It can include fresh, pickled and cooked vegetables, meat and cheese—presented hot or cold. In Italian restaurants the antipasti are often displayed on a table near the entrance to stimulate the diner's palate. The choice of antipasti is endless. Regional specialties abound: the stuffed artichoke here is typical of Liguria.

CARCIOFI RIPIENI

stuffed Artichokes

SERVES 6

This is a seasonal dish, with artichokes only available in the fall in most regions. Look for artichokes that are not too large and are a bright, uniform green color. The "leaves" should be firm and unshrivelled.

Ingredient

1 ½ cups (3oz / 90g) fresh bread crumbs
1 large onion, finely chopped
3 tablespoons finely chopped parsley
⅓ teaspoon freshly ground black pepper
approximately ½ cup (4 fl oz / 125mL) virgin olive oil.
1 cup (4oz / 125g) grated Parmesan cheese
2 garlic cloves, finely chopped
⅓ teaspoon salt
6 large globe artichokes

Method

1. Combine the bread crumbs with the cheese, onion, garlic, salt and pepper and mix wall. Set a side.
2. Trim the stem end from the artichokes. With sharp scissors, remove about 1 inch (2.5cm) from the tip of the coarse outer leaves. Discard any really tough outer leaves.
3. Rinse the artichokes in cold water and drain upside down for about 10 minutes. Gently spread leaves and insert a spoonful of the bread crumb mixture onto each leaf. Pour a little olive oil over the filling.
4. Arrange the artichokes in a saucepan just large enough to hold them. Add enough hot water to reach halfway up the artichokes, and add 2 tablespoons of the olive oil to the water.
5. Heat to boiling, then cover the saucepan, reduce heat and simmer for about 40 minutes or until the artichokes are tender. (Test the base of the artichoke with a skewer or cake tester; it is cooked if the flesh is tender.) Carefully remove from the saucepan and allow to cool.
6. Serve at room temperature.

MELANZANE ALLA NAPOLETANA

Eggplant Neapolitan Style

SERVES 4

If necessary, chill the Bel Paese until it is firm enough to grate or slice.

Ingredient

3 eggplants(aubergines), thickly sliced crosswise salt
½ teaspoon sugar
½ cup (2oz / 60g) Bel Paese cheese, thinly sliced or coarsely grated.
½ teaspoon salt
½ cup (2oz / 60g) grated Parmesan cheese
flour
olive oil
1 ¾ cups (14 fl oz / 430mL) tomato puree
½ cup (2oz / 60g) Mozzarella cheese, thinly sliced or coarsely grated.
½ teaspoon freshly ground black pepper

Method

1 Sprinkle the eggplant slices with salt, then leave for at least 30 minutes. Rinse well and pat dry.
2 Preheat the oven to 350°F (180℃).
3 Flour each eggplant slice lightly. Cover the base of a large skillet generously with olive oil. Heat the olive oil and cook the eggplant on the both sides over moderate heat until golden. Add extra oil as needed. Drain the cooked eggplant on paper towels
4 Stir the sugar into the tomato puree.
5 In a casserole dish, layer the eggplant, Bel Paese and Mozzarella cheese, and tomato puree mixture, sprinkling with salt and pepper. Parmesan and bake in the oven for 30 minutes, or until the topping is golden and the dish is bubbling.

PUREA DA FAVE

Puree of Broad Beans

SERVES 4

This recipe is best made with fresh beans, but dried beans, soaked overnight and simmered until soft, may be substituted. This puree is delicious spread on Italian bread.

Ingredient

1 lb (500g) shelled broad beans
2 small onions, diced
½ cup (4 fl oz / 125mL) virgin ollve oil
3 small potatoes, cut into chunks
½ teaspoon salt
salt and pepper, to taste

Method

1 Place the beans in a heavy-based saucepan, add enough cold water to cover and heat to boiling. Boil for 5 minutes, then drain and rinse the beans and return them to the saucepan.
2 Add the potatoes, onions and salt, and cover with cold water. Simmer until the water has evaporated and vegetables are very tender.
3 Puree the mixed vegetables through the coarse plate of a food mill (this eliminates the coarse outer skin of the beans) into a warmed bowl. Beat in about two-thirds of the oil, adding plenty of pepper to taste. Add more salt if necessary.
4 Spoon into a shallow dish, make a hollow in the top with a knife or the back of a spoon and pour in the remaining oil.
5 Serve at room temperature.

MOZZARELLA Mozzarella is a soft white unripened cheese. Originally made from water buffalo's milk (a type still available in parts of Italy and in some specialty food shops in the United States), today it is more commonly produced from cow's milk. While the freshest Mozzarella (also known as Bocconcini) can be eaten row, Mozzarella is very often cooked. It is traditionally used for pizza because of its excellent melting qualities. Mozzarella can also he used wherever a recipe calls for a soft cooking cheese, and it works well as a stuffing for vegetables or meat. Mozzarella is available packaged, or fresh, from the cheese counters of most large supermarkets and delicatessens. Fresh Mozzarella, usually sold in ball shapes, should be shiny white without any hint of dryness. It should be kept in the refrigerator and used within a week as it easily dries out, becoming rubbery and stronger in flavor.

Wine Notes

A drv rosé-style wine is generally an attractive versatile choice for Anipasto.

FRANCE : Try a Cabernet d' Anjou Rosé form the Loire Valley, made from Cabermet Franc, or perhaps one of the rather more robust Provencal Rosés.

USA : Choose a rosé-style Grenach from California.

AUSTRALIA : Select a Rosé from Mt Hurtle, Houghtons or Taltarni.

ITALY : If the Lacrimarosa a Irpinia Rosé is not available, try one of the light reds of Veneto, such as Bardelino.

MINESTRONE CON FOCACCIA

Thick Bean and Vegetable Soup with Focaccia

This classic soup is made with fresh and dried vegetables and thickened with pasta or rice, with countless variations. The Genoese flavor their soup with pesto rather than the Parmesan cheese, while in Tuscany they prefer to add olive oil. Serve in deep bowls with plenty of bread—focaccia goes well. This focaccia recipes comes from Tuscany. Traditionally eaten as snack, focaccia is served today with many different toppings.

SERVES 6~8

Use a hard wheat flour, if it is available

Ingredient

- 1 tablespoon active dry yeast or 1oz (30g) fresh yeast
- 4 cups (1 lb / 500g) all-purpose (plain) flour
- 1 tablespoon coarse sea salt
- 1 ½ cups (12 fl oz / 375mL) warm water
- ½ cup (4 fl oz / 125mL) virgin olive oil
- 1 teaspoon salt

Method

1. Mix together the dried yeast and water and allow to stand for about 15 minutes. Add 2 tablespoons of the oil and stir until the yeast is blended in. If using fresh yeast, blend together the yeast and water. then stir in the oil immediately.
2. Sift the flour and salt into a mixing bowl, then gradually stir in the yeast mixture. Mix well until all the ingredients are thoroughly combined. If the dough seems too dry, add a little more water, very gradually (The dough should feel rather sticky.)
3. Turn the dough onto a floured board and knead for about 8 minutes, or until the dough smooth and elastic when pressed.
4. Lightly oil a mixing bowl and place the dough in it. Cover lightly with a towel and leave to rise until doubled in bulk; this may take 1 ½ to 2 hours, depending on the warmth of the room.
5. Preheat the oven to 400°F (200℃).
   Turn the dough onto a lightly floured board, divide into two, and shape into two balls Gently role each into an oval or a rectangle with rounded ends. Place on baking sheets.
6. Press your fingertips all over the surface of the dough to make small indentations, and pour on enough of the remaining olive oil to generously cover the surface. Sprinkle on the coarse sea salt.
7. Bake for about 10 minutes, then reduce heat to 350°F (180℃) and bake for an additional 25 minutes, until well colored.

MINESTRONE

Thick Bean and Vegetable Soup

SERVES 6~8

To keep the zucchini fairly firm, add it at the same time as the macaroni and cabbage. This soup reheats very well.

Ingredient

- 1 tablespoon olive oil.
- 2 small onions, chopped
- 1 cup (6oz / 185g) dried beans, soaked for 12 hours
- 1 large carrot, sliced
- 1 small potato, diced
- 1 cup (4oz / 125g) shelled peas
- 3 tomatoes, peeled and chopped
- 1/3 teaspoon freshly ground black pepper
- 1/2 small cabbage, finely shredded
- 2 tablespoons chopped parsley
- 4 slices (rashers) lean bacon, diced
- 1 garlic clove, chopped
- 2 celery stalks, sliced
- 2 zucchini (courgettes), sliced
- 4 oz (125g) green beans, cut into 1 inch (2.5cm) lengths
- 1/3 teaspoon salt
- 10 cups (80 fl oz / 2.5L) water
- 1/2 cup (2 1/2 oz / 80g) elbow maccaroni
- 1 cup (4oz / 125g) freshly grated Parmesan cheese

Method

1 Heat the oil, add the bacon. onions and garlic and saute until slightly softened. Transfer to a large soup pot.

2 Drain the beans and add them to the soup pot with the celery, carrot, zucchini, potato, green beans, peas, tomatoes, salt, pepper and water. Simmer for about 45 minutes. Add the cabbage and macaroni and cook for an additional 20 minutes, or until the macaroni is well cooked.

3 Serve hot, sprinkled with the parsley and cheese, or serve the cheese separately.

CELERY Celery (Apium gaveolens) is native to Europe and once grew as a wild herb in the wetter regions of the Mediterranean. Today's crisp, crunchy variety was developed in the United States late last century. Celery can be eaten raw in salads, with dips, or as a snack. Celery can also be stir-fried, braised or lightly boiled. The aromatic green leaves impart a delicious flavor to soups and stews. Bunches of celery should be wrapped in plastic wrap and stored in the salad drawer of the refrigerator.

Wine Notes

This soup is best served with a fairly light red.

FRANCE : Choose from Chinon or Bouguell, the soft, fruity-red of the Loire Valley.

USA : Try a Merlot from the Pacific Northwest, such as Columbia Crest, which produces flavorsome reds with some degree of elegance.

AUSTRALIA : Select a good quality commercial red based on Shiraz, such as Rosemount Shiraz and David Wynn Shiraz Cabernet.

ITALY : Try a Bardolino or Valpolicella (from the Veneto region)—these light-bodied reds have a persistent, faintly bitter, yet attractive flavor.

RISOTTO ALLA MILANESE

Risotto, Milan Style

If pasta is the staple food of southern Italy, rice is the mainstay of the north. Risotto (literally rice in Italian) describes the dish made form the short grain rice grown in the Po valley. The characteristic creaminess of risotto is produced by the gradual release of starch as the rice is stirred. There are many differing interpretations of risotto, but this version from Milan is regarded as a classic.

SERVES 4

The rice needs to be watched closely to prevent from sticking

Ingredient

¼ teaspoon saffron threads
½ cup (4oz / 25g) unsalted butter
⅓ teaspoon freshly ground black pepper
2 ½ cups(13oz / 400g) Arborio rice salt
chicken stock
2 tablespoons water
1 onion, chopped
2 cups (16 fl oz / 500mL) dry white wine
2 ½~3 ½ cups (20~28 fl oz / 625~875mL)
1 ½ cups (6oz / 185g) grated Parmesan cheese, plus extra for serving

Method

1 Soak the saffrom m the water for at least 15 minutes.
2 Melt two-thirds of the butter in a heavy pan, add the onion and pepper and cook over low heat until the onion is golden brown.
3 Add the wine and simmer until it has reduced by half.
4 Add the rice and a little salt and cook for about 3 minutes, stirring constantly until the wine is absorbed. Add the saffron liquid and 2 cups of the chicken stock and cook gently, stirring continuously until all the stock has been absorbed.
5 Add all the remaining stock in small amounts as each quantity added is absorbed. Use just enough stock to ensure that the rice is cooked until tender but still firm stir often to prevent the rice from sticking.
6 Remove from heat and stir in the remaining butter and the cheese. Serve hot, and serve extra cheese at the table.

Wine Notes

A soft, rather fruity white is suitable here.

FRANCE : Try the Sylvaner form Alsace. Light and fragrant, it finishes with a pleasant tart.

USA : Choose a Johannisberg Riesling from the Columbia Valley, Washington.

AUSTRALIA : Try a soft and full Rhine Riesling from pathway.

ITALY : A riesling from the Oltreop Pavese region in Lombardy would be prefect. If hard to find, try Tocai Fnuliano form Friuli instead.

CARPACCIO

Raw Reef Slices

Piedmontese in origin, this dish was named after the famous Italian painter, Vitorre Carpaccio, by the owner of Harry's Bar in Venice. It has become very popular in restaurants worldwide while other raw meats or fish are sometimes used instead of beef. In Italy the prized beef of the Chinese breed is the first choice for this dish. Whatever beef is used, it should be as near perfect as possible, and the olive oil or the best quality available.

SERVES 6

If the meat and mushrooms are prepared too far ahead of serving time they will darken and look less attractive, but the flavor will not be spoiled. Cut the meat with a thin filleting knife when it is very cold. If you cannot find Parmigiano-Reggiano, use another variety of Italian Parmesan.

Ingredient

juice of 2 lemons
$\frac{1}{3}$~$\frac{1}{2}$ cup (3~4 fl oz / 90~125mL) extra-virgin olive oil
1 lb (500g) tenderloin (fillet) steak, very thinly sliced
8oz (250g) mushrooms
$\frac{3}{4}$ cup (3oz / 90g) shaved Parmigiano-Reggiano cheese
I garlic clove, slivered
$\frac{1}{3}$ teaspoon salt
$\frac{1}{3}$ teaspoon coarsely ground or crushed black peppercorns
leaves of Italian parsley, for garnish

Method

1 Place the lemon juice in a bowl, add the garlic silvers and leave for several hours. Remove the garlic and discard. Slowly drip the oil into the bowl, whisking as it drops in. Add the salt and pepper.
2 Arrange the beef slices attractively on a serving plate. Thinly slice the mushrooms and arrange them around the beef.
3 Pour the lemon dressing over the meat, and arrange the parsley leaves on top. Sprinkle the shaved cheese over the meat or serve separately.

Wine Notes

A quality dry red with a degree of elegance seems the most appropriate for this dish.

FRANCE : Choose a Bordeaux red such as a chateau-bottled wine from St Julien or Pauillac.

USA : Select a Californian Cabernet: Mondavi, Beaullieu and Heitz are world-renowned makers.

AUSTRALIA : Try any good vintage Cabernet Sauvignon and Cabernet blend form the Coonawarra.

ITALY : Try Chianti, the famous red of Tuscany. A good vintage Chianti Classico would be ideal.

RIGATONI ALLA NORMA

Pasta with Eggplant and Tomato Sauce

Pasta was once associated with southern Italy but Its popularity has spread to the north and, indeed, worldwide. It comes in countless varieties, both fresh and dried, and is eaten with hundreds of different sauces. This dish was created in Catania. Sicily, the birthplace of Vincenzo Bellini. It is named in honor of his most famous opera, Norma. Which he wrote in 1831 before he was thirty years old.

SERVES 6

In some recipes, the dish is returned to the oven and cooked for an additional 15 to 20 minutes, or until the cheese melts.

Ingredient

3 eggplants (aubergines), thinly sliced crosswise
12oz (375g) ripe tomatoes, peeled seeded and coarsely chopped
2 garlic cloves, finely chopped
⅓ teaspoon freshly ground black pepper
¾ cup (3oz / 9g) freshly grated Parmesan cheese
1 ½ tablespoons salt
½ cup (4 fl oz / 125mL) virgin olive oil
⅓ cup chopped basil
⅓ teaspoon salt
12oz (375g) rigatoni

Method

1 Sprinkle the eggplant slices with salt, place in a colander and leave to dram for 1 hour.
2 Puree the tomatoes.
3 Heat 3 tablespoons of the oil in a saucepan and add the tomatoes, basil and garlic. Add the salt and pepper and simmer over medium heat until the sauce becomes fairly thick.
4 Rinse the eggplant slices well and pat dry. Heat the remaining oil in a large pan. Fry the eggplant in the hot oil until each side is well browned. Drain on paper towels and sprinkle with salt and pepper.
5 Cook the rigatoni in a large saucepan of lightly salted boiling water until al dente, about 15 minutes. Drain well and place in a warmed serving dish. Arrange the eggplant on top, cover with the tomato sauce and sprinkle with the grated Parmesan.
6 Serve immediately.

PARMESAN Parmesan (parmigiano) is one of the most famous Italian cheese. It is ideal for cooking and melts easily while retaining Its distinctive, piquant flavor. It is grated over pasta dishes and also complements soups, sauces and souffles. If well-wrapped, solid Parmesan can be kept almost idefinitely in the refrigerator. Factory-grated Parmesan can be found on supermarket shelves, but the flavor is not as good as that of freshly grated Parmesan.

Wine Notes

Rosato (Rosé) from the slopes of Mt Etna is the local favorite with this dish, so choose a similar wine.

FRANCE : Try Tavel, the famous rose of the Rhôle Valley which is orange rather than pink.

USA : Grenache is a very successful rose grape in California; choose one from Gallo.

AUSTRALIA : Good quality dry roses are made by Houghtons, Mt Hurtle and Taltami, as well as many others.

ITALY : If the Etna Rosato of Sictly is unobtainable try one of the fine Tuscan Roses made from the Chanti grapes, Sangiovese and Canaiolo.

GNOCCHI DI PATATE CON PESTO

Pototo Gnocchi with Pesto

Gnocchi have been part of the Italian cooking repertorie since the days of ancient Rome vhen they were made with semolina. Today gnocchi (literally "dumplings") are still made with semolina in some areas, particularly m Sardinia. However, elsewhere potato is the more usual igredient. On the whole, gnocchi are kept simple so that their flavor can be enhanced by a fresh-tasting sauce, such as Pesto.

CNOCCHI DI PATATE

Basic Potato Gnocchi

SERVES 4

If the water is boiling too vigorously, it can cause the gnocchi to bread up. It might need a couple of attempts before the right temperature is achieved.

Ingredient

1 lb (1kg) floury potatoes
1 cup (8oz / 250g) all-purpose (plain) flour
1 teaspoon salt
tablespoon (½ oz / 15g) butter
2 eggs, well beaten
⅓ teaspoon freshly ground blacked pepper

Method

1 Preheat the oven to 350°F (180℃).
2 Peel and dice the potatoes, then boil in lightly salted water for 20 minutes, or until tennder. Mash until very smooth and blend in the butter.
3 Gradually work in the flour, beaten eggs and seasoning. Mix thoroughly but lightly.
4 Using floured hands, roll on a pastry board into finger-sized rolls. Cut into 1 inch (2.5cm) pieces.
5 Almost fill a large saucepan with water, heat to boiling, then reduce to a fast Simmer. Drop in the gnocchi one by one and cook for 3 to 4 minutes.
6 Remove with a slotted spoon as they rise to the surface and place in a heated oven proof dish. Dot the gnocchi with butter and place in the warm oven only until the butter melts.
7 Serve plain or topped with a sauce of your choice.

PESTO

SERVES 4

During the heady days of summer, when the fragrance of basil is everywhere, Pesto is a staple in every serious Italian cook's larder. It can be made in large quantities and stored.

Ingredient

1 ½ cups basil leaves
1 ¼ cups (5oz / 55g) pine nuts
¾ cup (6 fl oz / 180mL) virgin olive oil
1 lb (500g) Gnocchi (see recipe)
3 garlic cloves
1 ½ cups freshly grated Parmesan cheese
¼ teaspoon freshly ground back pepper

Method

1 Rinse the basil lightly, pat the leaves dry and strip form the stalks. Place the leaves in a food processor and add the garlic puree, gradually adding the nuts and cheese. Add the olive oil in a slow stream, then the black pepper.
2 Cook the gnocchi and drain well, retaining a couple of tablespoons of the liquid. Spoon the gnocchi into a heated dish, and set aside to keep warm. Stir together the reserved pasta liquid and the pesto and pour over the hot gnocchi. Toss well to ensure the gnocchi. Toss well to ensure the gnocchi are well coated.
3 Serve at once.

PINE NUTS Pine nuts are the kernels or edible seeds of a number of pine trees (genus Pinus) including stone and Mexican.
The stone pine has flourished In Mediterranean countries for centuries, and was prized by the Arab peoples as well as the Ancient Romans. In America different species bearing edible nuts have been cultivated for hundreds of years, and pine nuts feature in the diets of native Americans. The nuts are a pale yellow color and have a soft texture. They also have a high oil content and are a good source of vegetable protain. Toasted pine nuts can be added to sauces (the most famous being pesto), to stuffings for poultry and fish, and their flavor complements meat dishes. They are also added to salads, giving an attractive nutty flavor complements meat dishes. They are also added to salads, giving an attractive nutty flavor. They are available from large supermarkets and specialty food-stores. Pine nuts should be stored in an airtight container, preferably in the refrigerator.

Wine Notes

The choice of wine depends largely on the sauce served with the Gnocchi. A white wine will best complement the Pesto.

FRANCE : Pouillv-Fuisse or Macon Villages could be served.

USA : Choose a Chardonnay from California; it is probably the most versatile white wine style.

AUSTRALIA : Choose a Barossa Chardonnay a Hunter Valley Semilon or a quality Marsanne from South Australia.

ITALY : Choose a whife wine from Trentino, such as Chardonnay Toscano Blanco and Soave.

PENNE CON BROCCOLI

Pasta with Broccoli

Pasta was originally made in Sicily as early as the thirteenth century, when it was known as "maccaruni." There are several versions of this dish, using different lands of pasta and other ingredient such as diced cooked chicken and chopped livers. Sicilian pasta dishes are characterized by their unfailing combination of olive oil, tomatoes and fish. This Sicilian recipe, one of the more elaborate variations on the theme, offers a vibrant range of flavors.

SERVES 4

Although Pecorino cheese is the traditional choice for this dish, any hard, salty, grating cheese, such as Parmesan, can be substituted.

Ingredient

2 canned or bottled anchovy fillets milk
1 lb (500g) broccoli florets
1 small onion, sliced
1 ½ cups canned plum (Roma) tomatoes, chopped
⅓ teaspoon freshly ground black pepper
12oz (375g) penne
½ cup (2oz / 60g) grated Pecorino cheese
½ cup (2oz / 60g) olden raisins (sultanas)
⅓ cup (3 fl oz / 90mL) virgin olive oil
1 garlic clove, finely chopped
½ teaspoon salt
¼ cup (1oz / 30g) lightly toasted pine nuts
1 tablespoon choped basil leaves

Method

1 Soak the anchovies in a little milk for about 1 hour to reduce the saltiness.
2 While the anchovies soak, cover the raisins with a little hot water and allow to stand for 5 minutes.
3 Drain the anchovies and pat dry. Chop them coarsely and set aside.
4 Cook the broccoli In lightly salted boiling water until just tender. Drain well and set aside.
5 Heat 4 tablespoons of the olive oil in a large saucepan and cook the onion and garlic until softened.
6 Add the tomatoes to the onion in the pan. Cover the pan and simmer gently.
7 Heat the remaining oil in all small pan over low heat, add the anchovies and crush to form a smooth paste; stir into the tomato mixture.
8 Add the salt and pepper, adjusting quantities to taste, then add the drained raisins and the pine nuts, and stir until well blended. Add the broccoli and stir gently through the sauce. Remove from the heat and keep warm.
9 Meanwhile, cook the penne in boiling salted water until al dente, then drain and place in a deep serving dish.
10 Add the broccoli mixture to the dish containing the pasta.
11 Sprinkle on the shredded basil and the grated Pecorino.

12 Serve very hot.

BROCCOLI Broccoli (Brassica oleracea) is related to both cabbage and cauliflower and resembles the latter vegetable in shape. However, it ranges in color form green to purple-green, with one variety a bright lime green. Cultivated in southern Europe for over two thousand years, broccoli takes its name from the Italian word "broccolo", meaning cabbage sprout. Long a favorite of the Italians, broccoli was apparently served m the household of the emperor Tiberius. In Italy it is still a popular vegetable and is sometimes served simply cooked in olive oil, white wine and garlic. Italian immigrants took broccoli seeds to North America where it has become firmly established in the kitchen. Broccoli can be treated in the same manner as cauliflower: cut into florets, it can be steamed or boiled lightly, stir-fried, made into soup, or served raw in a salad or with a dip. An excellent source of vitamins A, C and B, and minerals, and so a popular vegetable with vegetarians, broccoli should not be kept longer than three or four days in the refrigerator. Buy it when It is very fresh: its florets should not have turned yellow, not should its stalks look brown. It is available fresh during most of the year and can also be bought frozen.

Wine Notes

A dry crisp but reasonablv full-bodied white would suit this dish.

FRANCE : Choose a white Bordeaux-many large firms have attractive "appellation Bordeaux" wines.

USA : Select a Sauvignon Blanc from the Napa Valley or Sonoma Country for definite flavor and 4 generally fresh, crisp style.

AUSTRALIA : Try a good Semillon from the Baross, Hunter Bailey of Magaret River regions.

ITALY : Choose Corvo Bianco, Sicily's best known white. It is medium bodied and well balanced, with an attractive vinosity.

SPAGHETTI ALLA BOLOGNESE

Spaghetti with Meat Sauce

Interpretations of this world-famous dish range form the basic to the elaborate, with much debate as to what constitutes an "authentic" Bolognese sauce (or ragù). The use of chicken livers and bacon in this version is typical of Bologna, where the sauce was originally created as a topping for tagliatelli, itself apparently inspired by the hair of Lucrezia Borgia. Today the sauce is also used in lasagne dishes.

SERVES 4

Sometimes the cheese is tossed through the pasta before the sauce is poured on. This sauce freezes very well, so it is worthwhile doubling the recipe and reserving half for future use.

Ingredient

1 tablespoon virgin olive oil
2 slices (rashers) streaky bacon, cut Into matchsticks
1 celery stalk, chopped
4oz (125g) ground (minced) beef
1 tablespoon tomato paste or thick tomato puree
1 Sprig thyme
1 cup (8 fl oz / 250mL) beef stock
2 tablespoons olive oil, optional
1 large onion, finely chopped
1 small carrot, chopped
1 garlic clove, chopped salt and pepper, to taste
2oz (60g) chopped chicken liver
1 bay leaf
$\frac{1}{2}$ cup (4 fl oz / 125mL) dry white wine
12oz (375g) spaghetti
$\frac{1}{3}$ cup (1 $\frac{1}{2}$ oz / 45g) grated Parmesan cheese

Method

1 Heat the olive oil in a large saucepan, add the onion and cook over moderate heat until soft. Add the bacon, carrot, celery, garlic and salt and pepper. Brown lightly, then add the meat and cook until the color changes. Stir in the chicken liver and cook until colored.
2 Spoon in the tomato paste, bay leaf and thyme. Stir in the wine and stock.
3 Cover and simmer for about 4 minutes, stirring occasionally. Remove the herbs and discard.
4 Meanwhile, cook the spaghetti m a large pot of boiling slated water for about 15 minutes or until al dente. Drain well.
5 If desired, stir the oil into the spaghetti and toss.
6 Spoon the hot sauce over the spaghetti and sprinkle with the cheese, or serve the cheese separately.

Wine Notes

A hearty red is the obvious choice with this dish.

FRANCE : Try a Bourgogne Rouge, such as those from Drouhin, Jadot and Bouchard Pere et Fils.

USA : Choose Hearty Burgundy, the immensely popular label of Emest and Julio Gallo.

AUSTRALIA : Try a Shiraz from the Barossa Valley or Mclaren Vale.

ITALY : Try a flavorful red such as Chianti, Montepulciano d' Abruzzo or a dry Lambrusco.

SOUTH AFRICA : Try a Pingtage form Simonsig, KWA and Nodorbum.

PANZANELLA

Bread Salad

Bread is treated with respect in Italy, and most towns produce their own varieties. Tuscany, in particular, boasts many styles of bread, generally unsalted. This lack of salt help the bread to stay fresh longer, but even stale bread never goes to waste—the area is rich in bread recipes, including bread salads. This delicious, fresh-tasting salad is perfect as an easy light summer meal or as an accompaniment.

SERVES 4

For best results. look for coarse-textured Italian-style white bread and leave it for a day or two before using. Balsamic vinegar does impart a beautiful and subtle flavor but, if it is not available, a good-quality red wine vinegar can be substituted.

Ingredient

- 8oz (250g) Italian bread, cut in thick slices or diced chilled wafer
- $\frac{1}{2}$ red bell pepper (capsicum), cut into chunks or Julienne strips
- 1 red onion, thinly shliced
- 1 tablespoon finely chopped basil
- 2 tablespoons chopped Italian parsley
- 1 tablespoons extra-virgin olive oil
- $\frac{1}{3}$ teaspoon freshly ground black pepper
- 2 large ripe tomatoes, peeled and chopped
- 1 small cucumber, peeled and coarsely diced
- $\frac{1}{2}$ green bell pepper (capsicum), cut into chunks or Julienne strips
- 2 teaspoons capers, rinsed and drained
- 1 garlic clove, finely chopped
- 5 tablespoons extra-virgin olive oil
- 1 teaspoon salt
- fresh basil sprigs, for garnish

Method

1. Place the bread in a bowl, pour on just enough of the water to cover and set aside.
2. Place the tomatoes, cucumber, bell peppers and onion in a large serving bowl with capers, basil, garlic and parsley.
3. Squeeze the bread as dry as possible and break into crumbs, and add to the bowl.
4. Whisk together the oil, vinegar, salt and pepper, and pour over the salad, Toss well, garnish with the basil and serve.

Wine Notes

A full-flavored white wine will go with this salad.

FRANCE : Try a Chenin Blanc from the Loire Valley; Coteaux de Saumur is a good example.

USA : Choose a Chenin Blanc form the Napa Valley or a Sauvignon Blanc from the west coast.

AUSTRALIA : Try a Verdelho such as those from Lindemans and Wyndham in the Hunter Valley and Sandalfor and Moonah Brook in Wastern Ausralia.

ITALY : The flowery, sometimes powerful, Vernaccia di San Gimignano is the local choice: those from Teruzzi & Puthod are the most readily available.

POLLO ALLA ROMANA CON POLENTA

Chicken Roman Style with Polenta

This dish from Rome combines the archetypal tastes of Italy—olive oil, garlic, onions, tomatoes and peppers. It is excellent with pasta or with polenta, which is one on the staple foods of northern Italy. Usually prepared in a special polenta pot, made of copper and shaped like a cauldron, boiled polenta is often served in lieu of bread. When reheated with butter and cheese or a tomato sauce, polenta becomes a more substantial side dish.

POLLO ALLA ROMANA

Chicken Roman Style

SERVES 6

Check the pot occasionally to ensure the liquid has not evaporated. If necessary, add more wine or water. If fresh plum (Roma) tomatoes are not available, canned Roma tomatoes may be substituted.

Ingredient

approximately 2 tablespoons virgin olive oil
2 onions, finely chopped
12oz (375g) ripe plum (Ramo) tomatoes, peeled and coarsely chopped
½ cup (4 fl oz / 125mL) dry white or red wine
½ teaspoon salt
1 quantity sliced Polenta (see recipe)
1 ½ tablespoons (1 ½ oz / 45g) butter, cut in small pieces
2 garlic cloves, unpeeled and crushed
4 lb (2kg) chicken pieces
3 green bell peppers (capsicums), seeded and cut into strips
2 teaspoons chopped oregano
⅓ teaspoon freshly ground black pepper
½ cup (4oz / 125g) grated Parmesan cheese

Method

1 Heat the oil in a large saucepan, add the garlic and onions and stir-fry until the onions are soft and golden. Remove the garlic cloves and discard. Push the onion to one side of the saucepan.
2 Wipe the chicken pieces and pat dry. Add to the pan. adding a little more olive oil, if necessary, and brown the chicken in batches. Return all the browned chicken to the pan.
3 Add the tomatoes, bell pepper strips, wine, oregano and salt and pepper.
4 Cover the saucepan and simmer over gentle to moderate heat until the chicken is tender, about 45 to 50 minutes.
5 Meanwhile, preheat the oven to 400°F (200℃).
6 Place the polenta slices in a buttered oven proof dish, sprinkling the grated Parmesan cheese between each layer. Dot the top surface with the butter.
7 Put the polenta in the oven until heated through, about 10 minutes.

8 To serve, place the chicken portions on serving plates and spoon over some of the sauce. Serve with the hot Polenta.

POLENTA

SERVES 6

Cooking the polenta in a mixture of white wine and water gives extra flavor.

Ingredient

2 ½ cups (20 fl oz / 625mL) water
6oz (185g) finely ground cornmeal (polenta)
½ teaspoon salt

Method

1 Heat the water to boiling in a large saucepan, then add the salt. Add the polenta and cook slowly for about 20 minutes, stirring constantly—or as often as possible. The mixture should be thick and smooth.
2 Rinse a tray with cold water, and spread the polenta mixture over it in al layer ½ inch (1.25cm) thick. Allow to cool.
3 Cut into slices, or dip your hands m flour and shape into dumplings the size of large walnuts.
4 Use as required.

OREGANO Oregano (Oreganum vulgare), also known as "Wild marjoram," is a member of the mint family and along with marjoram, was used extensively by the Mediterranean peoples many centuries ago for its medicinal, disinfectant and preserving qualties. Oregano, which has a stronger, more pungent flavor than marjoram, is a perfect complement to tomato-based dishes, pastas and pizzas, and is particular favorite served with lamb in Greece. Its flowers are used in the same manner as the leaves. As with most herbs, oregano can be grown at home in a pot and picked when needed. If purchased fresh, store m water m the refrigerator and use within a week. As with all herbs, the dried leaves have a stronger flavor than the fresh ones, and should, therefore, be used more sparingly. Indeed, oregano when dried remains truer to its original flavor than most herbs.

Wine Notes

This dish would typicallv be accompanied by a simple style of dry white.

FRANCE : Select a dry white from Entre-Deux-Mers. In general these wines show soft acidity and a fairly light Semillon-influenced flavor.

USA : Try a Californian Semillon or Chardonnay-a middle range, unwooded style.

AUSTRALIA : Choose a good blended white, featuring Semillon and Chenin Blanc from Houghtons, Wolf Blass or Yalumba.

ITALA : Of course it has to be Frascati. Its crisp, clean, dry style is perfect.

VITELLO TONNATO

Veal with Tuna Mayonnaise

Cattle are important to Lombardy's agricultural industry, and beef and veal feature prominently in the local cuisine. This dish, which is sometimes made with veal left over from a roast, has a surprising accompaniment of tuna fish. Tuna is one of Italy's most popular and versatile fish, as Vitello Tonnato proves. The dish is enjoyed in many regional versions throughout Italy, though milan and Piedmont claim it for their own.

SERVES 6

Although the sauce can be made in a food processor, the texture is much better when the ingredients are blended together with a mortar and pestle or by mashing with a fork.

Ingredient

2 lb (1kg) rolled shoulder of veal or
1 boned leg of veal
2 bay leaves
1 cup (8 fl oz / 250mL) dry white approximately
2 tablespoons capers, for garnish

1 carrot, sliced
1 celery stalk, with leaves, sliced 1 onion, chopped
½ teaspoon peppercorns
1 cup (8 fl oz / 250mL) water
lemon on slices, for garnish

TUNA DRESSING

4 canned or bottled anchovy fillets
⅔ cup (5 fl oz / 160mL) Virgin olive oil

4oz (125g) canned tuna, drained and flaked
2 tablespoons lemon Juice

Method

1 Tie the meat into a neat shape. Place it in a large saucepan and add the vegetables, bay eaves and peppercorns.
2 Pour on the wine and enough water to barely cover the meat.
3 Heat to boiling, skin, then reduce heat Cover and simmer gently for 1 ½ to 2 hours, or until the meat is tender. Allow the meat to cool in the liquid, then remove and slice thinly. Set aside. Discard the vegetables.
4 To make the dressing, mash together the anchovies and tuna, then gradually add the olive oil and blend together as for a mayonnaise. Gradually beat in the lemon juice.
5 Arrange the meat in slices in an overlapping design on a serving platter. Spoon over the dressing and garnish with the capers and lemon slices.

OLIVE OIL The Greeks and Romans prized the olive tree (Olea europaea) for its fruit—the edible olive was grown on Crete as early as 3500 BC—and olive oil was used to anoint the body during Homer's time. The oil was, and still is in some areas of the Mediterrancan, used medicinally for soothing aches. The oil was also used in Europe for many centuries as a fuel for lamps. There are a number of different grades of olive oil, but mostly only oils from the first pressing and sometimes the second are used in the kitchen. In some countries oils from the first cold pressing are then subdivided into four classes: extra-virgin, superfine, fine and virgin, with extra-virgin being the most flavorful and aromatic and also lowest in oleic acid (about 1 percent) and virgin being a little more bland and the highest in oleic acid (about 4 percent). Extra-virgin olive oil has the lowest smoking point and is best used for salads and uncooked foods rather than for cooking. Virgin olive oil is better for cooking as it stands up to heat better. The grades of superfine and fine are not in use everywhere. A grade of olive oil made from the second pressing and known as "pure" is less expensive and more widely available. It is renowned for its cooking qualities. The largest producers of olive oil are Italy and Spain, but most of the Mediterranean countries produce their own oil. In common wth grapes, olive harvests can vary each year, depending on climatic conditions. This has an effect on the oil—some yean the oil can be fruitier, more robust and more plentiful than others.
Olive oil should not be refrigerated, as It will solidify. Stored in a cool, dark place, it will keep for up to two years, though prolonged exposure to air can cause oxidization, and the oil will spoil.

Wine Notes

A dry sparkling wine is a most delicious accompaniment to this dish.

FRANCE : Choose a non-vintage Champagne (or vintage, if cost is no consideration).

USA : The Sonoma Green Valley "appellation" produces lean, racy styles in the European mode. Iron Horse vineyards are a well-established producer.

AUSTRALIA : Seppelts, Yellowglen and Croser make fine sparkling wines from cold climate grapes.

ITALY : Try one of the sparkling Pinots of Lombardy or neighboring Piedmont. Both districts produce elegant, sometimes austere Brut styles.

OSSOBUCO ALLA MILANESE

Veal Shanks Milanese Style

One of the most popular dishes served in Milan, Ossobuco is slowly braised to ensure the meat and bone remain intact. The diner is often presented with a special narrow fork (nicknamed the "tax agent") to extract the highly prized marrow Ossobuco is traditionally served with Risotto alla Milanese. (It is one of the very few times that Risotto is eaten as an accompaniment to a second course rather than as a first course on its own.)

SERVES 6

It may be necessary to allow two pieces per serving if the cuts are not meaty.

Ingredient

6 × 1 ½ inches (4cm) thick slices veal shank
1 carrot, finely chopped
1 garlic clove, finely chopped
3 tablespoons flour
⅓ teaspoon freshly ground black pepper
1 cup (8 fl oz / 150mL) dry white wine
3 ripe tomatoes, peeled, chopped and seeded
2 bay leaves
small piece lemon rind
3 tablespoons butter
1 celery stalk, sliced
1 small onion, finely chopped
½ teaspoon salt
4 tablespoons virgin olive oil
½ cup (4 fl oz / 125mL) chicken stock
1 tablespoon fresh chopped marjoram
⅓ cup chopped parsley

GREMOIATA
3 tablespoons finely chopped parsely
I garlic clove, very finely chopped
grated zest of 1 small lemon

Method

1 Preheat the oven to 350°F (180℃).
2 Trim any sinews or skin from the meat and discard the trimmings.
3 Melt the butter in a small pan, add the carrot, celery, garlic and onion and cook over moderate heat until the vegetables are soft and slightly brown. Set aside.
4 Mix together the flour, salt and pepper and sprinkle on the meat. Heat the oil in a large pan and fry the meat until browned on all sides. Arrange the vegetables in the base of a large casserole dish and spoon the meat on the top.
5 Pour the wine into the pan in which the vegetables were cooked and add the stock, tomatoes, herbs and lemon zest. Heat to boiling, cook until the liquid reduces by one-third, then pour it over the meat. The liquid should cover the meat halfway; if necessary, add in a little more water or chicken stock.
6 Cover the dish and bake m the oven for about 1 ½ hours, or until the meat is very tender.
7 Mix together the parsely, lemon zest and chopped garlic.

8 Serve the meat on individual plates. spoon over some of the liquid and vegetables from the casserole dish and sprinkle with the Gremolata mixture. Serve with plain boiled rice or Risotto alia Milanese.

PARSELY A Biennial plant. parsley (Petroselinum crispum), has been widely used for centuries. It was popular with the Ancient Greeks and Romans, who used It for medicinal purpose as a diuretic as well as in the kitchen. Its use spread throughout Europe and in the seventeenth century it was taken to American by British colorists. Today parsely is one of the most widely grown and used herbs. It is rich In vitamins A, B and particularly C. Parsely enhances other flavors and is one of the main components of bouquet garni. It goes with just about every savory dish and makes an attractive and delicious garnish It is also used in marinades. stocks, soups. sauces and vinegars, and can be added to butter to make a delicious spread. There are several varieties of parsley including the more wellknown curly-leaved, the broad-leaved, Hamburg parsely which has a tapering root that can be cooked like parsnip, and Italian parsely. However, it is also readily available, both fresh and dried. Fresh parsely is best stored in the refrigerator, either with its stems in water or wrapped in plastic and stored in the salad crisper.

Wine Notes

A medium-bodied red with lively fruit character would partner this dish well.

FRANCE : Choose a Rhone Valley red such as Chateauneuf-du-Pape. Generally this wine can be enjoyed whilst young and fruity. but the best, and most expensive, need bottle age.

USA : Try a flavorsome and spicy Californian Zinfandel from Rafanelli, Naile or Ridge Vineyards.

AUSTRALIA : Select a Shiraz from the Coonawarra region. There, the Shiraz grape generally yields medium-bodied, spicy wines with pleasant astringency.

ITALY : Barbera, from Lombardy or Piedmont, is an ideal match.

TIRAMISU

A popular and easy dessert in the Italian home involves soaking savoiardi (ladyfingers) in liqueur and serving them with different toppings. An early incarnation of this dish, a kind of rifle, was so popular with the nineteenth-century English travelers to Italy thai it became known as Zuppa Inglese (English soup). This modern version, from the Veneto, replaces custard with Mascarpone, with heavenly results. Tiramisu, meaning "pick-me-up," refers to the coffee mixed with the liqueur.

SEVERS 10

A spoonful of additional whipped cream may be used to garnish each serving.

Ingredient

2 teaspoons instant espresso coffee
1 lb (500g) Mascarpone cheese
½ cup (4 fl oz / 125 mL) coffee liqueur
1 ½ cups (12 fl oz / 375mL) whipping cream
21 ladyfingers (boudoir biscuits)
1 tablespoon boiling water
½ cup (3oz / 90g) confectioner's (icing) sugar
3oz (90g) grated dark chocolate
2 tablespoons milk

Method

1 Mix the coffee With the boiling water, and leave to cool.
2 In a large bowl. whisk together the Mascarpone cheese, two-thirds of the sugar, 3 tablespoons of the coffee liqueur and about two-thirds of the grated chocolate.
3 Whip the cream lightly in a separate bowl, then add the remaining sugar and whip until stiff. Fold the cream into the cheese mixture, ensuring it is lightly but thoroughly blended.
4 In a small bowl, blend together the coffee, the remaining coffee liqueur and the milk. Dip seven of the biscuits lightly into this mixture and place in the base of a glass serving dish, trimming the ends to fit if necessary.
5 Spoon half of the Mascarpone mixture over the biscuits. Dip another 7 biscuits into the coffee mixture and arrange on top. Add another layer of the Mascarpone mixture, and top with a final layer of bisquits.
6 Sprinkle the remaining grated chocolate over the top layer.
7 Chili for at least 4 hours to allow the biscuits to soften slightly and for the flavors to blend and mellow.

Wine Notes

A liqueur such as Kahlua or Tia Maria would be good, but there are some appealing wine options.

FRANCE : Petite Liqueur, the Moet et Chandon Champagne Liqueur, is rich enough for this dessert.

USA : Try a "slicky" (dessert wine) from one of the San Joaquin (Central Valley) specialists, one of the Special Bottling Ports of Ficklin or Quady's Black Muscat.

AUSTRALIA : Choose a fortified liqueur Tokay from Bailey's, Morris or Buller.

ITALY : Select a Marsala from Sicily. "Superiore" can vary from quite dry to very sweet, but it is always rich and nutty. Mirabella and Woodhouse are reliable producers who both export extensively.

PESCHE RIPIENE

Stuffed Peaches

Peaches are a popular summer fruit in Iialy. The white-fleshed, clingstone variety has a more delicate flavor and is usually eaten raw, perhaps sliced and macerated in a little wine or liqueur. For cooked dishes such as this one, the yellow-fleshed. freestone variety are used. Amaretto biscuits are made from almonds, which grow in southern Italy and Sicily, and their crunchiness contrasts wonderfully with the smooth texture of the peach.

SERVES 4

Amaretto biscuits are sold m specialty food stores and some supermarkets.

Ingredient

4 large, ripe but firm yellow-fleshed peaches
1 small egg yolk
1 tablespoon superfine (caster) sugar
Julienned orange zest, for garnish
6 Amaretto biscuits, crushed
1 tablespoon Amaretto liqueur
1 tablespoon butter, softened

Method

1. Preheat the oven to 375°F (190℃).
2. Peel and halve the peaches, remove the pie and scoop out and dice just a little of the flesh.
3. Crush the bisquiits, then mix with the diced peach flesh, egg yolk, Amaretto, sugar and butter.
4. Place the peach halves on a buttered baking sheet, and divide the filling among them. Bake for 30 minutes in the oven, until lightly browned.
5. Garnish with the orange zest before serving cold or at room temperature.

Wine Notes

Amaretto liqueur is the obvious accompaniment.
Alternatives need to be equally sweet and luscious.

FRANCE : Try a rich Muscat de Beaumes-de-venise from Domaine Durban or Paul Jaboulet.

USA : Try a dessert-style Muscat from California such as Muscat Canelli from St Francis, or Muscat California Alexandria from Sutter Home.

AUSTRALIA : Try a fortlfied white such as Frontignac from Grant Burge, or Verdelho from Hardy's or Sevenhilll.

ITALY : Choose Amaretto, the famous almond liqueur, or Frangelico, a delicious hazelnut liqueur.

JAPAN

World Cuisine

JAPAN has a classic cuisine that is now recognized as one of the most refined and unique in the world. As befits such status, its comparison with the other "greats" of the culinary world is inevitable. Analogies have resulted in one glib saying that Chinese food is for the delight of the stomach, French food for the delight of the nose, and Japanese for the delight of the eye.

That Japanese cuisine, in its highest form, is an ineffable feast for the eyes is indisputable. But that it is only a relatively flavorless exercise in fleeting beauty, surrounded by tediously ritualized etiquette, is a popular assumption that is certainly not warranted. At the everyday level, Japanese cooking is as down-to-earth as any other country's—as anyone who has heard the communal slurping at Tokyo noodle houses can weel appreciate.

The ultimate ideal of Japanese cuisine, whether fancy or down-home, is to charm all the senses but, unlike the cooking of many other countries, it does not seek to startle. And its major appeal is not through strong blends of herbs and spices. Indeed, it is committed to the delicate, natural flavors of the food itself and seems to enhance these flavors still further in the most delicate way possible.

For most Japanese, restaurants are the providers of the sort of artistic food that ranks as a highly visible symbol of integral qualities of the Japanese character and philosophy. In the past few years, country-style restaurants serving the regional foods of Hokkaido, Honshu and other Japanese provinces have proliferated throughout the big cities of Japan as the Japanese, like the rest of us, feel more and more cut off from their culinary roots. In Japan fast food means sushi bars—the aristocrat of "snack" foods—noodle bars, and the dreaded curry houses where the meals in question are uniformly brown and only vaguely spicy.

Historically, the Japanese have never experienced the luxury of food surplus, as only a relatively small percentage of the land is suitable for cultivation. And yet they have managed to create one of the world's finest cuisines by elevating simplicity and frugality to artistic and culinary virtues. Rice, fish vegetables, seaweed and fruits still form the major part of the Japanese diet, as they have done for centuries.

Politics, as well as culture, has left its mark on Japanese cooking, particularly as a result of Japan's vacillating policy of openness with, or seclusion from, the outside world. During the open periods, the Japanese adopted ideas and techniques they admired and then, during the periods of seclusion, made them uniquely their own by remolding and refining them to harmonize with the Japanese way of life.

Where food is concerned, while there are other Asian and European influences present, the fact that Japan was largely cut off from the world at the time when its cuisine was evolving has greatly contributed to the highly individualistic development of that cuisine.

The Japanese cook had to do without the spices from the East Indies, along with many foods that so influenced the cooking of other Asian countries and of Europe. Simplicity became the form of excellence, and what might have been an undesirable impoverishment served instead to form the basis of a cooking philosophy.

The Japanese have a respect for nature that borders on reverence. It is a deep feeling which permeates most aspects of their lives and which is most often manifested in the serving of food.

The idea of eating and enjoying foods in season is hardly a novel one, but to the Japanese the reasons for doing so are as much spiritual and philosophic as practical and sybaritic. They feel that by responding to the rhythms of the seasons they are united in a divine order and are in harmony with nature. The best compliment a host can pay his guests is to serve them the first of the season's finest foods.

Great emphasis is placed on freshness and quality in Japan, and many cooks shop every day to be certain of finding the best ingredients available. The major cooking methods they use are steaming and boiling. which gives the food great delicacy and lightness. Cooking times are brief, which ensures a higher retention of nutrients Even when the Japanese do fry, as in the renowned tempura, the results are still light and easily digestible.

The two great protein mainstays of the Japanese diet are fish and tofu (bean curd). both of which are low in calories and saturated fat. Obviously, some meat is eaten: sukiyaki and shabu sahbu, using beef, are two of the most popular dishes in Westernized Japanese restaurants. Pork and chicken are also used in recipes such as tonkatsu and chicken teriyaki.

The Japanese eat a wide variety of fresh vegetables and grains. Rice, of course, is the most important grain, but in some regions it is supplemented by millet. Eggs, many different kinds of noodles (particularly the nutritious buckwheat varieties), chicken and nori (edible seaweed) all contribute substantially to the modem Japanese diet as they did for previous generations.

Japanese often refer to their cooking as sappari, which means clean, neat, light and sparkling with honesty to the health-conscious world, this is a description of how all foods should be and it is the main reason, Japanese tourism aside, for the great mterest in Japanese cooking in the West.

HANA-EBI NO SUMASHI-JIRU

Clear Broth with Flower Shrimp

The seasons are paramount in Japanese cuisine, not just because of the seasonal availability of produce but also for aesthetic reasons. Certain dishes are only eaten at the "correct" time of year. In this delicately flavored broth, served in the spring, the shrimp are carefully prepared to represent flowers; a colorful assortment of seasonal vegetables and a garnish of kinome leaves from the Japanese pepper tree also celebrate the coming of spring.

SERVES 4

Lemon or lime rind can be substituted for the kinome leaves, which are difficult to find in the West.

Ingredient

- 8 shrimp (prawns)
- 2 cups (16 fl oz / 500mL) Niban Dashi (see glossary)
- 8 small carrots
- 1 tablespoon mirin (sweet rice wine)
- 4 cups (32 fl oz / 1L) Dashi (Japanese fish stock; see recipe)
- 2 tablespoons cornstarch (cornflour)
- 8 fresh asparagus stalks, trimmed
- 4 fresh shiitake mushroom caps, etched with a cross on top
- 2 teaspoons Japanese light soy sauce
- 2 teaspoons finely julienned lime or lemon zest

Method

1 Remove the shells from the shrimp, leaving tails in tact. Using a small sharp knife, make a shallow cut along the back of each shrimp and carefully devein. Make a small slit in the center of the body and pull the tail through the slit to create a resemblance to a flower.

2 Sprinkle the shrimp with the cornstarch. Heat the Niban Dashi to boiling, then add the shrimp. Reduce heat to a simmer and cook for 2 to 3 minutes, or until the shrimp flesh is opaque. Remove the shrimp with a slotted spoon or a small brass strainer.

3 Cut the asparagus into 2 inches (5cm) lengths. Peel the carrots, slice, and cut the slices into flower shapes with a small metal cutter.

4 Add the mushroom caps to the simmering liquid and cook for 2 minutes.

5 Cook the asparagus pieces and carrots in the simmering broth for 8 to 10 minutes. Remove the mushroom caps, carrot and asparagus with a slotted spoon or a small brass stainer Sprinkle with the mirin.

6 Divide the prepared shrimp, mushrooms, asparagus and carrots among 4 individual soup bowls. Add the dashi and soy sauce to the cooking liquid and heat to boiling. Pour the soup into the bowls and garnish with lime or lemon zest.

DASHI

MAKES 5 CUPS

Ingredient

3 Inches (7.5cm) piece of kombu (dried kelp)
5 cups (40 fl oz / 125L) water
1 cup cooked dried bonito

Method

1 Combine all the ingredients in a saucepan and heat almost to boiling over high heat.
2 Reduce the heat and simmer for 5 minutes, then strain through cheesecloth or muslin draped inside a colander.
3 May be refrigerated for several days.

Wine Notes

A dry, delicate sherry would be the perfect choice to serve with this broth.

FRANCE : Sherry is not a wine style reproduced in a serious way in France. Try instead Marc-de-Champagne, a spirit distilled from the remains of Champagne grapes, after pressing.

USA : The sherries of the Central Valley district have been maligned (with some justification) over the years, but a light dry style from a good winemaker would certainly be acceptable.

AUSTRALIA : Some excellent flor fino sherries are produced in the Barossa Valley and Riverland districts.

SPAIN : Manzanilla and fino are the styles to look for, being the lightest and driest in nature.

CHAWAN MUSHI

Chicken and Shrimp in Steamed Egg Custard

This remarkably delicate and delicious dish is considered a soup in Japan; Westerners would classify it as an egg custard. It is cooked and served in special bowls with lids and was traditionally eaten with chopsticks, but spoons are provided nowadays. Different ingredients may be added to the egg base, depending on individual taste and seasonal availability. Chawan Mushi is mainly a winter dish.

SERVES 4

The shrimp may sink into the custard; this will not affect the cooking of the dish. Because of its delicacy, no sauces are served with it. Chawan Mushi can also be served as a side dish with Sashimi.

Ingredient

- 2 ¼ cups (18 fl oz / 560mL) Dashi (Japanese fish stock)
- 2 chicken breasts, skinned and thinly sliced
- 3 eggs, lightly beaten
- 4 fresh shiitake mushroom caps, etched with a cross on top (or 4 dried shiitakes or 4 fresh cultivated mushrooms)
- 1 teaspoon mirin (sweet rice wine)
- 1 ½ tablespoons Japanese light soy sauce
- 1 teaspoon sake
- 12 ginko nuts or macadamias
- 4 shrimp (prawns), shelled and deveined, tails intact
- 4 small spinach leaves, blanched

Method

1. Combine the dashi, mirin and 1 teaspoon of the soy sauce and heat to boiling, then leave to cool.
2. Combine the chicken strips with the sake and remaining soy sauce. Allow to stand for 30 minutes.
3. Mix the eggs with the cooled dashi mixture and pour through a very fine strainer to create a satin smooth custard mixture.
4. Place a steamer (with water in base) over high heat.
5. While the water heats, divide the chicken and nuts among 4 individual ramekins or small bowls.
6. Pour in the custard to ½ inch (1.25cm) from the top, and skim off any bubbles from the surface.
7. Gently place a mushroom on top of each dish and arrange a shrimp beside it, tail up.
8. Wrap the steamer lid in a dish towel to absorb steam and prevent it from dropping back into the custard and spoiling the texture. (Replace the dish towel as it becomes saturated.) Leave the lid of the steamer slightly ajar to prevent overheating, which can also spoil the texture of the custard.
9. Reduce heat after 10 minutes, then steam for an additional 12 to 15 minutes.

10 When the custard is almost set, carefully garnish each dish with a blanched spinach leaf.
11 To test the custard, insert a cake tester, or toothpick; if clear juices flow, the custard is ready to be eaten.
12 Serve immediately.

Wine Notes

The challenge with this dish is to find a wine to match the texture of the custard.

FRANCE : The Anjou Coutaine district produces a flowery, dry style of Chenin Blanc; Condrieu from the Rhône Valley would be delicious too.

USA : Try to find a not-too-heavily oaked example of Viognier, a relatively new and uncommon variety in California.

AUSTRALIA : Try Marsanne, a wine of smooth texture, dry but not acidic, with a subtle flavor.

GERMANY : Choose a Sylvaner from the southern district of Baden-Württemberg.

NORIMAKI-ZUSHI

Sushi

The vinegared rice that forms the basis of all sushi dishes was not originally meant to be eaten; it was part of a preserving technique for a particular type of fish (carp), and was discarded as the carp was eaten. Gradually the custom of eating the rice and using dipping sauces developed. Now sushi has many different styles. In the style described here, the rice is rolled around the core ingredients and then wrapped in a cylinder of seaweed.

SUSHI RICE

MAKES 10 CUPS

It Is sometimes recommended in Japanese cookbooks that a helper stand by and fan the rice as the vinegar is added, so that the rice reduces to room temperature as quickly as possible. We do not regard fanning as an essential step!

Ingredient

3 ⅓ cups (20oz / 625g) short grain rice

4 cups (32 fl oz / 1L) water

VINEGAR MIXTURE

5 ½ tablespoons rice vinegar

5 tablespoons sugar

4 teaspoons salt

Method

1 Wash the rice under running water until water runs clear, then drain in a fine strainer for at least 1 hour.
2 Combine the vinegar mixture ingredients in a saucepan and cook very gently, stirring constantly until the sugar dissolves. Remove from heat and allow to cool.
3 Place the rice in a rice cooker or a saucepan with a tight-fitting lid, and add the water.
4 Cover tightly and heat to boiling. Boil over high heat for 2 minutes, then reduce heat. Cook gently over low heat for 15 minutes, or until all the liquid has been absorbed. Remove from heat and take off the lid.
5 Spread a clean dish towel over the top of the saucepan, replace the lid loosely and leave to stand for about 15 minutes.
6 Empty the cooked rice into a shallow wooden bowl (or other non- metallic bowl) and run chopsticks through the rice to separate each gram while gradually adding the cold vinegar mixture. Add only enough to moisten the rice well without making it too wet.
7 Traditionally the rice is covered and kept in a cool place (not the refrigerator) until it is to be used. In Japan, Sushi Rice is not kept for more than one day.

KOBABA-MAKI

Rolled Omelette

SERVES 4

Encased in both seaweed and thin Japanese omelette, this sushi dish is a good one to serve with the California Roll.

Ingredient

2 eggs
2 teaspoons sugar
1 cup prepared Sushi Rice (see recipe)
½ small cucumber
3oz (90g) pickled ginger
1 tablespoon salmon roe
little salt
2 sheets nori (dried seaweed), toasted
1 teaspoon toasted sesame seeds
2oz (60g) pickled turnip
¼ teaspoon wasabi (Japanese horseradish)

Method

1 Best the eggs lightly in a bowl, then add the salt and sugar.
2 Heat a nonstick 7~8 inches (18~20cm) pan over medium heat. Pour about half of the mixture into the pan and swirl so that it spreads evenly. Cook until the surface of the omelette is almost dry, then turn quickly with a spatula and cook the underside for only a few seconds. Remove from the pan and cool on a board. Repeat the process to make one more omelette.
3 Place one sheet of the seaweed on a bamboo mat and place one omelette on top.
4 Divide the Sushi Rice into two portions and spread one portion evenly over the omelette, pressing down lightly but firmly. Sprinkle half the sesame seeds on the rice.
5 Peel the cucumber and cut the flesh into strips. Place half the strips along the rice, top with half the pickled ginger and all the pickled turnip and spread on half the wasabi.
6 Using the bamboo mat, carefully roll up the omelette to form a long cylinder. Cut the roll into 2 inches (5cm) pieces. Make up the second roll in the same way, this time omitting the pickled turnip and sprinkling the salmon roe over the wasabi.
7 Arrange on a serving platter. Serve with pickled ginger and a bowl of dark soy sauce.

TEMAKA-ZUSHI

California Roll

SERVES 4

This modern variation of sushi, made with vegetables and cooked fish, is popular both in Japan and overseas. Use your hands instead of the usual bamboo mat to roll the nori around the rice.

Ingredient

2 sheets nori (dried seaweed), toasted
1 small cucumber
12 sugar peas (snow peas / mange-tout) or 12 zucchini strips
1 avocado
1 cup prepared Sushi Rice (see recipe)
1 teaspoon lightly toasted sesame seeds
3oz (90g) poached white fish cut into strips or smoked salmon

Method

1 Cut the seaweed sheets in half. Peel and pit the avocado and cut the flesh into strips. Peel the cucumber, slice lengthwise and discard the seeds. Cut the flesh into strips.
2 Spread each portion of seaweed with ¼ cup of the prepared rice, sprinkle a few of the sesame seeds over the rice, then place a quarter of the cucumber strips and 3 sugar peas on the sesame seeds.
3 Arrange a quarter of the white fish strips on top of each portion, then add a quarter of the avocado.
4 Using both hands, roll up the seaweed lengthwise to encase the rice.
5 Cut each roll into 2 inches (5cm) portions and arrange on a platter. Serve with pickled ginger and wasabi paste. Eat with your fingers.

RICE VINEGAR Rice vinegar is made from fermented rice in a process that is thousands of years old–one Chinese mention of it dates from 1100 BC. It is used in a number of Asian cuisines, particularly that of Japan. Japanese rice vinegar, known as su, has a mild sweetish flavor and is readily available from Asian food stores. Like Western vinegars, the more expensive brands tend to be of a superior quality. A mild white wine or Cider vinegar can be substituted if rice vinegar is not available.

Wine Notes

The vinegar in Sushi poses a few problem. A white wine with a strong, definite flavor would be the best choice.

FRANCE : Choose a white Graves or Entre-deux-Mers, or a dry white such as Sancerre or Pouilly Fumé.

USA : Try one of the new breed of powerful Sauvignon Blanc-Semillon blends emerging in California.

AUSTRALIA : Select a good Semillon from the Hunter Valley with rich vinosity and flavor.

ITALY : The Trebbiano variety has a strong, straightforward character which will work well.

SASHIMI

It Is said that this is the dish for which all Japanese yearn when they are abroad. It is prized for its texture as well as its delicate flavors. Every Japanese restaurant offers sashimi on its menu, sometimes as one course, but often as an entire meal in its own right. While in Japan beef and chicken are also eaten raw, sashimi is predominantly made from fish, of every variety; their preparation is carried out with almost ritual care. Other fish can be substituted for those used in this recipe.

SERVES 4

The fish used for Sashimi must be absolutely fresh. It is also important that you use the thickest possible fillets.

Ingredient

4oz (125g) garfish
4oz (125g) tuna
½ cup very finely shredded cucumber
1oz (30g) salmon roe, optional
Tosa Joyu (see recipe)
4oz (125g) ocean trout
4oz (125g) salmon
½ cup very finely shredded carrot
small portion wasabi (Japanese horseradish)

Method

1 Finely slice the fish, either vertically or at an angle.
2 Arrange small piles of mixed daikon, cucumber and carrot shreds on a Japanese-style serving plate.
3 Coil the garfish slices into a decorative shape. Reserve some of the slices of ocean trout to make a flower shape. Arrange the remaining slices of ocean trout, all the tuna slices and all the salmon slices on the plate.
4 Form the flower shape using the reserved slices of ocean trout. Turn the edges gently to represent petals.
5 Flatten and shape the wasabi into leaf shapes and place on the platter.
6 Serve immediately with individual bowls of Tosa Joyu. Only a hint of sauce is needed to enhance the Sashimi's flavor.

TOSA JOYU

Soy Dipping Sauce

MAKES ¼ CUP

Ingredient

4 tablespoons Japanese dark soy sauce
2 tablespoons dried bonito
1 tablespoon sake

Method

1 Combine all the ingredients in a small saucepan. Heat to boiling, stirring constantly, then remove from heat and strain. Allow to cool to room temperature.

WASABI Hotter than even the hottest chilies, wasabi is served sparingly as a condiment with a number of Japanese dishes and is a traditional accompaniment for Sashimi. Wasabi comes from the root of Wasabia Japonice, a plant which is native to Japan. The plant is difficult to grow, but in some parts of Japan it is successfully cultivated for its root, which is similar to the horseradish root. Hence, wasabi is sometimes known as Japanese horseradish. The root has a brown skin and pale green flesh and its flavor is more fragrant and less pungent than horseradish. A popular Japanese pickle, wasabi-zuke, is made by pickling wasabi in sake. This regional specialty comes from around Shizuoka. To prepare fresh wasabi for use as a condiment, peel and grate the root. Although the fresh root is not readily available in Western countries, wasabi is usually available in both paste (in tubes) and powder forms from Asian grocery stores. Powdered wasabi should be mixed with a little cold water and left for about 10 minutes before it is to be used to allow the flavor to develop; it should not be made further in advance or it will lose its heat. Wasabi paste should be stored in the refrigerator once opened. The powder should be stored in a container with a tight-fitting lid in a cool dry place.

Wine Notes

Sake is the popular and most appropriate beverage to serve with Sashimi; however, a light dry white wine of fairly simple flavor would lend itself to this dish.

FRANCE : Try a Muscadet or perhaps a dry Entre-ceux-Mers.

USA : Choose a lighter style of Sauvignon Blanc or an unwooded Chardonnay.

AUSTRALIA : Clombard-Sauvignon Blanc or a good generic dry white blend incorporating these.

CHILE : Choose from one of the many attractive Semillons and Sauvignon Blancs appearing on the market from Chile.

ZARU SOBA

Chilled Buckwheat Noodles

Japanese noodles (menrui) come in many types, shapes and sizes. The two most popular types are wheat noodles and buckwheat noodles, or soba. They may be eaten either in a soup or with a dipping sauce, as in this recipe. Chilled buckwheat noodles are very much a summer dish. Piled prettily on attractive plates, they are dipped in the sauce and eaten with chopsticks. In this version, small shrimp and mushrooms add extra flavor and interest.

SERVES 4

Although the delicate flavor of oyster mushrooms complements the almost nutty taste of buckwheat noodles, any mild-flavored mushrooms may be used. The oyster mushrooms are usually very lightly stir-fried in a little oil for 1 minute, but they are perhaps even more delicious served raw.

Ingredient

12oz (375g) soba (buckwheat) noodles, cooked until tender and drained well, then chilled
12 small cooked shrimp (prawns), shelled and deveined
4 lightly cooked oyster mushrooms, cut into strips
1 cup very finely shredded carrots, for garnish
1 tablespoon very finely shredded scallions (spring onions), for garnish
½ cup (4 fl oz / 125mL) Dashi (Japanese fish stock)
½ cup (4 fl oz / 125mL) Japanese light soy sauce
2 tablespoons grated ginger
Japanese dark soy sauce, for dipping

Method

1 Tip the chilled soba noodles into a basin and toss with the shrimp (whole or coarsely chopped) and the mushroom strips.
2 Arrange in piles on serving plates. Garnish with the chopped carrots and scallions.
3 Combine the dashi, soy sauce and ginger.
4 Give each diner a bowl of the dashi mixture and a bowl or Japanese soy sauce. Both are used for dipping.

SOBA NOODLES Made from wheat and buckwheat flours combined, saba noodles are light beige in color. Sometimes green tea or beetroot is added to the dough, giving color and extra flavor. Asian grocery stores in the West sell these noodles only in their dried form.

Wine Notes

This is a dish of light and delicate flavors, so the wine to serve with it should have similar qualities.

FRANCE : Choose a light non-vintage Champagne with an elegant, faintly nutty quality.

USA : Try a Riesling from the higher altitudes of California or perhaps from the Pacific Northwest, or try one of the quality Californian sparkling wines.

AUSTRALIA : Choose one of the beautiful finely balanced Rieslings from the cool districts such as Tasmania and southern Victoria.

GERMANY : A classical Kabinett Riesling from the Mosel would be perfect here. Serve well chilled.

TEMPURA

Tempura is a legacy of the Portuguese missionaries who came to Nagasaki late in the sixteenth century. Along with Christianity, they introduced their recipe for battered, deep-fried shrimp. The Japanese adapted it to include all manner of seafood and vegetables. They also lightened the oil and the batter and created their own dipping sauces. Tempura quickly caught on. In today's tempura restaurants, diners sit at low tables or at counters where the chef can be seen at work.

SERVES 2

To serve 4, add 1 lb (500g) firm white fish fillets, diced, and 4 scallops to the ingredients listed. Cook the seafood and vegetables in small batches to prevent the oil from cooling as the cold food is added. It is also a good idea to pass the oil through a fine wire strainer between each batch.

Ingredient

TEMPURA BATTER
2 eggs
2 cups (8oz / 250g) all-purpose (plain) flour
8 shrimp (prawns), shelled and deveined, tails intact
8 small pieces broccoli, thinly sliced
8 sugar peas (snow peas / mange-tout), trimmed
½ red bell pepper (capsicum), cut into strips
Sambai-Zu (see recipe)
1½ cups (l2 fl oz / 375ml) icy cold water
oil, for deep-frying
4 scallions (spring onions), cut into 2 inches (5cm) lengths
8 asparagus tips, halved
scallions (spring onions), finely chopped, for garnish, optional

Method

1 Break the eggs into a bowl, add the water and sift in the flour. Mix only until the ingredients are blended.
2 Heat the oil in a deep-fryer to 350°F (180℃).
3 Pat each piece of food dry, dip into the batter, then into the hot oil and cook quickly until pale gold and crisp.
4 Remove the cooked food from the oil with tongs and allow to drain on paper towels.
5 Arrange the Tempura on a platter; serve immediately with the Sambai-Zu.

SAMBAI-ZU

Rice Vinegar and Soy Dipping Sauce

MAKES ABOUT ⅔ CUP

Ingredient

3 tablespoons rice vinegar
5 teaspoons sugar
¼ teaspoon salt
3 tablespoons Niban Dashi (see glossary)
3 teaspoons Japanese dark soy sauce

Method

1 Combine all the ingredients in a saucepan and heat to boiling over high heat, stirring constantly.
2 Remove from heat and allow to cool before serving.

JAPANESE SOY SAUCE The Chinese started making sauces using soybeans about 3000 years ago, and the Japanese learned the skill from them. There are two main varieties of Japanese soy sauce (shoyu): light and dark. Light soy sauce, the thinner and saltier of the two, is used generally as a condiment and in cooking when soy flavor is desired but the natural color of the ingredients is meant to be preserved (as in seafood dishes). Dark soy sauce tends to be less salty but thicker and darker and is used in cooking when its dark color is desired. While dark and light soy sauces are made with fermented soybeans and wheat, a third type, called tamari, is made only with fermented soybeans. Japanese soy sauces tend to be a little sweeter than Chinese ones.

Wine Notes

A light pale beer, such as Miller Draft from the USA or one from Australia's Cascade Brewery, is hard to beat with Tempura, but a dry, crispy white wine would be fine.

FRANCE : Try Muscadet, a pleasant white wine.

USA : A Napa Valley Sauvignon Blanc would be a good choice.

AUSTRALIA : Choose a dry, varietal or blended white using Semillon, Sauvignon Blanc or Colombard.

NEW ZEALAND : Select a Sauvignon Blanc from Marlborough (South Island) of Hawkes Bay (Vorth Island).

SUKIYAKI

For a long time, because of their strong devotion to Buddhism, which forbids killing four-legged animals, the Japanese did not eat beef. In fact, it was not until the second half of the nineteenth century that beef was introduced into their diet by the British. It did not take long, however, for the Japanese to develop a taste for it and, in particular, for sukiyaki. Today there are many variations on the basic recipe, both individual and regional. This recipe comes from the Tokyo area.

SERVES 4

This dish calls for fine quality meat, a luxury in Japan. The Japanese prefer the beef to be well marbled with creamy fat which gives it richness and depth of flavor.

Ingredient

4 Japanese mushrooms (shiitake or other Asian variety)
½ Asian cabbage, cut into 2 inches (5cm) pieces
4 scallions (spring onions), cut into 2 inches (5cm) pieces
4oz (125g) tofu, cut into cubes
3 eggs, beaten
2~3 tablespoons sake, if required
1 cup shredded carrot
4oz (125g) rice noodles
1 ¼ lb (625g) beef tenderloin (fillet), sliced very thinly
2 bamhoo shoots, finely sliced
4 spinach leaves, rolled and shredded
2oz (60g) suet or beef fat or 2~3 tablespoons vegetable oil
1 cup shredded daikon (white radish)

SAUCE
½ cup (4 fl oz / 125mL) Dashi (Japanese fish stock)
⅓ cup (3oz / 90g) sugar
⅓ teaspoon salt
1 cup (8 fl oz / 250mL) Japanese dark soy sauce
¼ cup (2 fl oz / 60mL) mirin (sweet rice wine)

Method

1 If using dried mushrooms, place them in warm water and soak for 10 minutes.
2 Soak the rice noodles in warm water for 30 minutes or until tender, and then drain off as much water as possible.
3 Combine all the sauce ingredients in a saucepan and stir over low heat until the sugar dissolves.
4 Arrange the meat, cabbage, scallions, bamboo shoots, spinach, tofu, mushrooms and noodles attractively on a platter. Place the beaten eggs in a small bowl. Take the platter and the bowl to the table.
5 Heat a skillet over a table burner and use the fat or oil to cover the base of the pan.
6 Cook the Sukiyaki in two batches. Sauté half the beef and add half the scallions. When the beef is tender, pour over a little of the sauce, then add half of the cabage, bamboo shoots, mushrooms, noodles, tofu and shredded spinach leaves. Add a little sake if the mixture is drying out.

7 Repeat this procedure with the remaining ingredients when required.
8 Serve the shredded daikon and carrot as accompaniments.
9 The diners help themselves directly from the pan, dipping the individual hot morsels in the beaten egg before eating them. The heat of the food cooks the layer of egg adhering to it. However, in some countries health authorities do not recommend using raw egg. Pointed Japanese chopsticks or small tongs are used to transfer food from the pan.

TOFU Tofu is also known as bean curd, a name that describes it well, because tofu is made from pureed saybeans that are curdled to produce an easily digesten and nutritious "cheese." It originated inn China about 2000 years ago, and was taken to Japan 800 years later by Buddhist monks. It is an important and inexpensive source of protein in Asian cookery and is used in a multitude of ways; stuffed, diced, shredded and pureed. Because of its protein content, tofu is also valued by vegetarians. Available in Asian food stores, most health food shops and some general supermarkets, it is usually sold in blocks surrounded by liquid and will keep in the refrigerator for 3 to 4 days. It is also sometimes available in powdered form.

Wine Notes

Sake served warm in small ceramic cups would probably be the preferred accompaniment. However, try a full-flavored white, or a lighter style red wine.

FRANCE : A Beaujolais such as Chenas or Fleurie would be a good choice.

USA : Choose a good Fumé Blanc or a Chardonnay from any good Californian district—for example, Napa Valley or Sonoma.

AUSTRALIA : Try a dry Rosé; there are some good examples from McLaren Vale or Coonawarra.

NEW ZEALAND : Try a Chardonnay from Gisborne or Hawkes Bay.

SHABU SHABU

Shabu Shabu, like Sukiyaki, is classed as a "one-pot meal" or nabemono and is a popular choice during Japan's cold winter months. Some say the name of the dish descnbes the sound of the food pieces, held in chopsticks, being "swished" around in the pot; others say it translates as "shive shiver," alluding to the moving surface of the simmering stock. Either way, Shabu Shabu, traditionally cooked at the table, is a convivial dining experience.

SERVES 6

The Japanese chrysanthemum leaves are not essential, but they do add a distinctive flavor. They are sold in Asian grocery stores.

Ingredient

2 lb (1kg) tenderloin or sirloin (fillet or rump) steak, cut into wafer-thin slices against the grain of the meat
12 shiitake mushrooms, soaked in hot water for 30 minutes if dried
8 scallions (spring onions), cut diagonally into 2 inches (5cm) lengths
6 Asian cabbage leaves, torn into bite-sized pieces
½ cup Japanese chrysanthemum leaves, torn into bite-sized pieces (if available)
6oz (180g) tofu, cut into 1 inches (2.5cm) cubes
8oz (250g) bamboo shoots, halved and cut into crescent-shaped slices
1 sheet nori (dried seaweed), slashed in several places
cooking liquid (water or light beef stock)
Gama Dare (see recipe)
Ponzu (see recipe)

Method

1 Arrange the meat, mushrooms, scallions, cabbage, chrysanthemum leaves, tofu and bamboo shoots attractively on a large platter, spacing them so that guests may easily select each morsel with Japanese chopsticks.
2 Place the sheet of nori on the base of a large, flameproof casserole and fill to three-quarters full with water or a light beef stock. Heat to boiling over a table burner and simmer for about 5 minutes.
3 Each diner selects a portion of meat or vegetable, impaling it on the pointed end of the chopstick, dips it into the liquid and swishes it around for a few seconds to cook.
4 The liquid should be kept at a simmer all through the meal, and skimmed as needed.
5 Provide guests with individual bowls of each sauce.
6 The broth is often served separately after all the meat and vegetables are cooked.

GOMA DARE

Sesame Dipping Sauce

MAKES ABOUT 2 ½ CUPS

Ingredient

2~3 tablespoons sesame seeds ⅓ cup
(3 fl oz / 90mL) Japanese soy sauce
1 tablespoon sugar
¾ cup (6 fl oz / 180mL) Dashi (Japanese fish stock)
½ cup finely chopped scallions (spring onions)
2 tablespoons mirin (sweet rice wine) or dry sherry
1 tablespoon sake
1 cup grated daikon (white radish)

Method

1 In a dry pan, toast the sesame seeds until golden, shaking the pan constantly to prevent the seeds from burning.
2 Grind the seeds with a mortar and pestle or place them m a blender and process until flaky.
3 Combine the seeds with the soy sauce, mirin, sugar and sake, then gradually pour in enough dashi to create a sauce.
4 The sauce may be refrigerated, tightly sealed, for 2 to 3 days.
5 Fold in the grated daikon and sprinkle with the scallions before serving.

PONZU

Lime Sauce

MAKES ABOUT 2 ½ CUPS

A simpler version of Ponzu combines equal quantities of lime or lemon juice and dark soy sauce, while yet another blends tart orange juice with an equal quantity of dark soy sauce. However, because of its long cupboard life, it really is worthwhile to make this more sophisticated version and keep it on hand.

Ingredient

1 cup (8 fl oz / 250mL) lime juice, strained
⅓ cup (3 fl oz / 90mL) rice vinegar, or slightly more if a sharper flavor is preferred
1 cup (8 fl oz / 250mL) Japanese dark soy sauce
2 tablespoons Japanese tamari soy sauce
3 tablespoons mirin (sweet rice wine), heated to boiling point to remove alcohol small piece of kombu (dried kelp)

Method

1 Combine all the ingredients and allow to stand for at least 24 hours.
2 Strain the sauce through cheesecloth, then pour into a bottle.
3 Leave to mature in cool, dry place for at least 2 months. It will keep well for up to 12 months.

SHIITAKE MUSHROOMS Shiitake mushrooms are grown in both Japan and China. They take their name from the shii tree, one of the trees on which they grow; but they also grow on other trees, such as oaks. These dark-capped mushrooms with pale gills taste somewhat different to Western mushrooms. They are also far more juicy and very intense in flavor. They are used extensively in Japanese cookery, and also in some Chinese dishes. Traditionally, eating shiitakes was thought to bring good health. Fresh shiitakes are sometimes available in the spring and the fall. Dried shiitakes can be found in most Asian grocery stores. Before using them in a recipe, dried shiitakes should be soaked in either hot water for 30 minutes or, if preferred, in cold water for several hours. Stored in an airtight container, dried mushrooms will keep for up to one year.

Wine Notes

This dish is most successfully accompanied by sage, the Japanese brewed wine. As far as conventional wines go, a variety of styles could be explored.

FRANCE : Try a Beaujolais, a versatile and much-loved red wine. It need not be served chilled in cooler weather.

USA : Choose a Chardonnay of Fumé Blanc from Sonoma or the Napa Valley.

AUSTRALIA : Try a Chardonnay, Semillon or even a dry Rosé from Houghtons, Mt. Hurtle of Taltarni to partner this dish.

NEW ZEALAND : Choose a Chardonnay form the Hawkes Bay area.

AWAYUKI

Snowflake Dessert

Meals in Japan traditionally conclude with fresh fruit, beautifully presented, as is the Japanese way. But times are changing and simple sweets are now seen on restaurant menus. Interestingly, it was once considered unmanly for Japanese men to eat dessert. Sweet red bean paste, a common ingredient of Japanese sweets, is made from the red adzuki bean, a symbol of good luck. The best adzuki beans are said to come from Hakkaido.

SERVES 8

Agar-agar does not need to be chilled to set, but it does speed up the process of the dish is refrigerated.

Ingredient

4 cups (32 fl oz / 1L) hot water
½ cup (4oz / 125g) sugar
4 egg whites
fresh fruit
3 ½ oz (100g) agar-agar
¼ cup (2 fl oz / 60mL) milk
⅓ cup sweet red bean paste, optional

Method

1 Pour the hot water into a large saucepan and crumble in the agar-agar. Heat to boiling, then reduce heat and cook very gently for 10 minutes.
2 Add the sugar, wine and milk and stir until the sugar dissolves. Strain the hot liquid through fine sieve into a bowl, and set aside until lukewarm.
3 Beat the egg whites until stiff peaks form, then fold gently but thoroughly through the liquid. Pour into a 1 ½ inches (3.75cm) deep tray.
4 Chill until firm and cold. Cut the Jelly into diamonds or fancy shapes with cookie (biscuit) cutters. If desired, make small balls with the red bean paste and place on top of the Jelly shapes. Serve with fresh fruit.

Wine Notes

Traditionally, Japanese tea would be served with Awavuki. However, a sweet but not overly rich dessert wine would be a good choice.

FRANCE : A young Muscat-de-Beaumes-de-Venise is fragrant, soft and delightful and goes well with all but the very richest of sweet courses.

USA : A late-picked Johannisberg Riesling—try one from the Pacific Northwest region.

AUSTRALIA : Select a riesling in the Spätlese or Auslese style from the Eden Valley or from the Clare Watervale districts. They are generally fine and have a fresh acidity.

GERMANY : Try a Spätlese from the Mosel or Rheingau.

OHAGI

Rice and Bean Paste Balls

More a confection than a dessert, Ohagi is just one of a variety of Japanese sweets, or okashi. These are served in teahouses or eaten at home, over a cup of tea or nibbled as a snack. Okashi varieties are appropriate to the seasons; Ohagi, resembling bush clover, celebrates the fall; a winter favorite resembles a snowball; one spring sweet is pink and white, like cherry blossom; and a popular green summer sweet is called "moss in a stream."

SERVES 6

It Is possible to buy sweet red beans (adzuki beans) from an Asian grocery store and cook and grind them yourself; but it is much easier to buy the paste already prepared in a jar or can. To toast the flour, spread thinly and evenly on a baking sheet, place in a moderate oven (350°F / 180℃) and bake until evenly browned, about 15 minutes.

Ingredient

1 cup (5oz / 55g) sticky rice
1 cup (5oz / 55g) short grain rice
2 ¾ cups (22 fl oz / 680mL) water
½ teaspoon salt
6 tablespoons toasted soybean flour or rice flour
5 tablespoons superfine (caster) sugar
2 ½ cups (20 fl oz / 625mL) pureed sweet red bean paste

Method

1 Rinse the two types of rice under running water. Place the rice in a saucepan with a tight-fitting lid and add the water. Cover tightly and heat to boiling, then reduce heat and simmer for 15 minutes.
2 Remove from heat and spread the rice on a moistened cloth. Allow to stand for 10 minutes and then place the rice in a large bowl.
3 Sprinkle on the salt and thoroughly mix in. With a large wooden spoon or a fork, mash the rice grains until they are half crushed, but still remain coarse and well textured.
4 While the rice is still warm, moisten your hand with a little salted water and then shape the rice gently but firmly into walnut-sized balls.
5 Combine the flour and the sugar.
6 Cover each ball with a thin layer (about ¼ inch / 0.5cm) thick of the sweet red bean paste and then roll the balls in the flour and sugar.
7 If preferred, the bean paste may be used as the center filling, then covered with a thin layer of rice and rolled in the flour mixed with the sugar.
8 If these are served for afternoon tea, then one ball is served to each guest.

Wine Notes

Japanese tea is the traditional, and probably the best, accompaniment to this dish; however, here are some alternative wine choices.

FRANCE : Try Pinéau de Charentes (fortified, unfermented grape juice from the Cognac region usually served as an aperitif). Serve it chilled.

USA : Choose a light, sweet fortified wine, perhaps in the Madeira style, or try one of the fashionable and rather outlandish Grenache or Zinfandel dessert wines—the Bonny Doon winery is at the forefront of this genre.

AUSTRALIA : Choose and old oloroso sherry from Seppelts, Lindemans, Angoves or Mildara.

JAPAN : Japanese plum wine is sweet but not overpowering—Aka Dama from Suntory is the best known.

MEXICO

World Cuisine

MEXICO has seen a major change in its cuisine over the last ten to fifteen years as it emerges from the tamale-tortilla-taco straitjacket it occupied for such a long time. These days, cooks all over the world boast of their knowledge of minute regional differences rather than admit that they first "went Mexican" with the help of a chili-flavored packet mix. However belated, recognition and intense respect are only the proper due of a cuisine that reaches back thousands of years to ancient civilizations and that continues to astonish us with its depth of knowledge and sophistication.

A systematic form of agriculture came into being in Mexico around 7000 BC, coinciding with similar beginnings in the Middle East. The first cultivated crops were chillies, peppers, avocados and squashes, followed by corn and a virtual seed catalog of bean varieties. But perhaps the greatest gift we have received from these early Mexicans is the cultivated tomato which first came to prominence in the Central American diet in around 800 BC. The Spaniards introduced many new foods and new cooking techniques (particularly frying) to the New World but the inherent value and character of the native cuisine was not lost; it emerged and changed, but as vigorous as ever.

Mexican cooking is almost a byword for diversity, as the mountainous terrain hampered travel between areas, but there are linking threads that join up the different strands in each part of the country. The wheat and cattle of the north have a great influence on the cooking of the area from beef stews with chilies to flat wheat tortillas. The cuisine of central rural Mexico revolves around fruits, grains, sheep and pigs, while on the extensive coastlines, east and west, fish soups, broiled (grilled) jumbo shrimp, ceviche (the raw pickled fish dish) and baked oysters shine on seafood-filed menus.

The chilies of Mexico deserve a book to themselves. They range in size from baby's thumbnail offerings to big, thick specimens measuring nine inches (twenty-two centimeters). They vary in color from light to dark green, yellow to scarlet to almost black, running the gamut of flavors from sweet to exceptionally hot. The hundreds of names border on poetry—serranos, poblanos, jalapeños, guajillos, anchos, pasillas—and varieties that are mild in one part of the country frequently turn fiery a few hundred miles away.

Mexicans use two types of tomatoes in a large number of sauces: the green husk tomato, a rather small green-yellow fruit that releases its flavor only after it is cooked, and the standard red tomato. The cornmeal flour used to make tortillas can thicken sauces but many popular Mexican dishes are made slick and smooth with ground pumpkin seeds, almonds or walnuts.

Corn is the staple of Mexican cooking and it appears in as many distinctive ways as imaginative cooks have ideas. Most city-dwellers buy their tortillas ready-made but country cooks still buy ground cornflour—masa harina—to make their own. The flour is mixed to a dough with water, then formed into small balls which are flattened into rounds before receiving a final squashing in a tortilla press. Traditionally, tortillas are baked briefly on a comal or griddle iron. Tamales use the same masa harina flour but lard and stock are beaten into the mixture until it is light and fluffy. This blend is then smeared over corn husks, topped with a spicy meat, chicken or vegetable filling, before being tightly folded and steamed.

Tortillas can be eaten simply as bread or used to wrap around guacamole, fried mixtures of chorizo sausages and vegetables, frijoles refritos (refried beans), salsa verde or whatever is on hand. Crisp-fried tortillas smothered with lettuce, refried beans, cheese and chili sauce are tostadas. Equally ubiquitous is guacamole, the familiar blend of mashed avocado, tomato and onions that dates from Aztec times, and appears at most Mexican meals as regularly as salsa verde, the fresh, highly piquant sauce of chillies, green tomato and onion.

Sopas secas (literally "dry soups") occupy the same place on the Mexican menu as pasta does on the Italian, as the second course of a full meal. In the majority of cases, rice is the main ingredient. Widely eaten in Mexico, it was introduced during the colonial period. Easily the most cooked rice dish in Mexico is arroz a la Mexicana—a red-tinged blend of tomatoes, rice and onions—a great standby of home and restaurant cooks. It is often spiced up with chillies or served with an egg dish as an accompaniment.

The scenic Mexican coastlines span vast swathes of the Pacific Ocean, the Gulfs of Mexico and California and the Caribbean Sea, throwing up a host of fish dishes as simple as broiled (grilled) fish with a dab of chili sauce or as complicated as the traditional Christmas Eve dish involving dried salt cod. Mexico also produces large harvests of dried shrimp that, of course, have the twin benefits of long storage and the ability to be transported inland. Dried shrimp fritters are widely eaten.

The most accessible meat in many peasant societies is chicken because hens are so cheap and easy to raise. Many Mexican dishes use steamed, shredded chicken, particularly in regional variations of tacos and tostadas. Moles, those unique Mexican stews with numerous and varied ingredients, lift both chicken and turkey to the top of the culinary tree.

Pork is probably the most popular meat in Mexico, except in the cattle-breeding north. Every bit of the pig is eaten—ground up for sausages, fried as crackling for snacks, left in large joints for roasting, or cut up in stews Picadillo, the popular minced meat dish, can be made from either pork or beef, Chorizo, the definitive Mexican sausage, can be made from either coarsely or finely ground pork, which is then colored with herbs, mixed with nuts, and made fiery or mild, longer or shorter, depending on the region.

The ancestry of Mexican desserts is easy to trace—just a straight line back to the egg—yolk rich extravaganzas of Spain and Portugal. Flan, a rich caramel custard, is the most widely known and eaten Mexican dessert, but the national roll-call includes many fruit-based desserts using limes, pineapples and coconuts. Many Mexicans, however, stick to the habit of the Aztecs who preferred to end their meals with the fresh fruits harvested throughout the year: a great idea that has withstood the test of time and taste.

Tequila (a spirit distilled from fermented agave pulp) is a potent and well-known Mexican drink. It forms the basis of the popular cocktail, the margarita.

Many visitors to Mexico stay near the coast, spending their time at resort enclaves filled with silver jewelry, chili-inspired food, mariachi bands and bougainvillea-drenced patios. Sipping a potent piña colada or coco loco and eating a spicy arroz a la Mexicana in the skin-dampening heat is all life should be about.

NACHOS AND GUACAMOLE

Nachos, though not part of the classic Mexican repertoire, combine many Mexican favorites: tortillas, guacamole and frijoles refritos, or refried beans. Tortillas are the bread of Mexican cuisine. Guacamole is an avocado mixture eaten in Mexico with every meal except breakfast; its name is a combination of the Aztec words for avocado and sauce. Frijoles refritos have been popular since Spanish colonists arrived m Mexico and introduced frying, as well as the pig (and thus the supply of lard).

NACHOS

SERVES 4

Nachos are often made without the Frijoles Refritos outside Mexico.

Ingredient

6 ½ oz (200g) tortilla chips or corn chips
1 ½ cups (6oz / 185g) grated Cheddar cheese
½ cup Guacamole (see recipe)
½ cup (4oz / 125g) sour cream
1 ½ cups Frijoles Refritos (see recipe)
⅓ cup well-drained, canned jalapeño chilies, sliced
⅓ cup (2oz / 60g) black olives, sliced

Method

1 Preheat the oven to 350°F (180℃).
2 Spread the individual chips with a thin layer of Frijoles Refritos.
3 Arrange a layer of the chips in the base of a shallow ovenproof serving platter, and sprinkle lavishly with some of the grated cheese. Continue layering the chips and cheese until they are all used.
4 Top with the jalapeño slices and heat in the oven until the cheese melts, about 10 minutes.
5 Garnish with extra chips and a little of the sour cream and olives. Serve at once, with the Guacamole and remaining sour cream and olives in separate bowls.

GUACAMOLE

Avocade Dip

SEVERS 4

Do not use the food processor for this recipe, as the texture of the dip should be quite coarse. Serve the Guacamole with tortilla chips of corn chips.

Ingredient

2 large ripe avocados
1 or 2 small jalapeño chilies, sliced or finely chopped
1 teaspoon chopped cilantro (coriander) leaves (more if desired)
½ cup diced tomato
1 small onion, finely chopped or grated
2 teaspoons lime or lemon juice
salt, optional

Method

1 Cut the avocados in half and scoop out the flesh. Mash with a fork.
2 Combine the avocado flesh, tomato, chilies, onion, cilantro and lime juice. Add a little salt if desired and serve at once.

FRIJOLES REFRITOS

Refried Beans

SERVES 6

Resist the temptation to mash the beans with a food processor, as the result will be rather gluey. Substitute bay leaves or summer savory if epazote is unavailable.

Ingredient

2 cups (12oz / 75g) dried pinto beans
10 cups (80 fl oz / 2.5L) water
3 teaspoons salt
1 ½ teaspoons chopped epazote leaves
1 small onion, finely chopped
½ onion
1oz (30g) lard (pork fat)
3 jalapeño chilies
½ cup (4 fl oz / 125mL) olive oil
½ cup (2oz / 60g) crumbled sharp tasting Cheddar cheese, optional

Method

1 Rinse the beans, then place in a bowl and cover with water. Soak for at least 4 hours. Discard any skins or beans that float to the surface.
2 Drain well and place the beans in a heavy saucepan. Roughly chop the half onion and add with the water and lard to the pan. Cover and simmer gently over medium heat for 1 ½~2 hours or until the beans are tender. Check often to ensure the beans are still covered with water, and in necessary add hot water.
3 When the beans are tender, add the salt, chilies and epazote, and cook, uncovered, for an additional 15 minutes.
4 Drain the beans, reserving the cooking liquid. Refrigerate the cooked beans for several hours to allow the flavors to blend.
5 Heat the oil in a large pan, add the onion and stir-fry for about 5 minutes. Add half the cooked beans and half the cooking liquid, and mash to a soft paste. Gradually add the remaining beans and liquid and mash to a coarse consistency.
6 Continue to cook over medium heat until most of the liquid has evaporated; stir often to prevent sticking.
7 If serving as a separate dish, spoon onto a warmed serving plate and sprinkle with the coarsely crumbled cheese if desired.

AVOCADOS The avocado is the delicious fruit of a large deciduous tree (Persea americana) that is native to South America. Archaeological evidence shows that the Mexicans' enjoyment of it began at least 7000 years ago and that it was still important in their cuisine when the Spanish arrived in the early 1500s. The Spanish planted sapling in several tropical countries, and its popularity has become widespread. There are many varieties of avocado, ranging from tiny seedless ones known as cocktail avocados through to large pear-shaped ones. The avocado can be enjoyed in many ways: by itself or with a light dressing; as an interesting addition to salads; and lightly cooked with seafood or chicken. Both the flesh and the leaves are used in Mexican cuisine. As cooking avocados can cause a bitter flavor to develop, cook for as short a time as possible. Unripe avocados can bag at room temperature at home. Brush the avocado flesh with lemon juice to prevent it from discoloring after the skin has been removed.

Wine Notes

Full-bodied whites such as Chardonnay work well with these flavors.

FRANCE : Choose a white Burgundy style, such as Macon-Villages or Saint-Veran or one of the "new wave" full-bodied whites from Provence or Languedoc.

USA : Try one of the many excellent, full-bodied Californian Chardonnays.

AUSTRALIA : McLaren Vale in South Australia produces excellent, flavorsome Chardonnays.

NEW ZEALAND : Select a good Chardonnay with some richness of flavor say from the Hawkes Bay district.

HUEVOS RANCHEROS

Ranchers' Eggs

With the arrival of the Spanish, the chicken was added to Mexico's food resources. Previously only the wealthy ate meat, while the working Indians would eat mostly fish or vegetables, both of which were in abundance. The introduction of the chicken made possible many of the egg dishes which are now enjoyed. Originally served to the field workers during their morning's labor, Huevos Rancheros is a popular and substantial snack at any time.

SERVES 4

To reduce the spiciness of the sauce, discard the chili seeds before adding the flesh. Always wash your hands after handling chilies, as chili juice can sting the eyes.

Ingredient

⅓ cup (3 fl oz / 90mL) oil
2 jalapeño chilies, finely shredded
4 medium tomatoes, finely chopped
4 corn tortillas
grated Cheddar cheese, optional
1 small white onion, finely chopped
1 garlic clove, finely chopped
salt and pepper, to taste
4 eggs

Method

1 Heat 2 tablespoons of the oil in a small saucepan and cook the onion, chilies and garlic until the onion is soft. Add the tomatoes and cook for 3 to 4 minutes over moderate heat. Add the salt and pepper and cook for an additional 3 minutes.
2 Meanwhile, heat the leftover oil in a skillet, add 1 tortilla and fry for 2 to 3 seconds, or until the tortilla is heated through (they do not have to be crisp). Drain on paper towel. Cook the remaining tortillas in the same way.
3 Fry the eggs in the same pan used for the tortillas, adding extra oil if needed. You may need to cook the eggs in two batches.
4 Place the tortillas on 4 serving plates, top each with an egg and spoon on the sauce. Sprinkle with the cheese if desired.

Wine Notes

These are most often consumed with tomato juice or tequila, but a lively red would be a good choice.

FRANCE : Choose a Beaujolais or a Mâcon Supérieur red.

USA : Try an attractive, lightish red from California using varieties such as Dolcetto, Barbera or Sangiovese.

AUSTRALIA : Select a soft red with a berry flavor such as a Merlot, a Malbec or a blend of these from Coonawarra or the Barossa Valley.

CHILE : Good inexpensive reds are new coming from Chile. Merlot is a popular variety.

CEVICHE

Marinated Raw Seafood

The Mexican coastline extends for many thousands of miles, bordering both the Pacific Ocean and the Caribbean Sea. It is not surprising that seafood is important in local cuisine. There are many versions of this ancient Mexican dish, believed to have originated in South America, but the principle is the same: the acid of the citrus juice "cooks" the fish. Any very fresh, firm-fleshed fish—such as pompano, red snapper or sole—may be used.

SERVES 4~6

Although most Mexican recipes use raw chilies, the canned variety, which have a more mellow flavor, are very good in this recipe.

Ingredient

- 1 lb (500g) mixed seafood, including scallops, shrimp (prawns) and firm fish fillets, cut into strips.
- 1 onion, finely chopped
- ⅓ cup (3 fl oz / 90mL) virgin olive oil
- 1 tablespoon wine vinegar
- ½ teaspoon salt
- 6 lettuce leaves or other salad green 2 limes, cut into slices, for garnish
- 1 ⅓ cups (11 fl oz / 340mL) lime or lemon juice
- 2 canned or fresh jalapeño chilies, finely chopped
- 1 large tomato, skinned, seeded and coarsely chopped
- 1 teaspoon chopped oregano leaves
- freshly ground black pepper, to taste

Method

1 Rinse the fish and lightly pat dry. Shell the shrimp and remove the black vein. Trim and clean the scallops.
2 Combine the seafood in a non-metallic bowl and pour in the citrus juice. Cover and refrigerate for 4 hours, lightly stirring occasionally, then drain off the liquid.
3 Combine the chilies, onion, tomato, oil, vinegar, oregano, salt and pepper. Add to the seafood and mix well. Return to the refrigerator until ready to serve.
4 Arrange the lettuce leaves on individual plates, then arrange piles of the marinated seafood on top and garnish with the lime slices.

Wine Notes

The herby, piquant flavors of this dish require a wine with some character, yet it must not be too heavy for the essentially light seafood theme.

FRANCE : Select a Sancerre or Pouilly Fumé, both are crisp, but definite in flavor.

USA : Try a Sauvignon Blanc, or a Colombard or Semillon from a good Napa, Sonoma or San Francisco Bay area winemaker.

AUSTRALIA : Choose one of the very good Margaret River (Western Australia) Chenin Blancs.

NEW ZEALAND : Try a Sauvignon Blanc, particularly from the Marlborough district.

ENCHILADAS DE POLLO Y DE CARNE

Chicken and Beef Enchiladas

There are many recipes for enchiladas, varying even within regions. Beef is more likely to be used for the filling in the north of Mexico, while chicken features in the enchiladas of the center and south. The traditional corn tortillas, which still dominate the central and southern regions, are replaced in the north by wheat flour tortillas, developed after the Spanish settlers introduced wheat in that area.

ENCHILADAS DE POLLO

Chicken Enchiladas

SERVES 4~6

Enchiladas are usually eaten on their own at suppertime, but they can also be served as an accompaniment to other dishes, as a breakfast meal, or as a tasty snack at any time of the day. The tortillas may become soggy if the enchiladas are not served as soon as they are prepared.

Ingredient

ENCHILADA SAUCE

4 tablespoons virgin olive oil
1 large onion, chopped
1 red bell pepper (capsicum), cored, seeded and finely chopped salt and pepper, to taste
6 large tomatoes, skinned and chopped
¾ teaspoon cumin

FIILING

8oz (250g) cooked chicken, diced
⅓ cup (2oz / 60g) toasted almonds, chopped
2 eggs, beaten
generous pinch cinnamon
oil, for shallow-frying
1 tablespoon chopped raisins
2 tablespoons chopped green olives
2 tablespoons water
12 small tortillas (about 4~5 inches / 10~12cm in diameter)

GARNISH

1 tomato, cut into wedges
red onion slices
finely shredded lettuce

Method

1 To make the sauce, heat the oil in a pan, add the tomatoes, onion, cumin and red pepper. Stir-fry until the vegetables are tender, then add the salt and pepper. Remove from heat and keep warm.
2 Combine the chicken, raisins, almonds and olives in a bowl and mix well.
3 Beat the eggs with the water and cinnamon until light and foamy.
4 Dip each tortilla into the egg mixture. Place a portion of filling into the center of each tortilla, roll up and fasten firmly with toothpicks.

5 Heat the all in a large skillet. Cook the tortillas quickly over moderate heat for about 2 minutes on each side, or until golden brown. Drain well on crumpled paper towels and remove the toothpicks.
6 Arrange the tortillas on a serving plate and spoon the warm sauce on top. Decorate with the tomato, lettuce and onion.

ENCHILADAS DE CARNE

Beef Enchiladas

SERVES 4~6

A strong-tasting crumbly cheese such as Coon may be substituted for the Cheddar.

Ingredient

Enchilada Sauce (see recipe)
12 corn tortillas
2 cups (8oz / 250g) grated Cheddar cheese plus 1 cup (4oz / 125g), extra, optional 1 lb (500g) ground (minced) beef, cooked
2 tablespoons olive oil
2 onions, finely chopped

Method

1 Preheat the oven to 375°F (190℃).
2 Heat the sauce in a small pan.
3 In another pan, heat the oil and briefly fry the tortillas. Drain on paper towels.
4 Mix together the onion, 2 cups of the cheese and the beef.
5 Dip each tortilla into the hot sauce. Place some of the beef mixture on each tortilla and roll up. Place, seam side down, in a shallow baking pan. Cover with the remaining sauce, then sprinkle the extra cheese on top, if using. Bake for 20 minutes, then serve.

CUMIN Cumin (Cuminum cyminum) is an annual herb, rather similar in appearance to caraway or fennel. Its long seeds are strongly scented and give a spicy, slightly bitter taste. It is a native of the Mediterranean region, and was known to the people there from ancient times (the Egyptians used it to preserve the bodies of their rulers, in the process known as mummification). Cumin seeds can be used whole or ground, and are essential in curry powders and Mexican chili powders. Cumin is also a popular pickling spice. It is very popular in the cuisines of Mexico, India and North Africa. Both the seeds and the powder are generally available in supermarkets.

Wine Notes

This dish just cries out to be accompanied by beer! Try Corona from Mexico or Lone Star from Texas. A soft, spicy red would be the best wine.

FRANCE : Select a Mâcon Supérieur, Côtes du Rhône or Bandol from the South.

USA : Choose a soft, full-bodied spicy Zinfandel from California.

AUSTRALIA : Try a young McLaren Vale Shiraz.

NEW ZEALAND : Try a Merlot from Hawkes Bay or Gisborne.

TACOS WITH PICADILLO

Tacos are yet another use to which the Mexican cook puts the tortilla. Tacos are a traditional antojito—a spur-of-the-moment snack—and the fillings can range from a simple chili sauce to the elaborate Picadillo, an exotic combination of meat, fruit and spices. Sometimes the tortillas used for tacos are lightly fried or toasted before they are filled and folded in half. These are often known as soft tacos, and differ from the deep-fried tortilla which is the usual taco shell.

TACOS

SERVES 8

Other Simpler fillings can also be used in tacos. Another way of serving is to present all the ingredients in separate bowls and allow the diners to assemble their own tacos.

Ingredient

Pleadillo (see recipe)
2 onions, finely chopped
1 cup (4oz / 25g) grated Cheddar cheese
torn lettuce leaves, for garnish
24 taco shells
3 tomatoes, finely chopped
2 tablespoons black olives, for garnish

Method

1 Spoon enough of the Picadillo into each taco to two-thirds fill it, then add a little of each of the other ingredients, except the garnishes.
2 Arrange the filled tacos on a tray and garnish with the lettuce and olives.

PICADILLO

SERVES 6~8

The unusual combination of flavors works wonderfully. It may be served as a main course or as a filling for tacos, empanadas, or perhaps large chilies or bell peppers. Lard was used in earlier versions of this dish, but it is now more common to use oil.

Ingredient

3oz (90g) lard (pork fat) or ⅓ cup (3 fl oz / 90mL) oil
2 large onions, finely chopped or minced
¼ cup (2 fl oz / 60mL) lemon or lime juice
4 poblano or other hot chilies, finely chopped or shredded
2 bay leaves or avocado leaves
½ teaspoon ground cinnamon
salt, to taste
2 lb (1kg) lean ground (minced) beef
⅓ cup (3 fl oz / 90mL) dry sherry
6 tomatoes, skinned and chopped
⅔ cup (3oz / 90g) stuffed green olives, sliced
2 teaspoons chopped capers, optional
½ teaspoon ground cumin
⅓ teaspoon freshly ground black pepper

1. Heat two-thirds of the lard in a large heavy pan Add the meat and onions and cook over high heat until evenly browned.
2. Lower heat and add the sherry and citrus juice. Cook for 5 minutes.
3. Stir in the tomatoes, chilies. olives, capers, bay leaves and raisins and simmer for another 20 minutes.
4. Heat the remaining lard in a small pan, add the garlic, cumin and cinnamon, and fry for 3 to 4 minutes, then add to the meat with the pepper and salt. Simmer an additional 5 to 10 minutes. Check the seasoning, then transfer to a serving plate.

TORTILLAS Corn tortillas have been the daily bread of Mexico for centuries. They are made from a simple mixture of masa harina (specially treated corn), water and salt, that can either be patted into flat disks by hand or rolled into balls and flattened in specially designed tortilla presses. Flour tortillas, typical of northern Mexico, are made with flour instead of masa harina plus lard, and are rolled out instead of pressed. Fresh tortillas are usually found only at specialty Mexican food stores, but ready-made commercial tortillas and masa harina mix are stocked in many supermarkets. Mexicans use tortillas in a variety of ways, including as a bread rolled around fillings, and as a base for toppings.

Wine Notes

A fairly bold red goes well with Tacos—strong but simple in flavor, and certainly not expensive.

FRANCE : Choose from the vin de pays reds of the southern regions such as Costiéres du Gard.

USA : Select a robust example of Grenache, Mourvédre or Syrah from California.

AUSTRALIA : Choose a Shiraz or any good, flavorsome blend from the Barossa Valley.

NEW ZEALAND : Try a Cabernet Sauvignon or Cabernet Merlot blend from the North Island.

ITALY : Montepulciano d'Abruzzo with its rustic, flavorsome characteristics is ideal.

ENSALADA DE NAVIDAD

Christmas Salad

While Mexico is rich in vegetables—Cortés was astounded by the variety displayed in the markets of the Aztec capital, Tenochtitlan—salads appear only occasionally on the dining table. The following salad is traditionally served after midnight mass on Christmas Eve. The Catholic faith was introduced into Mexico by the earliest Spanish colonists, and its influence is still strong today.

SERVES 6

A traditional version of this recipe tosses the salad ingredients together. The pomegranate seeds add a distinctive tang and a touch of the exotic to this festive salad. If these seeds are unavailable, simply omit, or substitute shredded, unsprayed wild rose petals.

Ingredient

1 head romaine (cos) lettuce
2 small beets (beetroot)
¼ medium pineapple, peeled, cored and diced
1 large banana, sliced or coarsely diced
3 teaspoons pomegranate seeds
1 large carrot
4oz (250g) jicama or 1 cooking apple, peeled and diced
⅓ cup (2oz / 60g) roasted almonds

DRESSING

1 tablespoon salad oil or light olive oil
½ teaspoon sugar
1 tablespoon lime or lemon juice
pinch of salt and pepper

Method

1. Rinse the whole lettuce leaves and then dry them.
2. Crisp the lettuce leaves in a plastic bag in the refrigerator until required.
3. Cook the carrot until just tender. Cook the beets separately until tender crisp. Coarsely grate each.
4. Arrange the lettuce leaves on a serving platter with the beets, carrot and fruit.
5. Combine the dressing ingredients in a small jar, seal and shake vigorously. Pour over the salad.
6. Garnish with the chopped nuts and pomegranate seeds.
7. Serve at once.

POMEGRANATES The pomegranate (Punica granatum) is native to the Mediterranean area and southern Asia. It is sometimes shown in ancient Chinese paintings, mentioned in the Bible and in stories of Mohammed. The pomegranate's sweet-tart seeds and pulp are enjoyed on their own and in drinks, salads, sauces, as well as with chicken, meat and fish dishes. The seeds are also used in Mexican cuisine as a garnish, because of their beautiful appearance.

Wine Notes

The perfect choice to serve with this dish is Sangria, the Spanish red wine punch which is now also popular in Mexico. It is a very refreshing drink in hot weather.

SANGRIA : For each person, combine a glass of dry red wine with a tablespoon of lime juice and a teaspoon of sugar. Add a few cubes of fruit and chill. Oranges are often used; you may also try pineapple, apple or pear if desired. When ready to serve, pour into a goblet and garnish with a sprig of mint.

CHILI CON POLLO

Chili with Chicken

Most chicken in Mexico are free-range, and as a result are more flavorful than the average European or North American chicken. However, their flesh is tougher and they do not lend themselves to roasting or broiling (grilling). The traditional method of cooking chicken in Mexico is stewing or braising it slowly until the meat can be pulled off the bone. It is then shredded or finely chopped and added to countless dishes.

SERVES 4

If you can, buy ground chicken for this dish; otherwise use finely chopped chicken thigh or breast fillet meat. Chili con Pollo is also a good filling for tacos and enchiladas.

Ingredient

4 cups cooked red kidney beans or 2 × 14 oz (450g) cans of beans
2 tablespoons olive oil
1 lb (500g) finely chopped or ground (minced) chicken
2 small onions, finely chopped
2~3 small hot red chilies, seeded and finely shredded
1 large tomato, peeled and chopped
2 garlic cloves, finely chopped
1 bay leaf or 1 avocado leaf, torn into pieces
salt and pepper, to taste
2 tablespoons chopped cilantro (coriander), for garnish
¾ cup (6oz / 80g) light sour cream

Method

1 Rinse the beans in cold water and drain.
2 Heat the oil in a large skillet over moderate heat, add the chicken, onions and chilies, and cook only until the chicken meat becomes opaque. Add the tomato, garlic, bay leaf and salt and pepper. Simmer for an additional 8 to 10 minutes, or until the meat is cooked through.
3 Add the beans, and stir over moderate heat until warmed through.
4 Spoon onto serving plates, garnish with the chopped cilantro and the whole leaves.
5 Serve a bowl of sour cream separately.

Wine Notes

A richly flavored white wine will best accommodate the chicken-chili combination.

FRANCE : Select a wine from an appellation such as Rully, Saint-Véran or Montagny.

USA : Choose a Fumé Blanc or Chardonnay from the Napa Valley in California.

AUSTRALIA : The Chardonnays of Pathaway are some of Australia's most flavorsome and rich.

SPAIN : Try the Torres Gran Viña Sol.

ARROZ A LA MEXICANA

Mexican Rice

Rice was introduced to Mexican cuisine in the mid-1500s by Spanish traders sailing from the Philippines back to Spain. Sautéed rich, sopa seca (dry soup), is served between the appetizer and the main course in a traditional Mexican meal. It can also be eaten as a light meal by itself. This recipe for Arroz a la Mexicana comes from Puebla. In Veracruz, plantain would be included, while in Michoacan the rice is fried in chicken fat.

SERVES 4~6

Do not cook the rice in advance as it will not absorb the flavors properly.

Ingredient

2 cups (11oz / 340g) long grain rice
1 small onion, grated or very finely chopped
1 red bell pepper (capsicum), cored, seeded and chopped
1 tablespoon cumin
3 small whole chilies, optional
2 ½ cups (20 fl oz / 600mL) chicken stock
salt and pepper, to taste
4 tablespoons olive oil
1 garlic clove, finely chopped
1 large tomato, peeled, seeded and finely chopped
1 tablespoon finely chopped cilantro (coriander) or parsley
¼ cup (1oz / 30g) green peas, optional

Method

1 Rinse the rice in a colander under running water. Place in a bowl and cover with hot water. Allow to stand for 30 minutes before draining well. Leave in a colander for an hour to dry out.
2 Heat the oil in a heavy pan and add the rice, onion and garlic. Cook over low heat until the onion has softened, stirring to coat all of the rice grains with oil.
3 Mix in the red pepper, tomato, cilantro, cumin and chilies, if using. Add the stock and peas, if using, cover tightly and cook for 15 minutes over moderate heat, stirring from time to time until the liquid is absorbed and the rice is fluffy. (If more tender rice is preferred, add a little more stock at this stage and cook until all the additional liquid is absorbed.)
4 Remove the chilies. Add seasoning as required and serve.

Wine Notes

Choose a soft, fruity style of wine, preferably a light red.

FRANCE : Many regions have their own attractive rosés differing in style and variety. Choose one from Provence or Anjou.

USA : Try one of the popular light reds from California. Zinfandel, Barbera Gamay, Pinot Noir and Merlot are the most common varieties.

AUSTRALIA : Try a light fresh red in the Beaujolais style, for example Mitchelton's Cab Mac.

ITALY : Dolcetto d'Alba and Barbera d'Ati from Piedmont have a soft, grapey quality.

PESCADO ESTILO YUCATECO

Fish Yucatan Style

Throughout Mexico we find recipes for whole fish cooked in various ways. This reflects Mexico's immense coastline, and the many hundreds of tons of fish caught fresh each day. Each region—even each port—is justifiably proud of the way fish is prepared locally, often in a simple fashion to retain the flavor of the fish. In this version, from Yucatan, the fish is wrapped in banana leaves. If banana leaves are unavailable, wrap the fish in heavy foil.

SERVES 6

Any firm-fleshed fish, like pompano, red snapper or sole, would be suitable.

Ingredient

1 whole fish, about 5 lb (2.5kg), cleaned
1 tablespoon salt
4 tablespoons virgin olive oil
1 poblano chili, finely shredded
1 cup (6 ½ oz / 200g) pumpkin seeds, optional
1 banana leaf
2 hard-cooked (hare-boiled) eggs, sliced
3 tablespoons lime juice
1 teaspoon freshly ground black pepper
2 small white onions, thinly sliced
½ green bell pepper (capsicum), chopped
2 tablespoons shredded cilantro (coriander) leaves
¼ cup (2 fl oz / 60mL) orange juice
2 limes, cut into wedges

Method

1 Preheat the oven to 350°F (180℃).
2 Wipe the fish all over with a damp cloth. Rub the lime juice all over the skin and inside the cavity. Sprinkle with the salt and pepper.
3 Heat the oil in a large pan, stir-fry the onion, chili, green pepper, pumpkin seeds and half the Cilantro leaves. Cook until the vegetables are softened but not browned.
4 Place the fish on an oiled banana leaf and spread the onion mixture evenly over the fish. Pour the orange juice over the fish. Fold the leaf over the fish to make a package, fastening with toothpicks if necessary.
5 Place in an ovenproof pan and bake for 30 to 35 minutes, or until the fish flakes easily when tested with a fork.
6 Serve in the opened banana leaf or transfer to a serving platter. Garnish with the sliced eggs and remaining cilantro. Serve with the lime wedges.

LIMES The lime tree (Citrus aurantifolia) is thought to have originated in India and Southeast Asia. Spanish explorers introduced limes to Europe and to the Americas. Lime rind and juice can be used in both sweet and savory dishes. Varieties of limes differ in color, size and even flavor. The yellow-skinned Mexican limes (also known as West Indian or Key limes) are smaller and their flavor is less sharp than the Tahiti (also known as Persian) limes.

Wine Notes

The interesting combination of flavors in this dish is best suited to a soft but flavorsome white wine.

FRANCE : Try wines of Alsace which are France's most appropriate. Try Gewurztraminer or Piont Gris.

USA : Select a Gewurztraminer with some depth; fine examples come from the Mendocino -Lake County area.

AUSTRALIA : Choose an aromatic, full-bodied Rhine Riesling or Traminer-Riesling blend from the Barossa Valley or Clare Valley.

NEW ZEALAND : A Marlborough Sauvignon Blanc would be a good choice.

MOLE POBLANO DE GUAJOLOTE

Turkey with Poblano Sauce

Complex moles (or sauces), like this one, are a feature of southern Mexican cooking. The origins of this world-famous dish are well known: almost 400 years ago the nuns of the Santa Rosa convent in Puebla created it to impress a group of dignitaries, including the viceroy of Mexico. The recipe has been simplified over the years but Mole Poblano de Guajolote is still featured on special occasions, such as weddings and baptisms.

SERVES 8~10

If you cannot find the suggested combination of chilies in your local market, substitute a mixture of available chilies. Don't forget that these chilies need to be soaked overnight before sauce preparation can begin.

Ingredient

1 young turkey, about 8 lb (4kg), cut into serving portions
6 garlic cloves
1 small onion, quartered
1 tablespoon salt
½ teaspoon black peppercorns

SAUCE
15 mixed chilies (pasillas, mulatos and anchos)
1 ½ lb (750g) ripe tomatoes, peeled and finely chopped
4 large garlic cloves
½ cup (3oz / 90g) raisins or currants
½ teaspoon ground cinnamon
1 tablespoon sugar
pinch ground cloves
3oz (90g) semisweet (dark cooking) chocolate, broken into pieces
½ cup (4 fl oz / 125mL) light oil or 4oz (125g) lard (pork fat)
1 onion, chopped
¾ cup (4oz / 125g) roasted peanuts
½ teaspoon black peppercorns
½ teaspoon aniseed, optional
1 tablespoon salt
⅓ cup toasted sesame seeds

Method

1 Soak the chilies overnight in enough water to cover. The next day, drain the chilies, discard the stems and grind the chilies (including the seeds) to a paste.
2 Place the turkey pieces in a large flame-proof casserole, add just enough water to cover. Add the onion, garlic, salt and peppercorns. Heat to boiling, skim the surface and reduce heat.
3 Cover and simmer gently. Pierce with a fork to test for tenderness after 1 ½ hours. When the turkey pieces are tender, drain, and reserve 2 cups of the stock. Pat the turkey pieces dry with paper towels.
4 Heat half the oil in a heavy pan. Add the turkey pieces and fry, turning to brown evenly. Drain away any excess oil.

5 In a food processor, blend together all the sauce ingredients except the prepared chili paste, sesame seeds and chocolate. If necessary, add a little stock from the turkey pieces to form a smooth paste.

6 Heat the remaining oil in another saucepan. Add the chili paste, sauce mixture and sesame seeds and reduce heat to low. Add the chocolate, stirring constantly until thoroughly blended. Stir in the reserved stock, cover, and cook gently until the liquid thickens. Pour over the turkey pieces and leave over a low heat for 20 minutes, or until the turkey pieces are heated through.

7 An alternative version of this recipe presents the turkey is brushed all over with butter and lime juice, then baked at 350°F (180℃) for 2 hours, or until the juices run clear when pierced with a knife. The turkey is carved into serving-sized portions and the sauce is poured over them.

CHOCOLATE One of the most loved of all ingredients—indeed, claimed by some to be addictive—chocolate finds a place in the cuisine of many countries. It is manufactured from the beans of the cacao tree (Theobroma cacao), which is native to South America. Theobroma is Greek for "food of the gods." In 1519 Hernando Cortés, the Spanish conquistador, was offered a beverage made from pounded cocoa beans, spices and a little honey by the Aztec king Montezuma II. Nine years later he returned to Spain with some of the beans in his possession, thus kicking off what would become several centuries of European and American culinary experimentation. Nowadays, of course, chocolate is available in many different forms and qualities and is an integrated ingredient in many recipes.

Wine Notes

Finding a wine to go with chocolate may seem difficult, but the chocolate flavor is not particularly pronounced in this dish. A soft, spicy red wine will be suitable.

FRANCE : Try Gigondas, the ever-improving appellation of the southern Rhône.

USA : Try a zesty, berryish and slightly jammy Zinfandel from California. Its fruit-driven qualities mark it as a good choice for this dish.

AUSTRALIA : Australia produces some delightful Sparkling Burgundies. They are rather idiosyncratic wines which are not really much like anything else. Choose one from Great Western in Victoria.

NEW ZEALAND : Try a Sparkling Burgundy from the North Island, or try a soft fruity red, perhaps one featuring Merlot.

TORTA DE CIELO

Almond Sponge Cake

This cake is rich in eggs, almonds and sugar and is typical of the dessert recipes introduced by the Spanish nuns who came to Mexico in the early colonial period. Before the nuns' arrival, meals usually concluded with fruit, such as pineapple, papaya or passion fruit. This delicate almond sponge is traditionally served at first communion parties and weddings. The literal translation of the Spanish name is "Cake of Heaven."

SERVES 6~8

Decorative garnishes such as pomegranate seeds and unsprayed wild rose petals may be used.

Ingredient

½ cup (2oz / 60g) all-purpose (plain) flour
6 eggs, separated
¾ cup (6oz / 185g) sugar
½ teaspoon almond extract (almond essence)
¾ cup (3oz / 90g) blanched, finely ground almonds
1 tablespoon brandy or Kahlúa
1 tablespoon confectioners' (icing) sugar

Method

1 Preheat the oven to 350°F (180℃).
2 Sift the flour into a small bowl, then add the ground almonds.
3 In a large bowl beat the egg whites until soft peaks form. At high speed, gradually beat in ¼ cup (2oz / 60g) of the sugar, mixing until glossy peaks form.
4 In another bowl, beat together the egg yolks with the remaining sugar, Kahlúa and almond extract.
5 Using a rubber spatula, fold the almond / flour mixture and the egg yolk mixture into the whipped egg whites. Pour the mixture into a buttered and floured 9 inches (23cm) spring form pan and bake for 40 minutes, or until the cake springs back when pressed lightly with a finger.
6 Place the cake pan on a wire rack to cool. When it is cool, gently remove it from the pan. To serve, dust the surface of the cake with the confectioners' sugar.

Wine Notes

A light fortified sweet white is delicious with this sponge cake. Hot chocolate would also be good.

FRANCE : Try to find a white vin doux naturel (sweet dessert wine) from around Roussillon.

USA : Choose a sweet Madeira-style wine from California's Central Valley district.

AUSTRALIA : Select a fortified Frontignac or Tokay fro Victoria's Rutherglen district.

SPAIN : Look for a sweeter style of sherry like oloroso.

FLAN A LA MEXICANA

Mexican Caramel Custard

Rich and meltingly delicious, this dessert combines the milk, eggs and sugar of the Old World with the vanilla pods of the New, reflecting the merging of cultures that occurred during the time of Spanish rule in Mexico. The cross-pollination worked both ways: this recipe was created in Spain and then became popular throughout Mexico. This flan is the perfect ending to a spicy meal.

SERVES 6

It Is essential to cook the custard in a waterbath to ensure that the texture of the custard is satiny smooth. For a particularly sinful version of this recipe, substitute light cream for half the milk.

Ingredient

1 cup (8oz / 250g) sugar
1 vanilla pod or 1 teaspoon vanilla extract (vanilla essence)
orange zest, for garnish, optional
3 ¾ cups (30 fl oz / 930mL) milk
3 eggs
6 egg yolks

Method

1 Preheat the oven to 350°F (180℃).
2 Cook half the sugar in a heavy-based pan over low heat until it caramelizes. Pour the caramel into two 8 inches (20cm) flan pans, tilting so the soft caramel swirls around the sides. Set aside.
3 Combine the milk, remaining sugar and vanilla pod or extract in a heavy saucepan. Heat to boiling then reduce heat and cook for 8 minutes, stirring often.
4 Remove the saucepan from heat and allow to cool slightly
5 Beat the whole eggs and the egg yolks together until foamy, then stir in the milk mixture. Strain the resulting custard and pour into the prepared pans. Place them in a baking pan half-filled with hot water, and bake for about 50 minutes, or until just firm to the touch. Set the pan aside to cool to room temperature.
6 To unmold, dip the base of each pan into hot water and leave for a couple of minutes. Invert each pan onto a serving platter and gently shake to release.
7 Garnish with the orange zest if desired.

Wine Notes

A sweet dessert wine of the Sauternes style is a natural choice for this dessert.

FRANCE : Sauternes is France's truly great dessert wine. Try a moderately priced Monbazillac or Loupiac.

USA : Look for a late-harvest Riesling or Semillon, preferably a botrytis-affected style with its extra concentration of flavor, from the Sonoma area.

AUSTRALIA : Choose a botrytis-affected (noble rot) dessert wine made from Semillon or Rhine Riesling from Padthaway or the Eden Valley.

HUNGARY : Tokaji Aszu carries a "sweetness rating" on the label, in the form of "putts" or"puttonos"; 3, 4, or 5 "putts" are sweet and rich; 5 "putts" is particularly ambrosial.

MOROCCO

World Cuisine

MOROCCO throws up images so disparate that they belong to several centuries and as many cultures. One foot in the Orient, one foot in the West—the stance of Casablanca will always be associated with the 1940s mood and staccato dialog of the Humphrey Bogart movie; but port cities are never a true reflection of any county.

Morocco is set apart by the fact that it is the only Arab country with a truly grand cuisine—not merely good but great. A casual stroll through the produce sections of the country's major souks gives a wraparound image of large mounds of spices, several orchards of preserved lemons, large vats of olives, the largest dates most of us have ever seen and sweetmeats sold in multiples of 2 pounds (1 kilogram) in weight. The flat, round unleavened Arab bread is piled high on stands and carts, and it is always fresh from the oven. Nougat and nut brittle are sold by artisans whose families may have been in the business for generations.

Tajine dishes—high, cone—shaped and topped with lids—are displayed for sale next to the traditional two-tier couscous cookers of clay and metal. Nearby, stall-holders serve their customers mint tea to help ease the way for a sale. The scene is a constant reminder to visitors that they have come to Morocco for the food as much as for the breathtaking scenery.

As in Asia, streetside food stalls fill the double bill of providing cheap fast food and looking picturesque for the tourist cameras. Hard-cooked (hard-boiled) eggs make a popular Moroccan snack, and street vendors dish them up with the most common condiments—salt and cumin. These two flavorings are again on call at the stalls selling hot chickpeas and fava (broad) beans by the small mound. Tiny lam's liver or minced meat kebabs spiced up with hot peppers and pushed into a pocket of Arab bread, bowls of lentils accented with garlic and onion, chickens impregnated with saffron, tajines and fruity meat stews are all sold on the sidewalk, or what passes for one, while the bigger operators provide tables and chairs.

Moroccan meals generally begin with a line-up of salads, many of which contain cooked vegetables like carrots and cauliflower which are livened up with piquant marinades. Variety meats such as cooked liver are frequently found tucked in with cooked and uncooked vegetables to add contrast. Other popular first courses are bean soups and olives which are eaten with the flatbread much in the same way that we use butter. The salads are left on the table throughout the meal for guests to continuously enjoy as they please.

Harira, the most commonly eaten soup in Morocco, deserves a much greater press than it has received so far. A pungent, thickened broth combines diced lamb, chickpeas and lentils with lighter ingredients such as tomato, onion and parsley. Its relative obscurity probably stems from the fact that it has traditionally been eaten as the first dish to break the fast each evening during the holy month of Ramadan. These days, however, it is turning up more and more on Moroccan restaurant menus.

Morocco is famous for Its olive oil, the best of which comes from the Souss area in the south. Smen, a clarified butter like the Indian ghee but flavored with herbs, is also a much-used fat in Moroccan cooking. Harissa, a fiery blending of hot ted peppers, olive oil and garlic, is the chain that links the cuisines of Morocco, Tunisia and Algeria. But the candidate for most unique ingredient in Moroccan cooking is the preserved lemon, pickled in coarse salt and lemon juice, or olive oil. Only the peel and a little of the juice from the pulp are used to infuse an army of Moroccan dishes with a sweet sharpness that is hard to define.

Charmoula is the basis of many of the Moroccan sauces. A mixture made with olive oil and lemon juice and seasoned with cilantro (coriander), saffron, sweet and hot peppers and garlic, it invariably turns up in any dish featuring fish or poultry.

Tajines, the famous stews of Morcco, depend mostly on lamb or chicken. Served in the tall conical dish from which they derive their name, tajines are placed in the center of the table for everyone to share on family occasions, but in most Moroccan restaurants individual diners order their own and the dish is placed next to them. Favorite spices for tajines are sweet and hot red peppers, saffron, cumin and cilantro.

Friday is the great Muslim rest day and the time for many to enjoy couscous, Morocco's most famous dish. Whether the main meat ingredient is lamb, chicken or fish backed up by a mighty selection of vegetables, the backbone of couscous is large-grained semolina steamed over a rich stock well seasoned with a mixture of saffron, onions, ginger and peppers.

In the legendary La Mamounia restaurant in Marrakech, m'choui has to be ordered a whole day in advance before you can live out your kasbah fantasy of Berber-style roast lamb eaten amid the Arabian nights' decor. Traditionally, m'choui is slow-roasted in the open air until the meat is so tender that it can be pulled off with the fingers. Seasoned with cumin, hot peppers and salt, it needs no other accompaniment than large chunks of crisp Arab bread. In Morocco, m'choui is also made with antelope, young camel or mountain goat.

Even in the everyday surroundings of your own home, the serving of bisteeya. the many-layered wonder it seems sacrilegious to call a pie, almost demands the presence of a waiter dressed in a fez and babouches (the ornate, backless Moroccan slippers). In Western kitchens, most cooks use Greek phyilo pastry but in Morocco the genuine paper-thin pastry article is warkha, a labor-intensive composite of small circles of fried pastry patted into one large sheet. Pigeon is the original ingredient in this savoury mille feuilles, punded with eggs, almonds and raisins, chopped into bite-size pieces. Historians believe that bisteeya can be traced back to ancient Persia via the Moorish occupation of Spain.

Moroccans are famous for their sweet tooth but they eat pastries, cakes and rice confections on special occasions, religious and family celebrations, rather than as a dessert course. Bisteeya the pastry marvel, also comes in a sweet version, laced with ground almonds, cinnamon and sugar, and is known as keneffa. Rice pudding, so popular throughout the MIddle East, frequently accompanies fresh fruit at the end of a meal.

But perhaps the neatest definition of Moroccan culture and by extension its food came from the country's long-reigning king, Hassan II. "Morocco is like a tree nourished by roots deep in the soul of Africa which breathes through foliage rustling to the winds of Europe. Yet Morocco's existence is not only vertical. Horizontally it looks to the East, with which it is bound by ties of religion and culture. Even if we wished to sever those ties—and we do not wish to—it would be impossible." A quick glance at a typical Moroccan menu is confirmation of these deep-rooted influences.

MEZE

Appetizers

Moroccan appetizer selections can be feasts in themselves. The more important the occasion, the more elaborate and varied the choices. The selection almost always includes olives, of which there are myriad varieties in Moroccan markets—from tiny, glossy black specimens to great purple beauties. Many of the dishes, including both of these given here, are commonly made in advance to give the flavors time to mingle.

ZAYTUNE M'CHARMEL

Olives with an Herbed Marinade

SERVES 12

Black, green and purple olives are all very good choices for this recipe. If using dried black olives, soak them in water for at least 8 hours, then drain them and pat dry before macerating them in the herbs and oil.

Ingredient

1 lb (500g) olives
6 tablespoons finely chopped parsley
⅓ teaspoon ground cumin
⅓ teaspoon freshly ground black pepper
⅓ cup (3 fl oz / 0mL) extra-virgin olive oil
2 garlic cloves, slivered
½ teaspoon chili powder
1 tablespoon finely chopped Preserved Lemon

Method

1 Combine all the ingredients in a large bowl, toss together, cover, and allow to marinate for at least 48 hours before serving. If not using them immediately, store in the refrigerator. The olives will keep for 3 weeks.

MISHSHI

Stuffed Vegetables

SERVES 6

Sometimes 2 chopped hard-cooked (hardboiled) eggs are added to the filling.

Ingredient

3 large ripe tomatoes
1 large beet (beetroot), cooked and finely chopped
2 tablespoons chopped cilantro (coriander)
2 tablespoons lemon juice
⅓ teaspoon freshly ground black pepper
⅔ cup (5 fl oz / 160mL) mayonnaise
1 tablespoon chopped green bell pepper (capsicum)
red onion slices, for garnish, optional
2 small red onions, finely chopped
⅓ cup Italian parsley
½ cup (4 fl oz / 125mL) extra-virgin olive oil
½ teaspoon salt
6 canned artichoke hearts, well drained
1 tablespoon chopped red bell pepper (capsicum)
1 tablespoon chopped yellow bell pepper (capsicum), optional

Method

1 Cut the tomatoes in half crosswise, then spoon out the seeds and discard. Scoop out the pulp and chop finely, reserving the shells.
2 Scoop out the center of the artichoke hearts and chop finely, reserving the shells.
3 Combine the chopped tomato, onions, beet, parsley and cilantro.
4 Mix together the olive oil, lemon juice, salt and pepper and stir into the bowl.
5 Mix together the mayonnaise and the chopped bell peppers.
6 Divide the tomato mixture between the tomato halves and the artichoke hearts, top each with a little of the mayonnaise mixture, and chill.
7 Garnish with red onion slices, if desired, and serve.

RED ONIONS The onion (allium cepa) is a biennial member of the lily family. It was mentioned as far back as 4000 years ago in the records kept by Sumerian scribes. Credited by the ancient Chinese and Indian cultures with promoting a healthy life, the onion became an integral part of world cuisine. There are several varieties of onion, differing in size, color and pungency, though they all possess an intrinsic sweetness that emerges during cooking. The onion gently browned in oil is the basis of many casseroles from diverse cuisines. It can also be braised, boiled, stuffed, added to sauces and used as a garnish, either raw or cooked. The small red onion is a particular favorite of Mediterranean and North African cooks, and being sweeter-tasting and more juicy than the more common, large yellow or brown onion, it is used as often raw as cooked. The small red onion is not as readily available away from the Mediterranean as other varieties, but the larger red Spanish onion, also mild enough to be eaten raw, is widely available and is a good substitute. Fresh onions should be kept in a well-ventilated, cool spot where they should remain in good condition for up to a month.

Wine Notes

Montilla, Spain's inland cousin of sherry (from coastal Jerez), is the perfect partner. Something in this style, therefore, would be ideal.

FRANCE : France has no real sherry alternative, so choose a Sancerre from the Loire Valley for its pungent, grassy aroma and flavor.

USA : Select a Napa Valley Fumé Blanc from Sterling, Silverado or Robert Mondavi.

AUSTRALIA : Try a good fino sherry. Mildara, Angoves, Seppelts and Lindemans have products of uniformly high quality which span all price ranges.

SPAIN : Choose Montilla, if it is available or a good fino or manzanilla sherry.

HARlRA

Lamb and Vegetable Soup

Moroccan soups are typically spicy and rich. Harira, made from lamb, vegetables and pulses, is enjoyed all year round, but it has special significance during the holy month of Ramadan. Then the tradition is for Harira to be served at the moment the sun sets, signaling the end of the day's fast for Moslems. It is often accompanied by a selection of light tidbits such as fresh dates, sweet cakes and dried fruits.

SERVES 8

Some cooks add ½ cup cooked rice during the last 15 minutes of cooking; others add ½ cup cooked noodles. If rice or noodles are added the lentils are often eliminated. Remember, the flavor should be very peppery and quite lemony.

Ingredient

2 tablespoon butter
1 lb (500g) lean lamb, diced
1 ½ teaspoons turmeric
¾ teaspoons ground cinnamon
½ teaspoons sweet paprika
2 celery stalks, with leaves, chopped
½ cup dried chickpeas, soaked overnight, then cooked, or ¾ cup canned chickpeas
4 tablespoons chopped parsley.
1 lb (500g) large ripe tomatoes, peeled and chopped
2 tablespoons flour mixed with ½ cup (4 fl oz / 125mL) water
2 large onions, chopped
4 chicken giblets, chopped
1 ½ teaspoons freshly ground black pepper
½ teaspoons ground ginger
6 cups (48 fl oz / 1.5L) water
½ teaspoons salt
⅓ cup red lentils, soaked for several hours and drained
1 tablespoon chopped cilantro (coriander), optional
lemon wedges

Method

1 In a large saucepan, melt the butter and add the onions. Cook over moderate heat for 3 to 4 onions. Cook over moderate heat for 3 to 4 minutes, or until softened.
2 Add the lamb and giblets and cook gently for about 20 minutes, or until lightly browned. Turn often so they do not stick to the saucepan. Add the spices and cook for another 5 minutes.
3 Add the water, celery, salt, chickpeas and lentils to the pan. Simmer for about 1 hour, or until the lentils are tender.
4 Add the parsley, cilantro and tomatoes and cook over moderate heat for about 15 minutes. Stir in the flour and water mixture and heat to boiling, stirring constantly.
5 Serve in individual bowls, accompanied by lemon wedges, to be squeezed into the soup.

LENTILS The lentil (Lens esculenta) is a small annual legume related to the pea. There are several varieties of lentil, and the seeds vary in color from green to brown to bright orange-red. Known to have been cultivated since ancient times, lentils have been found in settlements near Lake Biel in Switzerland which date from the Bronze Age. Also, they were imported form Egypt by the Ancient Romans. Red lentils, thought to be the oldest variety, have been found m China, in tombs from the Han dynasty. Today lentils are widely used in many parts of Asia, the Middle East and North Africa. An excellent source of vegetable protein and some of the B vitamins, lentils have long been a staple part of the diet for people with limited access to meat and are becoming very popular with vegetarians. Lentils are also low in fat and do not contain any cholesterol. Lentils do not need to be soaked before cooking, but if they are it speeds up the cooking time. They are most frequently used in soups and stews. The pureed dahl of India is famous. Salads too can be enhanced in color and texture by adding cooked lentils. The cuisine of India, Pakistan and Bangladesh also uses flour ground from lentils. Lentils are readily available. They will keep indefinitely, stored in a cool, dark place.

Wine Notes

A good, dry sherry would be the ideal choice for this dish–otherwise choose a full-bodied white.

FRANCE : Try a dry, botrytis-affected white Bordeaux made by some of the Sauternes chateaux, such as R, from Chateau Rieussec.

USA : Choose a New York State Chardonnay from winemakers such as Gold Seal, Benmarl, Wagner and Hargrave.

AUSTRALIA : Try an amontillado sherry; Lindemans and Seppelts excel as producers of this matured and full-bodied style.

SPAIN : Select Montilla, a wine made from the Pedro grape, from the region around Cordoba.

SLAYAD

Salads

Vegetables and fruit are plentiful, luscious and inexpensive in the Moroccan markets, and salads—bursting with color, flavor and texture—are served with every meal. These varied combinations of raw and lightly cooked vegetables and fruit are beautifully presented. They are served as a first course and then are left on the table throughout the remainder of the meal, providing a piquant contrast to the rich dishes that follow.

MTBOJA

Roasted Bell Pepper, Tomato and Onion Salad

SERVES 6

You will find that the skins can be removed quite easily after the roasted peppers have been placed in the plastic bag for about 20 minutes.

Ingredient

3 large red bell peppers (capsicums), cut in half lengthwise
3 tablespoons flat Italian parsley
2 tablespoons white wine vinegar
⅓ teaspoon salt
3 large tomatoes, peeled and seeded
2 small red onions, peeled and diced
⅓ cup (3 fl oz / 90mL) extra-virgin olive oil
1 garlic clove, finely chopped
⅓ teaspoon black pepper

Method

1 Preheat the broiler (griller), then roast the peppers on both sides until the skins are charred, about 15 to 20 minutes. (The time will vary depending how much juice the peppers hold.)
2 Remove the membranes and seeds and discard. Place the peppers in a plastic bag and seal. Set aside for 20 minutes, then remove the skin and coarsely dice the flesh.
3 Coarsely dice the flesh of the tomatoes. Place the peppers, tomatoes and diced onions in a serving bowl. Toss in the parsley leaves.
4 Mix together the olive oil, wine vinegar, garlic, salt and pepper, and pour over the vegetables.
5 Toss the salad and serve.

LEMON, ONION AND PARSLEY SALAD

SERVES 4

Although limes are not commonly used in this dish in Morocco, they make a beautiful alternative.

Ingredient

5 thin-skinned lemons
⅓ cup Italian parsley, coarsely chopped
1 olive, for garnish
1 white or red onion, peeled and sliced or slivered
½ teaspoon salt

Method

1 Peel four of the lemons, discard the seeds and dice the flesh.
2 Mix together the diced lemon, onion, parsley and salt. Cover and chill.
3 To serve, slice the remaining lemon thinly, arrange the slices on the edge of a serving dish and pile the lemon mixture in the center. Garnish with an olive, if desired. Serve at once.

ORANGE DATE AND ALMOND SALAD

SERVES 4

Moroccan oranges are sweet and very juicy. They are delicious just as they are, and superb in salads and sweet dishes. Look for oranges with a thin, brightly colored skin. Orange-flower water is available from pharmacies and Asian grocery stores. Rosewater can be substituted. Pomegranate seeds offer a pretty alternative to dates.

Ingredient

inner leaves of a romaine (cos) lettuce
1 tablespoon lemon juice
2 tablespoons superfine (caster) sugar
8 fresh dates, pitted and sliced lengthwise
3 navel oranges
1 tablespoon orange-flower water
½ teaspoon ground cinnamon
¼ cup almond slivered or chopped

Method

1 Wash and dry the lettuce leaves, place in a plastic bag and chill in the crisper drawer of the refrigerator.
2 Peel off all the orange skin with a small knife, ensuring all white pith is removed.
3 Separate the segments and remove the membranes over a bowl to catch the juice.
4 Place the segments in a bowl. Squeeze out and save any juice remaining in the orange membranes.
5 Mix together the orange juice, lemon juice, orange-flower water, sugar and cinnamon. Spoon the mixture over the orange segments and chill until required.
6 Arrange the lettuce leaves on a serving dish, then place the orange segments on top. Sprinkle with the dates and almonds.

DATES The date palm (Phoenix dactylifera) is known to have grown on the banks of the Middle Eastern rivers as long ago as 50000 BC and has been in cultivation in the Middle East for the past 7000 years. Referred to as the "tree of life" by the peoples of the region, it provided them with one of the most nutritious of foods—the date is over 50 percent carbohydrate and is rich in iron and fiber. The date palm also provided weaving and building materials, sap, from which drinks were made and shade from the hot Arabian sun; in addition, the pits of dates were used as charcoal. Today the date continues to be one of the big cash crops of the Middle East and North Africa. In these regions a handful of dates, a loaf of bread and a glass of tea are considered a meal for a farmer or shepherd. The Arabs adopted the Persian custom of combining fruit with meat, and the date has become an important ingredient in the tajines and salads of North Africa. Dates are also used in the curries and chutneys of India. Now grown in California as well as the Middle East, fresh dates should be eaten as soon as possible. However, dates do freeze well, losing none of their flavor or texture. Dried dates can be eaten as they are, or used in cakes, puddings and cookies. They are also delicious pitted and stuffed with a mixture of nuts and cream cheese. The dried date has special place on the Western table at Christmas but is also available year-round. Stored in an airtight container, dried dates will keep for up to six months.

Wine Notes

A dry, soft and fruity style of white is the most successful style to match with the diverse flavors here. Don't serve an expensive wine.

FRANCE : Choose an Alsatian white such as a Riesling or a Tokay (made from Pino Cris)

USA : Try a Riesling from Washington State, from makers such as Hogue Cellars and Columbia Cellars.

AUSTRALIA : Select a Petaluma Rhine Riesling from the Clare-Watervale district, or a Plantagenet Rhine Riesling from Mt Barker would be a good choice.

SOUTH AFRICA : Try a fresh, flavorsome Paarl Riesling from Nederburg or Boschendal.

SAMEK KEBAB M'XOBSA

Fish Brochette and Moroccan Flatbread

Fish is often prepared in Morocco with a marinade called charmoula, made with olive oil, lemon juice and such seasonings as garlic, paprika, cilantro and saffron. The broiled fish is traditionally served with salad, and accompanied by plenty of Moroccan flatbread. This bread does not keep well and the custom was that each morning the household cooks would prepare their dough and then take it to the communal village over for baking.

SAMEK KEBAB

Fish Brochette

SERVES 4

Monkfish and daurade are popular choices in Morocco, but any firm white-fleshed fish will work well.

Ingredient

⅓ teaspoon saffron threads
1 ½ lb (750g) thick white fish fillets
1 garlic clove, finely chopped
1 tablespoon chopped fresh cilantro (coriander) leaves
½ teaspoon sweet paprika
½ teaspoon hot paprika, plus extra for serving
2 tablespoons lemon or lime juice
2 tablespoons water
1 red onion, finely chopped
¼ cup chopped Italian parsley
¾ teaspoon sea salt, plus extra for serving
⅓ teaspoon cumin
⅓ cup (3 fl oz / 90mL) virgin olive oil
Italian parsley sprigs, for garnish

Method

1 Soak the saffron threads in the water
2 Cut the fish into 1 inch (2.5cm) cubes and place in a bowl.
3 Mix together the strained saffron water and the remaining ingredients except for the parsley sprigs.
4 Spoon the mixture over the fish cubes, mix thoroughly but lightly, and cover the bowl. Chill for at least 4 hours
5 Press the fish cubes onto skewers and broil (grill) over hot coals or under a preheated broiler (griller). Cook for about 4 minutes on each side, or until cooked through but not dry. Spread any remaining marinade over the fish cubes as the brochettes are turned.
6 Garnish with the parsley sprigs and serve with small bowls of extra sea salt and hot paprika.

XOBSA

Moroccan Flatbread

SERVES 8

Small well-washed river pebbles are traditionally used as a base for the bread while it bakes. If they are unavailable, just lightly oil the oven trays before adding the dough rounds. The dough's rising time will vary with the warmth of the surroundings; leave until doubled in bulk.

Ingredient

¾ cup (6 fl oz / 180mL) lukewarm water
3 teaspoon sugar
2 cups (8oz / 250g) all-purpose (plain) flour, sifted
1 tablespoon active dry yeast
1 teaspoon salt

Method

1 In a large bowl, mix ½ cup of the water with the yeast, sugar and salt and stir well. Allow to stand for 15 minutes, or until small bubbles appear. Stir again, then add the sifted flour, mix in well and knead for 5 minutes. Add the rest of the water gradually, kneading until a firm dough is formed. Shape into a ball, cover lightly and set aside in a warm place for 1 hour.
2 Preheat the oven to 400°F (200℃).
3 Divide the dough into two portions and shape each piece into a ball. Roll each piece on a lightly floured board until it is very thin and leave to rise again for about 1 hour.
4 While the dough rises, prepare the baking sheets. If using pebbles, cover the entire surface of 2 baking sheets With them and heat them in the oven for 30 minutes. If not using pebbles, lightly oil the baking sheets.
5 Carefully place the flatbreads onto the heated pebbles or sheets. Reduce heat to 300°F (150℃) and bake the bread for 30 minutes.
6 Remove the baking sheets from the oven and lift the bread from them.
7 Serve the bread broken into pieces.

PAPRIKA Paprika is a bright orangish red to brick-red powder obtained by grinding the pods of several different bell peppers. Its flavor can range from mild and sweet to almost as pungent and hot as cayenne pepper. It is used to flavor stews, sauces and soups, and as a garnish it adds color to pale foods including fish, eggs, cheese and potatoes. The best paprika is sold to be made in Hungary, where it is the national spice, but it is also produced elsewhere, such as in Spain, South America, and in California in the United Slates. Because paprika turns brown when exposed to sunlight, it is best stored in a cool, dark place in an airtight container.

Wine Notes

A dry white with some spiciness of flavor is best suited to this dish.

FRANCE : Try a Muscadet, the famous white from round Nantes. Muscadet de Sevre-et-Maine is the best subregion, and sur lie has the most character.

USA : Choose a tasty, enticing Sauvignon Blanc from Beaulieu, Beringer or Caymus in California.

AUSTRALIA : Select a Semillon-Sauvignon Blanc blend from Western Australia's southern districts. Try Cape Mentelle, Capel Vale or Amberley.

ITALY : Look for a Pinot Grigio from the Alto Adige, Collio and veneto regions.

CHERMOULI

Baked Fish

Although Morocco has a long coastline fronting both the Mediterranean Sea and the Atlantic Ocean, fish is rarely served beyond the coastal strip, and each fishing port has built up, over centuries, a localized cuisine. Even today these artificial boundaries are in force. Recipes from the Saft region, on Morocco's Atlantic coast, are particularly interesting, often featuring such ingredients as fennel, rice and, in particular, saffron.

SERVES 6

Use any firm-fleshed fish such as sea bass or bream. Use dried saffron for the seasoning on top of the fish–a dry mixture is required.

Ingredient

⅓ teaspoon saffron threads
1 ¼ cups (8oz / 250g) short grain white rice
⅓ teaspoon salt
⅓ tablespoon (1 ½ oz / 45g) butter softened
1 onion, finely chopped
1 large, firm-fleshed fish, about 5 lb (2.5kg)
⅓ teaspoon dried saffron, extra
2 lemons, sliced
2 tablespoon water
¼ cup finely chopped parsley
⅓ teaspoon freshly ground black pepper
juice of 1 large lemon
2 teaspoon finely grated lemon zest
¼ cup (2 fl oz / 60mL) olive oil
salt and pepper

Method

1 Soak the saffron threads in the water.
2 Fill a medium-sized saucepan with lightly salted water and heat to boiling, and the rice and cook for about 20 minutes, or until cooked. Drain well and fluff up with a fork. Set aside.
3 Preheat the oven to 400°F (200℃).
4 Mix together the parsley, salt, pepper, saffron water, cinnamon, butter, lemon juice, half the onion, and lemon zest. Stir into the rice.
5 Wipe all over the fish, including inside the cavity, with paper towel. Spoon the stuffing into the fish, then close the cavity. Place the fish in an oiled baking dish.
6 Mix together the remaining onion, the oil dried saffron and salt and pepper, and spoon over the top of the fish.
7 Cover the fish lightly with aluminum foil and bake for 1 hour. Remove the foil and bake for an additional 20 minutes, or until the skin is crisp and the flesh flakes easily when lightly touched with a fork.
8 Carefully transfer the fish and stuffing to a preheated serving dish and arrange the lemon slices on the dish. Cut the fish into serving portions and serve each with some of the hot stuffing and lemon slices.

Wine Notes

A pale, dry rosé is the popular wine style served with fish and shellfish in Morocco.

FRANCE : Choose a Rose from Provence or Languedoc in the south of France.

USA : Select a dry Grenache Rose or a Cabernet Rosé from I Lohr in Monterey.

AUSTRALIA : Try Holystone, a Pinot Noir-Chardonnay blend, or Taltarni's Rosé des Pyrenees.

PORTUGAL : Look for a Rosé from the Bairrada region—Nobilis is a good export brand.

TAJINE DE'AL HOMES

Tajine of Chickpeas with Herbs and Spices

Although tajine recipes may be successfully prepared in an ordinary casserole dish, the term "tajine" refers to the shallow, brown, earthenware pot with a conical, pointed lid in which this dish is traditionally cooked. In most Moroccan households tajines are still cooked over a charcoal burner, the indirect, slow heat helping produce the rich, aromatic flavor that is the essence of a good tajine.

SERVES 6

If you do not have a tajine, use a shallow saucepan with a heavy bottom.

Ingredient

- 4 cups (1 $\frac{1}{2}$ lb / 750g) dried chickpeas, soaked overnight
- 3 large tomatoes, peeled, seeded and chopped
- 1 tablespoon chopped cilantro (coriander)
- $\frac{1}{3}$ teaspoon ground cumin
- $\frac{1}{3}$ teaspoon ground ginger
- $\frac{1}{3}$ teaspoon freshly ground black pepper
- $\frac{1}{4}$ teaspoon sweet paprika
- 2 $\frac{1}{3}$ teaspoon salt
- 1 large onion, finely chopped
- 3 tablespoons chopped Italian parsley
- $\frac{1}{3}$ teaspoon saffron threads, soaked in 2 tablespoons water
- $\frac{1}{3}$ teaspoon ground cinnamon
- $\frac{1}{4}$ teaspoon hot paprika
- $\frac{1}{3}$ cup (3 fl oz / 90mL) virgin olive oil

Method

1. Drain the chickpeas, then rinse. Add 2 teaspoons of the salt and the chickpeas to plenty of boiling water, and cook until tender. Strain the chickpeas and rub off as much skin as possible.
2. Place the chickpeas in a tajine with the onion. Add the tomatoes, chopped herbs, strained saffron liquid, spices and the remaining $\frac{1}{3}$ teaspoon salt and mix well.
3. Add the olive oil, then place the tajine over low heat, cover and simmer for 15 to 20 minutes, or until the flavors have developed and the mixture is heated through.
4. Serve immediately.

Wine Notes

A flavorsome dry white would suit this dish.

FRANCE : Choose an Alsatian Sylvaner with its slightly perfumed aroma.

USA : Try a good Californian French Colombard or Sauvignon Blanc.

AUSTRALIA : Select a Semillon-Sauvignon Blanc from the Barossa Valley or Western Australia.

SOUTH AFRICA : Look for a Steen (also known as Chenin Blanc) form KWV.

DJEJ DE'AL HOMES

Chicken with Chickpeas

Chickpeas, eaten since the time of the pharaohs in ancient Egypt, are synonymous with Arab cuisine. Together with lentils and other pulses, chicken have been a dey source of protein when meat was in short supply. Chicken too plays an important part in Moroccan cookery and features in many Moroccan recipes. The flavors and textures of chicken and chickpeas combine well together, as shown by this classic Moroccan dish.

SERVES 6

Freshly chopped cilantro (conander) leaves are sometimes added to this recipe. If you enjoy this distinctive flavor, add a tablespoon with the parsley. The use of canned chickpeas will not affect the flavor, and they are certainly more convenient.

Ingredient

1 roasting chicken, about 3 lb (1.5kg)
½ teaspoon ground ginger
½ teaspoon freshly ground black pepper
½ teaspoon turmeric
⅓ cup (3oz / 90g) butter
4 red onions, finely chopped
4 cups (32 fl oz / 1L) chicken stock
2 teaspoon coarse salt
½ teaspoon sweet paprika
½ teaspoon ground cumin
½ teaspoon ground cinnamon
1 tablespoon olive oil
1 cup cooked or canned chickpeas
½ cup finely chopped parsley

Method

1 Wipe the chicken, pat dry and cut into serving portions.
2 Mix together the salt ginger, paprika, pepper, cumin. turmeric and cinnamon. Rub the spice mixture into the chicken portions and leave for at least 2 hours.
3 Melt the butter and oil in a large saucepan, and sauté the chicken pieces and the onions until golden.
4 Add the chickpeas and chicken stock to the pan and simmer for 1 hour, or until the chicken is tender
5 Stir in the chopped parsley. Serve the chicken and chickpeas and sauce with cooked rice. Serve immediately.

CHICKPEAS Grown throughout the Middle East, India and southern Europe, the chickpea (Cicer arietinum) is an excellent source of carbohydrate and protein. It is considered indispensable in North African cooking and is an important part of a vegetarian diet. Used in soups, stews, pureed and as a garnish, the chickpea is available dried or precooked in cans. Dried chickpeas must be soaked for up to twelve hours before cooking.

Wine Notes

Serve a spicy white with some body with this dish.

FRANCE : Choose a Pinot Gris from Alsace. This variety is often labeled as Tokay d'Alsace.

USA : The Pacific Northwest produces some unusual, high quality whites. Try a Pinot Gris from Oregon or an Aligoté from Washington.

AUSTRALIA : Try a Western Australian Verdelho, from either Moondah Brook or Sandalford, with a distinctive, rather aromatic quality.

SOUTH AFRICA : Choose the grapey, dry style of Chenin Blanc (sometimes labeled as Steen) from KWV or Simonsig.

DJEJ M'QUALLI

Chicken with Green Olives and Preserved Lemon

This tajine recipe comes from Tetouan in Morocco's north and, like most Moroccan tajines, it is meltingly tender and fragrant with spice. Preserved lemon, a staple condiment used in the cuisine of the Middle East and North Africa, adds its distinctive flavor and texture. This dish is usually accompanied by cooked couscous, and is served in the center of the table so that diners can help themselves.

SERVES 4

The preserved lemons should be prepared at least 3 weeks in advance; otherwise buy them premade from an Asian food store. Use a meat mallet or a rolling pin to crush the olives.

Ingredient

- ⅓ teaspoon saffron threads
- 1 roasting chicken, about 3 lb (1.5kg)
- 1 tablespoon peanut oil or light olive oil
- 1 large red onions, finely chopped
- ⅓ teaspoon ground ginger
- ⅓ teaspoon hot paprika
- peel of 1 preserved lemon, cut into strips (see recipe)
- 1~2 tablespoon lemon juice
- extra olives, for garnish, optional
- 2 tablespoon water
- coarse salt
- 5 tablespoon (2 ½ oz / 75g) butter
- 2 garlic cloves, finely chopped
- ⅓ teaspoon ground cinnamon
- 1 cup (8 fl oz / 250mL) water
- 8 green olives, crushed
- 2 tablespoon finely chopped Italian parsley leaves

Method

1. Soak the saffron threads in the 2 tablespoon water.
2. Rub the salt on the inside and outside of the chicken and allow to stand for 1 hour. Rinse well and pat dry.
3. Heat the oil and butter in a casserole dish just large enough to hold the chicken. When the oil mixture is sizzling hot, add the chicken and cook until brown on all sides. Add the onions, garlic, strained saffron water, spices and 1 cup water.
4. Cover the casserole dish and cook over low heat for 1 ¼ to 1 ½ hours, or until the chicken is tender, turning the chicken from time to time. If the liquid evaporates during cooking, add a little more water as required.
5. About 10 minutes before the end of the cooking time, add the strips of preserved lemon peel and olives. Adjust the seasoning if necessary. Add the lemon juice to taste, and the chopped parsley.
6. To serve, place the chicken on a heated serving dish. Strain the sauce from the casserole over the chicken, using the lemon peel and olives as garnish. If desired, extra olives may be added for garnish. Serve with couscous.

HAMDA M'REQYDA

Preserved Lemons

To reduce the salty flavor, some Moroccan cooks lightly rinse the salted lemon slices under running water and drain them for several hours before placing in the jars. For variation, use limes instead of lemons.

Ingredient

20 small lemon
3 teaspoon sweet paprika
2 tablespoon coarse salt
extra-virgin olive oil or peanut oil

Method

1 Scrub the lemons, then pat them dry and cut into slices or wedges. Sprinkle the cut surfaces generously with salt and leave for 24 hours—preferably in a colander. (This allows the juices to run off and reduces the bitterness)
2 Arrange the lemons in jars, sprinkling paprika between layers. Pour enough oil over the lemons to completely cover them and seal the jars firmly.
3 Leave for about 3 weeks before eating for the flavors to mellow and blend and the lemons to develop a rich golden hue.

CINNAMON Cinnamon is the dried inner bark of Cinnamomum zeylanicum, an evergreen tree which belongs to the laurel family. The Egyptians were using cinnamon as early as 1450 BC. The Romans valued the spice as a basis for incense, and during the Middle Ages cinnamon, along with other spices, was so highly sought after that it had a value equal to gold or gemstones. Today cinnamon is a indispensable spice. In North African and in some Asian cuisines, cinnamon is used to flavor savory dishes. In Western kitchens it is used mainly to flavor sweet dishes, such as cakes or puddings; it is also added to cooked fruit, and used with drinks; it has a natural affinity with chocolate, and is one of the spices in mulled wine. Cinnamon is available as rolled sticks (or quills) of dried bark or In powder from supermarkets. As with all spices, the delicate flavor of cinnamon will evaporate when exposed to air, so it should be kept in an airtight container out of the light.

Wine Notes

The strong flavors of the lemon peel and the olives will challenge any wine.

FRANCE : Try a southern French red such as a Côtes-du-Rhône or vin de pays.

USA : Choose a Zinfandel from the Napa Valley, but not the rosé style known as Pink Zin.

AUSTRALIA : Select a Shiraz from either the Hunter Valley in New South Wales or from McKaren Vale in South Australia.

ITALY : Try a rustic southern Italian red, such as Montepulciano D'Abruzzo.

TAJINE DE'AL LHALME M'CHSARGEL

Couscous with Lamb and Quinces

The word couscous is synonymous with the magic of North Africa. Originating with the Berbers, the name is used interchangeably for both the semolina grains and the finished dish. Today, there are many regions of the world where couscous dishes are served, but it is the couscous of Morocco that is prized above all others. Here it is combined with lamb and quinces: cooking meat and fruit together is another keynote of North African cuisine.

SERVES 6

Couscous is most easily prepared in a special two-part pot made of stainless steel, tin, enamel or even pottery, called a couscoussier. Its top half is a colander or steamer in which the grains of couscous are placed, and the bottom half is a stew pot in which the meat and vegetables simmer, producing the steam that cooks the couscous above. If you do not have a couscoussier, use a steamer with a tight-fitting lid.

Ingredient

⅓ cup (3oz / 90g) butter
1 teaspoon ground ginger
⅓ teaspoon saffron threads, soaked in
2 tablespoons water
3 lb (1.5kg) lean lamb, diced
1 ½ cups couscous
1 lb (500g) quinces, peeled, cored and sliced
½ teaspoon ground cinnamon
3 onions, grated
½ teaspoon freshly ground black pepper
⅓ teaspoon cayenne pepper
2 tablespoon chopped Italian parsley
2 cups (16 fl oz / 500mL) water
4 onion, chopped
approximately ⅓ cup (3oz / 90g) sugar

Method

1 Heat one-third of the butter in the base of a couscoussier, then add the onions, ginger, pepper, saffron liquid, cayenne and parsley and cook gently for 2 minutes.
2 Raise the heat and add the lamb. Sauté until the lamb has changed color but has not browned.
3 Pour in the water and heat to boiling. Lower the heat, cover and simmer for about 1 hour. Make sure the water does not evaporate.
4 While the lamb is cooking, prepare the couscous Place the couscous in a large bowl, cover with cold water, stir once, then drain immediately. Stir again once or twice, then leave for 15 minutes, or until the grains begin to swell.
5 Separate the grains lightly with your fingertips, then tip half the grains into the top section of the couscoussier. Place this over the simmering lamb, after adding the chopped onions to it. Leave until steam rises, then add the remaining couscous.
6 Steam the couscous, uncovered, for about 30 minutes. Occasionally loosen the grains with a fork to prevent lumping

7 Remove the top half of the couscoussier from the heat and tip the couscous onto a large shallow platter. Separate the grains with damp fingers. Add the remaining butter to the couscous and lightly rub it in with the palms of your hands, tossing the couscous at the same time.
8 Prepare the quinces while the meat and the couscous cook. Place them in a saucepan and barely cover with water. Add the sugar and simmer for about 15 minutes or until just tender, then drain.
9 To complete cooking, add the quinces to the lamb. Then slowly trickle the couscous into the top of the couscousier, cover and steam for 20 minutes, tossing the grains with a fork from time to time.
10 Taste the lamb mixture and adjust the seasoning to taste. You may need more sugar.
11 Place the couscous in a ring around the edge of a large serving dish. Spoon the lamb and quinces into the middle and pour on the sauce. Sprinkle with the cinnamon.

COUSCOUS Couscous is a cereal product made from semolina, which is coarsely ground drum wheat. The grains of semolina are sprinkled with flour and water, then rubbed, either by hand or machine, into tiny pellets. Couscous was made in the deserts of North Africa for centuries by the Berber tribes, though they originally made it with millet, not wheat. Rich in carbohydrates, couscous is most easily prepared in a special pot called a couseoussier; as described in the recipe, the couscous grain cook in the top half of the bottom half. In morocco couscous is likely to be combined with lamb or mutton, chicken or fish. Couscous may also be steamed over water and served like pasta as an accompaniment to other main dishes, or it can be mixed with honey, fruit or nuts and served as a dessert. While couscous is still made by hand in North Africa, and this handmade variety can by bought from same gourmet or Middle Eastern food stores. The machine-made variety is more readily available.

Wine Notes

An aromatic, full-bodied white with plenty of fruit flavor will complement this dish well.

FRANCE : Try a spicy Alsace Gewurztraminer, or Dopff du Moulin's blended Chateau du Moulin.

USA : Choose a Washington State Riesling or Gewurztraminer from makers such as Hogue Cellars and Chateau St Michelle.

AUSTRALIA : Try a white from Eden Valley in South Australia, such as Flazman's Vineyard Traminer or Orlando's St Helga Rhine Riesling.

SOUTH AFRICA : Try a Gewurztraminer, Steen or Riesling from Nederburg or Bergkelder.

M'CHOUI

Roasted Lamb

This is one of the dishes for which Morocco is famous. Originated by the Berbers, a Beduin tribe, m'choui is traditionally made by spit-roasting a whole lamb over a bed of charcoal: the outside becomes extremely crisp, but the inside remains juicy and tender. The guests would pull off the meat with their fingers and season it with salt, pepper and cumin. M'choui can also be adopted for the household oven, using smaller cuts of meat.

SERVES 8

Although the modern-day preference is for lamb that is quite pink, for this recipe it is essential that the lamb be cooked until it is almost falling apart.

Ingredient

1 large leg of lamb, about 3 ¾ lb (1.75kg)
2 garlic cloves, finely chopped
1 teaspoon sea salt, plus extra for serving
1 teaspoon sweet paprika, plus extra for serving
½ teaspoon ground cinnamon
mint and basil sprigs, for garnish
1 cup (8oz / 250g) butter, at room temperature
1 teaspoon ground cumin, plus extra for serving
½ teaspoon cayenne pepper

Method

1 Trim all excess fat from the lamb. Slash the meat in a number of places with a small pointed knife.
2 Mix together the butter, garlic, salt, cumin, paprika, cinnamon and cayenne pepper. Blend well, then rub into the meat, ensuring that it penetrates the slashes as deeply as possible. Cover the meat lightly and chill for at least 2 hours, up to 12 hours, to allow the flavors to permeate the meat.
3 Preheat the oven to 450°F (230℃).
4 Place the lamb in a baking dish, fat side up. Bake in the oven for 15 minutes, then reduce heat to 350°F (180℃) and continue cooking until the meat can be easily pulled from the bone with a fork, about 2 hours. Baste frequently with the juices from the baking dish.
5 To serve, place the meat on a large carving board or a metal platter and garnish with sprigs of fresh herbs.
6 Serve extra sea salt, cumin and pepper in small bowls so diners may season their meat to suit their personal taste.

CAYENNE PEPPER Cayenne pepper is made from ground, dried chili peppers. The pepper, indigenous to America, was first introduced to Europe at the end of the fifteenth century by Christopher Columbus' physician, Chanca. The Portuguese explorer Magellan took the pepper to Africa and Asia where it has flourished. Cayenne pepper is widely used in North African, Mexican and Indian dishes to add bite. It also features in some mustards and pickles. Store it in an airtight container out of direct sunlight.

Wine Notes

Cabernet Sauvignon, either straight or blended, is a good partner with most variations of lamb.

FRANCE : Try a good cru bourgeois such as Chateau Fourcas Hosten from Listrac or Chateau Patache d'Aux from Bégadan.

USA : Choose a Californian Cabernet from Beaulieu Vineyards or Louis Martini.

AUSTRALIA : Select a Coonawarra Cabernet such as Rouge Homme or St Hugo from Orlando.

SOUTH AFRICA : Choose a Cabernet from Nederburg, Kanonkop or Meerlust. They are typical of the best South African Cabernet producers.

RGHAIF

Sweet Flaky Pancakes

These flaky, airy deep-fried pancakes are made with a folded dough, similar to puff pastry or the French delicacy milles feuilles. They were traditionally served at breakfast or as a snake at any time of day. They can be stuffed, often with a savory filling, but they are often enjoyed as a dessert, served warm with honey and melted butter or sprinkled with walnuts, lemon juice and honey.

SERVES 6

The Rghaif can also be served well dusted with confectioners'(icing) sugar.

Ingredient

4 cups (1 lb / 500g) all-purpose (plain) flour
1 teaspoon white sugar
salad oil
1 tablespoon active dry yeast
about $1\frac{3}{4}$ cups (14 fl oz / 430mL) lukewarm water

Method

1 To make the "starter," mix 6 tablespoons of the flour with the yeast and sugar and sprinkle onto $1\frac{1}{4}$ cups (10 fl oz / 310mL) of the lukewarm water. Whisk until well blended. Place in a warm spot for 15 minutes, or until the mixture begins to froth.
2 Sift the remaining flour, then add the frothing starter and about 7 tablespoon of the lukewarm water to create a soft dough. Knead the dough vigorously, adding more water if necessary to make a soft, elastic dough (It may be slightly sticky).
3 Divide the dough into 18 balls. Roll each ball in oil until the surface is coated. Roll out each ball into a 9 inches (23cm) circle. Fold two opposite edges of each circle toward the center, then fold in the other edges to create a rectangle 6×8 inches (15×20cm). Fold the dough from the narrow end into the center of each rectangle. Repeat with the opposite side, then roll out to form rectangles about 4×6 inches (10×15cm).
4 Pour the oil into a large pan to a depth of $\frac{1}{2}$ inch (1.2cm) and heat gently until it sizzles. Fry the pastries one at a time, until golden brown and crisp on all sides, about 2 to 3 minutes each side.
5 Serve with melted butter or sugar and honey.

Wine Notes

Serve a sweet dessert wine with this dish.

FRANCE : Choose a generic Sauternes such as Loupiac or Mombazillac. Coteaux du Layon from the Loire is another possibility.

USA : Try the Christian Brothers Chateau La Salle, or Beringer's Sonoma Valley botrytis-offected Nightingale sweet white.

AUSTRALIA : Try Noble Riesling from Brown Brothers or Noble Gold from Wolf Glass.

SOUTH AFRICA : Look for a Noble Late Harvest label from Nederburg or the De Wetshof Edeloes.

KENEFFA

Sweet Bisteeya with Milk and Almond Sauce

Bisteeya, a pie made with the thinnest sheets of pastry conceivable, is one of the famous dishes of Morocco. The pastry, known as warka or warkha, is highly complex to make. Even in Morocco many buy their warkha ready made, and strudel pastry or phyllo sheets may be substituted. The classic bisteeya comes from Fez and is made with pigeons. There are many other regional varieties, and this dessert bisteeya comes from Marrakech.

SERVES 6

Cover the sheets of phyllo or strudel pastry that you are not using with a damp cloth; this will prevent them from drying out and cracking.

Ingredient

- 10 sheets of strudel or phyllo pastry
- 1 ½ cups (8oz / 250g) blanched whole almonds, toasted
- 4 tablespoons cornstarch (cornflour)
- ½ cup (4oz / 125g) superfine (caster) sugar
- 2 tablespoons orange-flower water
- light salad oil, for frying
- 3 tablespoons confectioners' (icing) sugar
- ½ teaspoon ground cinnamon
- 4 cups (32 fl oz / 1L) milk
- 4 tablespoons ground blanched almonds

Method

1. Separate the leaves of pastry. and cut, using small scissors and a plate as a guide, into 9 inches (23cm) rounds.
2. Pour oil into a large pan to a depth of ½ inches (1.2cm) and heat over moderate heat for 4 to 5 minutes.
3. Fry the pastry rounds, turning once, until crisp but not browned. Remove the pastry rounds from the pan very carefully with kitchen tongs and drain on paper towels. Set aside.
4. Finely chop or crush the whole almonds with a rolling pin and mix with the confectioners' sugar and cinnamon. Set aside.
5. Blend the cornstarch with about ¾ cup (6 fl oz / 185mL) of the milk
6. Combine the remaining milk with the superfine sugar in a saucepan and heat to boiling. Gradually stir in the cornstarch paste, mixing constantly to prevent lumps from forming. Cook until the mixture has thickened.
7. Add the ground almonds and orange-flower water and whisk until very smooth, about 1 minute.
8. Remove from heat and set aside to cool, then chill for about 1 hour.

9 To assemble the dessert, place 2 of the pastry rounds on a large serving dish and sprinkle with half of the chopped toasted almond mixture. Place 3 pastry rounds on top and spoon over 4 tablespoons of the almond cream. Cover with 2 more rounds and sprinkle on the remaining chopped almond mixture. Arrange the remaining pastry sheets on top and spread on 3 tablespoons of the almond cream.

10 The remaining almond cream may be spooned around the dessert or served in a separate bowl.

11 Serve at once.

Wine Notes

Try a sweet, perhaps lightly fortified wine of the Muscat type.

FRANCE : Choose Muscat de Frontignan, de Lunel or de Mireral from near Montpellier.

USA : Select a Muscat Canelli from Charles King in the Napa Valley or one of the Quady Winery Central Valley Muscats.

AUSTRALIA : Try Baileys Muscat Rouge or D'Arenberg's Muscat of Alexandria.

SOUTH AFRICA : Choose Muscat from Bergkelder or KWV in the Cape region.

RUSSIA

World Cuisine

RUSSIA

is much an enigma today as it has ever been—perhaps more so since it swept away the Communist regime before anything else materialized to take its place. Everything is in flux, it seems, except the food. In tourist hotels, the dishes remain highly conservative: borscht, blini with caviar, chicken kiev and ice cream.

There are two images of Russian food which are prevalent in the Western mind. The first is derived from cookbooks mainly written by emigres-the beef stroganov, chicken kiev and samovar genre that harks back to the upper middle-class and aristocratic origins of the writers' families. In contrast with this image is the impression, fuelled by television and tourist horror stories, that people have to spend the majority of their time in food lines or paying outrageous prices at the "private enterprise" markets that have sprung up allover the former Soviet Union. There are no queues there, because the prices are too high for the average wage-earner.

The Russians stick closely to tradition when it comes to cooking. Russians do not devour cookbooks as other cultures might, searching for new ways to enhance their menus. They simply do not see the need for change and prefer less lavish versions of the old favorites rather than anything that is foreign or new-fangled.

The Russian word zakusit has two different meanings: the first, to bite into something; the second, the food eaten after a fiery gulp of vodka. Both of these interpretations could well apply when it comes to zakuski, the famous Russian appetizers that resemble the first course of a Swedish smorgasbord. Originally, visitors were welcomed with trays of vodka and zakuski. Today, zakuski are eaten at the table as a prelude to a meal: one or two items on regular nights of the week—a salad or piece of sausage—or as big a spread as the budget will allow on special occasions—cabbage salad, beetroot salad, caviar—stuffed egg or pirozhki, tiny half-moon pies filled with hard-cooked(hard-boiled)eggs or meat.

Beets(beetroot) have been part of the Russian diet since the beginning of recorded history. Salads and soups based on this hardy vegetable, one of the few able to survive the harshness of the Russian winter, have long been a highlight of many an otherwise colorless winter meal. Borscht is the definitive Russian soup and there are as many variations as there are cooks. Sometimes it is little more than beets and stock; at other times it may include tomatoes, cabbage, potatoes and meat together with beets.

The Russians say "Shchi da kasha, mat masha" — "Cabbage and buck wheat, that's our mother." In the summer months, fresh cabbage is used; in winter the principal form is sauerkraut. Kasha, or buckwheat groats, was the great filler of the serfs in Tsarist Russia. In many areas when conditions were especially difficult, it was all they had to eat. These days many vegetarians in other countries eat kasha as an accompaniment to vegetable main courses because the crunchy, porridge-like grain is high in nutritive value.

Beef stroganov was named for the illustrious Stronanov family of Imperial Russia. Actually it is rarely prepared in Russian homes today for the obvious reason—the astronomical cost of tenderloin(fillet) steak. In the West, however, it is an icon of Russian cooking and as such can be found in the high-call tourist hotels and restaurants of St. Petersburg and Moscow.

Kotliery, whether of minced chicken, pork or fish, are one of the most popular dishes in Russia and come in all shapes and sizes. Pojarski was the owner of a nineteenth century restaurant near Moscow who made his fortune through chicken patties of his own invention. Aleksander Pushkin bought some of Pojarski's patties and judged them to be so good that he even included a mention of them in a poem. True patriots do not count them as real Russian food because minced patties were introduced into Russia in the nineteenth century by French cooks, but their popularity cannot be denied.

Much of Russia's culture, including the alphabet and religion, can be traced back to Byzantium, and the lavish meals served at the Orthodox Easter recall this heritage.

One of the most famous sweet dishes—Pashka is the richest of cream cheese desserts. Traditionally, pashka was blessed at a Russian Orthodox midnight resurrection service before being eaten at home.

Every romantic novel set in Russia includes a scene with a samovar but these days a Journey throughout the country yields hardly a sighting unless you are in a remote area. Most people are surprised to learn that the samovar was not a tea dispenser—only a gloriously ornate receptacle the boiling water needed to dilute the often strong tea. This was made in the tiny pot called the zavarka which was usually placed on top of the samovar. In a much more plebeian way, this system is still in use today. With a poorly-made tin kettle taking the place of the samovar, tea is pured into cups, followed by a splash of boiling water from the kettle.

Any talk of Russian cuisine must hark back to air-brushed daydreams of the past grandeurs of the nobility: whole cherry trees placed on picnic tables for guests to pick at for dessert. the floating fish boats with overflowing tanks moored on the Neva river in St. Petersburg and the great layered kulebyaka pies—salmon, rice and eggs, piled high in a pastry wrapping—that ranked as take-out foods for the aristocracy, especially during their summer holidays in Odessa, where they were supplied by the gourmet shop, Yastchouk. All long gone now but nonetheless worth remembering, especially when standing outside Peter the Great's ornately restored Winter Palace on the outskirts of St. Petersburg.

BORCHT

Beet Soup

Russia, Poland and Ukraine take credit for the origin of Borcsht. There are many versions with greatly differing ingredients and degrees of sweetness to distinguish them. As a Russian saying has it, there are as a many ways of serving Borscht as there are grandmothers in Russia. It can be elaborate, like the version prepared by French chef Antonin Careme for the Russian court in the last century, or prepared simply, like the recipe offered here.

SERVES 6

For a heartier dish, use beef shank (shin) or chuck steak to make the stock and add the diced meat to the soup.

Ingredient

- 2 beets (beetroot)
- 2 potatoes, peeled and cut into chunks
- ½ teaspoon salt
- 1 small onion, sliced
- 1 tablespoon tomato paste
- ⅓ teaspoon freshly ground black pepper
- 2 garlic cloves, finely chopped
- 1 tablespoon finely chopped dill
- 2 cups shredded red or white (green) cabbage
- 6 cups(48 fl oz / 15L) very rich beef stock
- 3 large ripe tomatoes, peeled and chopped
- 2 tablespoons oil
- 1 carrot, sliced
- salt, to taste
- extra lemon juice, optional
- 2 tablespoons finely chopped parsley
- sour cream, optional
- juice of 1 lemon

Method

1. Boil the beets in a stainless steel, glass or ceramic saucepan for at least 1 hour, or until tender, or bake in a moderate over (350°F / 180℃) for 1 ¼ hours, or until tender. When they are cool enough to handle, trim off the stems, peel and julienne.
2. Heat the stock to boiling in a large saucepan, add the potatoes and tomatoes and season with the salt. Reduce heat and simmer for about 15 minutes, or until the potatoes are almost cooked.
3. Meanwhile, heat the oil in a large skillet, add the onion and carrot and sauté over medium heat for 5 minutes. Add the cabbage and contniue cooking until the cabbage has softened, about 5 minutes. Add these vegetables to the saucepan.
4. Toss the julienned beets in the lemon juice and stir them into the soup. Simmer for 5 minutes.
5. Add the tomato paste and season with the salt and pepper, adding a little lemon juice if desired. Simmer for an additional 10 minutes.
6. Remove the soup from the heat and sprinkle in the garlic and chopped herbs. Let stand for 10 minutes before serving. Serve the sour cream separately, if using.

Wine Notes

A fruity red might suit this rich soup, or perhaps a full-bodied Gewurztaminer.

FRANCE : Try a rich, soft Beaujolais such as Saint-Amour or Cote-de-Brouilly.

USA : Try one of the "new wave" Napa Valley blended reds, such as a Beaulieu Berryessa or Sutter Homes Soleo, featuring Zinfandel, Gamay and Barbera.

AUSTRALIA : Choose a fruity soft Pinot Noir-Shiraz blend; good examples come form Elderion in the Barossa Valley and Montara near Ararat, Victoria

ITALY : A Merlot form the Veneto or the Trentino-Alto-Adige regious would be suitable choice.

SUP IZ VISHNI

Cherry Soup

In Russia soup is synonymous with the first course, and the origins of some Russian soups can be traced back for centuries. Soups with a sour base are an important part of this culinary tradition. Fresh sour cherries, such as English Morello, are perfect in this recipe. If fresh cherries are not available, bottled cherries that have not been excessively sweetened may be substituted, although the resulting dish will not be quite as good.

SERVES 6

Although it is not usual in home cooking, some restaurants slightly thicken the soup by stirring in some arrowroot mixed with water before the soup is simmered.

Ingredient

2 lb (1kg) sour cherries
small piece cinnamon stick
1 ½ cups (12 fl oz / 375mL) water
juice of 1 orange
1 tablespoon julienned orange zest
4 cloves
2 cups (16 fl oz / 500mL) light, dry red wine
⅔ cup (5oz / 155g) sugar
1 tablespoon lemon juice
½ cup (4oz / 125g) sour cream or smetana (see glossary)

Method

1 Pit the cherries, reserving any juice.
2 Tie the cloves and cinnamon stick in a piece of muslin and place in a non-metallic saucepan. Add the cherries, reserved juice, wine, water and sugar. Heat to boiling, stirring occasionally. Reduce the heat, cover the saucepan and simmer for about 30 minutes.
3 Reserve about 1 cup of the cherries. Tip the remaining cherries and half the cooking liquid into a food processor and puree.
4 Return the puree and the reserved cherries to the saucepan, and add the orange juice, lemon juice and half the orange zest. Simmer over low heat for 10 minutes.
5 Remove from heat, taste, and add more sugar if the soup is too sharp. Discard the cinnamon stick and cloves. Allow the soup to cool, then chill for at least 3 hours.
6 Add a spoonful of sour cream to each bowl before serving and garnish with the remaining orange zest.

Wine Notes

Soups are difficult to partner with wine and this unusual dish is particularly challenging.

FRANCE : Select a sweet aperitif wine such as a red Pineau des Charentes.

USA : Choose a dessert wine made form Riesling or Muscat grapes form California or Washington State.

AUSTRALIA : Try an aromatic, late-picked Traminer from Seppelts of Eden Valley, or and unusual variety such as Taminga from Trentham Estate, or Orange Muscat from Brown Brothers.

GERMANY : Try the cherry-based spiri, Kirsch; some good examples come from the Black Forest.

ZAKUSKI

Appetizers

Appetizers—simple and elaborate, hot and cold—are an important component of Russian cuisine. In the country houses, the zakuski table with its splendid array of luscious food was set up in the antechamber to the dining room, completely separate form the meal to be served. Today, Zakuski are offered to guests while the cook adds finishing touches to the main meal. They can be canapes, or more. substantial—variety is the key to Zakuski.

BLINI S IKROI

Blini with Caviar

SERVES 6

For a lighter texture, substitute all-purpose flour for one-third of the buckwheat flour. To keep the amount of oil in which the blini are cooked to a minimum, dip half a potato in oil and rub it lightly over the pan.

Ingredient

1 ¼ cups(10 fl oz / 310mL) water
2 teaspoons active dry yeast
3 cup (12oz / 375g) buckwheat flour
1 egg, separated
1 cup (8oz / 250g) sour cream, lightly whipped
½ cup (4 fl oz / 125mL) milk
2 teaspoons sugar
⅓ teaspoon salt
butter of light salad oil for cooking
½ cup caviar or lumpfish roe, red of black

Method

1 Warm the water and milk until they are lukewarm.
2 Blend together the yeast and sugar with a small amount of the warm liquid in a bowl and stir until the sugar has dissolved. Add the remaining liquid, then set aside until the mixture begins to foam a little. Add half the flour, stirring until smooth.
3 Cover with a cloth or a plastic bag and allow to rise until doubled in bulk. The rising time can vary between 45 minutes and 2 hours. Add the salt, egg yolk and the remaining flour, beating well. Set aside and allow to rise for an additional 1 ½ to 2 hours, until doubled in bulk.
4 Whip the egg white until stiff, then fold into the mixture, which will be quite stiff.
5 Heat a small, heavy-based pan over moderate heat and add a very small amount of butter. Spoon in about 2 tablespoons of the batter and cook for 4 minutes, or until golden brown, then turn with a spatula and cook for 2 to 3 minutes. Lightly butter the pan after cooking each blini.
6 Keep the blini warm. Serve with bowls of caviar and lightly shipped sour cream. The blini can be eaten folded over a filling of caviar and sour cream or topped with the sour cream, then the caviar.

MARINOVANNYE GRIBY

Pickled Mushrooms

SERVES 8

These mushrooms will keep for up to 3 weeks (or longer), if they are covered with the pickling liquid and refrigerated.

Ingredient

1 ¼ cups(10 fl oz / 310mL) white wine vinegar
1 teaspoon black peppercorns
1 bay leaf, torn in several places
2 sprigs dill
1 lb (500g) button mushrooms
⅓ cup (3 fl oz / 90mL) water
3 cloves
2 garlic cloves, peeled and crushed
1 teaspoon salt
1 tablespoon light oil

Method

1 Combine the vinegar, water, peppercorns, cloves, bay leaf, garlic, dill and salt in a large saucepan and heat to boiling.
2 Wipe the mushrooms and trim their stems. Drop the mushrooms into the vinegar mixture. Reduce heat to low and simmer for 10 minutes, stirring several times. Allow to cool.
3 Discard the cloves and pour the mushrooms and liquid into a container with a tight-fitting lid. Pour the oil onto the surface. Cover tightly and leave in the refrigerator for at least 1 week.
4 To serve, strain off most of the liquid and serve as part of a zakuski spread or as an accompaniment to cold meats.

PIROZHKI

Small Pastries with Savory Filling

MAKES ABOUT 48

Pirozhki may be chilled for up to 12 hours before being baked

Ingredient

PASTRY
2 teaspoons active dry yeast
⅔ cup (5 fl oz / 160 mL) lukewarm milk
1 egg, beaten
3 ½ cups(14oz / 435g) all-purpose (plain) flour
2 teaspoons sugar
1 cup (8 oz / 250 g) butter, melted and cooled to room temperature

FILLING
3 tablespoons oil
2 lb (1kg) lean ground (minced) chicken, veal or beef
3 tablespoons light (pouring) cream
¾ teaspoon salt
⅓ teaspoon ground nutmeg
2 large onions, finely chopped
3 hard-cooked (hard-boiled) egg, finely chopped
¼ cup (2 fl oz / 60mL) chicken or beef stock
1 ½ tablespoons all-purpose (plain) flour
½ teaspoon freshly ground black pepper
2 tablespoons finely chopped parsley
milk or water, for sealing pastries

Method

1 Combine the yeast and sugar in a larger bowl and blend in the lukewarm milk. Allow to stand for 5 minutes or until slightly frothy.
2 Pour in the butter and beaten egg and beat with a wooden spoon.
3 Sift in the flour in several batches, stirring well after each addition. Adjust the amount of flour as necessary to form a workable dough.
4 On a lightly floured surface, knead the dough until it has a soft, smooth texture, adding a little more flour, if necessary, in the kneading process. Shape into a ball, cover lightly and let stand for 15 minutes.
5 Preheat the oven to 425°F (220℃)
6 To prepare the filling, heat the oil in a large pan, add the onions and cook over moderate heat until softened. Add the meat and cook until the color changes. Remove from heat and drain off excess juices. Add the remaining filling ingredients, adjust the seasoning, and set aside.
7 To make the pastries, break the dough into pieces, roll thinly and cut into 48 round, each 3 inches (7.5cm) wide. Place a spoonful of the filling on one side of the rounds, leaving a small rim around the edge. Brush the rim with milk, fold the pastry over and pinch the edges together or press with a fork. Arrange on a lightly greased baking sheeter and bake for about 20 minutes.
8 Serve hot or warm.

CAVIAR Caviar is the roe of the female sturgeon, and 98 percent of the world's supply comes form sturgeon that return from the ocean to the Caspian Sea to lay their eggs. No other fish roe can rightly be called caviar. Caviar has been prized by the Russians for centuries but only became popular outside the region in the 1920s when White Russian emigres introduced it to French society. Since then it has become a sought-after delicacy. Once the caviar has been collected and cleaned, it is placed in brine and packed in cans or jars. Cavior comes in two forms: pressed, which is made from small damaged eggs, and the more expensive whole grains. Caviar is traditionally served cold, often over ice, and accompanied by sour cream and bread; or it is used in canapes or as a garnish. There are three main types of sturgeon from which caviar is produced: Beluga, which gives the largest, dark gray and the most expensive eggs; Ossetra which has smaller yellowy brown eggs; and Servruga with very small green-black eggs. Once the cans are opened, caviar should be kept cold and eaten within two weeks. Caviar is sold in specialty food shops.

Wine Notes

In Russian Zakuski are accompanied by icy cold vodka. Moscow produces excellent vodka, such as Stolichnaya Cristall. Other choices are Absolut from Sweden and Wyborowa from Poland. Champagne or quality sparkling wines are good alternatives.

FRANCE : Select as good a Champagne as the budget will allow.

USA : Try one of the excellent sparkling wines being produced in California by combined French-American winemaking operations.

AUSTRALIA : Choose a "flagship" model from a good winemaker, such as Seppelts Salinger.

RUSSIA : Look for one of the good sparkling wines from around Rostov.

SALATY

Salads

Last century visitors to the sumptuous country houses of wealthy Russians could assuage their hunger at any time of day at the zakuski table, which was always set with substantial tidbits that have become classic hors d'oeuvres. Salads of all kinds were also included, and today these salads complement nearly every Russian meal. They are often made with cooked vegetables and include a pickled ingredient, such as cucumbers.

VINEGRET

Cooked Vegetable Salad

SERVES 6

Canned or bottled beets can be substituted for home-cooked fresh ones. However, if home-cooking the beets, do not cook them in an aluminum saucepan.

Ingredient

1 lb (500g) beets (beetroot)
2 large carrots, cut into small dice
2 dill pickles (pickled cucumbers), cut into dice
3 scallions (spring onions), finely chopped
⅓ teaspoon freshly ground black pepper
3 potatoes
1 onion, finely chopped
2 cups (8oz / 250g) cooked peas
salt, to taste

DRESSING
1 teaspoon dry mustard
⅓ cup(3 fl oz / 90mL) vegetable oil
½ teaspoon sugar, optional
2 tablespoons red wine vinegar
salt and pepper, to taste
dill sprigs, for garnish

Method

1. Place the beets in a saucepan of lightly salted boiling water and simmer until tender—this could take at least 1 hour, depending on the size and age of the beets. When cool enough to handle, remove the skin and cut the beets into cubes.
2. Cook the potatoes in lightly salted water for about 15 minutes, then add the carrot and cook until both are tender. Cut the potatoes into cubes.
3. In a large bowl, combine all the vegetables with the salt and pepper. Toss together lightly.
4. To make the dressing, whisk together the mustard and vinegar in a small bowl, then gradually whisk in the oil, salt and pepper. Whisk in the sugar if the dressing tastes too sharp.
5. Pour the dressing on the vegetables and toss again to coat evenly.
6. Chill until serving time. Serve garnished with dill sprigs.

SALAT IZ SVYOKLY I KHRENA

Beet and Horseradish Salad

SERVES 5

When time is limited, make this salad with canned or bottled beets, but not those packed in vinegar. Use prepared horseradish if fresh is not available.

Ingredient

1 lb (500g) young beets (beetroot), tops removed
6 tablespoons white wine vinegar
1 tablespoon sugar
1 bay leaf
1 teaspoon peppercorns
3 tablespoons water
2 tablespoons coarsely grated horseradish
4 tablespoons sour cream, optional

Method

1. Place the beets in a saucepan, cover with water and boil gently until tender. The length of cooking time varies with the size and age of the beets—usually it would take at least 1 hour. The beets are cooked when they are easily pierced with a cake tester.
2. Allow the beets to cool, then slip off the skin. Grate the beets coarsely or cut into thin slices.
3. Meanwhile, heat the vinegar to boiling with the sugar, bay leaf and peppercorns, then remove form heat. Add the water.
4. Spread half the beets out in a serving bowl, then spread the horseradish over the top, and then layer over the remaining beets. Pour over the vinegar marinade and chill for 24 hours.
5. Drain off the marinade and add the sour cream to the top of the salad, if using.
6. Serve with hot or cold meats.

RASSOLYE

Herring and Potato Salad

SERVES 4

Remember to soak the salt herrings well in advance. Use regular horseradish if red horseradish is not available.

Ingredient

4 small salt herrings
1 beet (beetroot) cooked, peeled and diced
1 small white onion, grated or very finely chopped
4 new potatoes, boiled and diced
1 dill pickle (pickled cucumber), sliced
1 tablespoon chopped fresh parsley, for garnish

DRESSING

3 teaspoons wholegrain mustard
1 tablespoon white wine vinegar
1 teaspoon red horseradish, well drained
½ teaspoon hot mustard
¾ cup (6oz / 185g) sour cream
salt and pepper, to taste

Method

1. Soak the herring in cold water for 6 to 8 hours. Drain and rinse well, then pat dry and cut into ½ inch (1.25cm) pieces. Place in a large bowl and add the diced potatoes, beet, cucumber and onion.
2. To make the dressing, mix together the mustards with the vinegar. Gradually stir in the sour cream and the horseradish. Season with the salt and pepper.
3. Spoon the dressing over the salad and toss lightly but well.
4. Pile onto a serving plate, garnish with the chopped parsley and serve with dark rye bread.

BEETS The beet (Beta vulgaris), also known as the beetroot, is a member of the beet family which includes the sugar beet (used in the sugar industry) and the mangewurzel (grown as feed far livestock). The beet has been eaten by peaple around the Mediterranean for centuries, although it was the leaves of the smaller, wild beet that were prized. Today's cultivated beet is eaten for its chick root; the leaves are often discarded, although they can be treated like spinach. Small beets are delicious grated raw and eaten in salads. However, beets are most often boiled or roasted whole, and then served as a vegetable with sauces—orange is a good taste partner—or in soups such as borscht. Cooked beets are also commonly used cold in salads or hors d'oeuvres. Beets can be bought fresh, from supermarkets and greengrocers. They should be kept in the refrigerator and used within a week. They are widely available ready-cooked or pickled, in jar and cans.

Wine Notes

These salads contain just about every enemy of wine. On home soil they would be consumed with icy cold vodka, possibly with a beer chaser. As the salads are likely to be part of a zakuski table or served with a main meal, you could choose a wine that is complementary to the other foods. Don't waste a superlative wine an the salads—the vinegar would "kill" it. Choose rather an inexpensive domestic Riesling style.

KULEBYAKA

Russian Fish Pie

This dish was originally very elaborate, consisting of layers of crepes, salmon, rice, mushrooms and other delicacies. In the 1800s it was served on the tables of the country estates as well as in Moscow restaurants. The French chefs who had been employed at the Russian court and Russian emigres later took the recipe to France where it rapidly gained a following. Simpler modern versions are often adaptations of the French recipes.

SERVES 8~10

This dish is most commonly made with salmon, but any firm-textured fish may be substituted. Start with a whole fish or cutlets. If preferred, mix all the filling ingredients together instead of arranging them in layers.

Ingredient

PASTRY

4 cup (1 lb / 500g) all-purpose (plain) flour
1 ½ cups (12oz / 375g) butter, cut into small dice
chilled water
⅓ teaspoon salt
1 egg

FIllING

10 cups (80 fl oz / 2.5L) water
3 onions
2 celery stalks, including leaves, chopped
2 bay leaves
1 teaspoon black peppercorns
½ cup (4oz / 125g) butter
juice of 1 large lemon
salt and pepper, to taste
½ cup (2oz / 60g) short grain rice
1 ½ cups (12 fl oz / 375mL) dry white wine
2 carrots, thickly sliced
3 sprigs parsley
1 teaspoon salt
2 lb (1kg) salmon
8 oz (250g) mushrooms, coarsely chopped
3 hard-cooked (hard-boiled) eggs, finely chopped
1 cup (8 fl oz / 250mL) rich chicken stock
2 tablespoons chopped dill

GLAZE

1 egg, separated
2 tablespoons milk

Method

1 To prepare the pastry, sift together the flour and salt into a bowl or onto a marble slab. Add the butter and rub in lightly with your fingertips until the mixture is the texture of bread crumbs.
2 Make a well in the center and add the egg, working it into the mixture with your fingertips. Add sufficient chilled water to create a firm-textured dough. Shape into a ball, divide in two, wrap in plastic and chill for about 30 minutes.
3 To prepare the filling, pour the water and the wine into a large saucepan or fish cooker. Add half an onion to the saucepan with the carrots, celery, parsley, bay leaves, salt and peppercorns.
4 Heat to boiling, then reduce heat and add the salmon. Cover the pot and simmer for about 15 minutes, or until cooked.
5 Remove the fish, discard the skin and bones, and flake the flesh. Discard the vegetable.
6 Finely chop the remaining onions.
7 Melt half the butter in a heavy pan over medium heat and add the chopped onions. Cook until soft and transparent. Then remove the onion from the pan and set aside.

8 Heat the remaining butter in the same pan, and sauté the mushrooms over low heat. Spoon into a bowl and stir in the lemon juice.
9 Mix together the onions, mushrooms, hard-cooked eggs and salt and pepper.
10 Heat the chicken stock to boiling, add the rice, and cook, covered, over medium heat for about 15 minutes, or until the rice is tender. Fluff with a fork.
11 Add the flaked salmon and chopped dill to the rice, mix well and season to taste. Set aside until quite cold.
12 Divide the dough into two portions, one slightly bigger than the other. Roll out the smaller portion on a lightly floured surface to make a rectangle about 9×15 inches (23×37cm). Roll carefully around a rolling pin and transfer to a well-buttered baking sheet.
13 Spread one-third of the salmon and rice over the dough, leaving a border of about 1 inch (2.5cm) around the edges. Spoon on one-third of the mushroom, onion and egg mixture and spread evenly. Top with another layer of the salmon mixture and continue layering until all the ingredients are used.
14 Roll out the remaining dough into a rectangle large enough to cover the filling. Brush the pastry edges with egg white. Place the sheet over the filling and carefully pinch the edges of the pastry to ensure it is well sealed. Trim off any excess pastry, scraps and reserve. Make several slashes in the top of the pastry to allow steam to escape.
15 Roll out the remaining scraps of dough and make decorations of leaves or other shapes. Brush with the remaining egg white and arrange on the pastry top.
16 To glaze, beat the egg yolk with the milk and brush over the surface of the pie. Chill for 30 minutes.
17 Preheat the oven to 400°F (200℃).
18 Place the Kulebyaka in the oven and bake for about 1 hour, or until the crust is golden brown.
19 Serve hot or cold, thickly sliced.

SALMON Salmon, the "king of fishes," has long been prized for its flavor and nutritional value. It is a migratory fish that spends its adult life in the ocean but returns to freshwater spawning ground to breed. There are two main types of salmon, the Atlantic and Pacific. With increasing pollution of rivers worldwide, wild salmon are becoming more rare and, so, more expensive. Salmon farming has been carried out for many years, making the fish more accessible. The best eating salmon is under three years old and is often served whole or in cutlets. Its firm flesh and rich, strong flavor encourage a simple approach to cooking, such as poaching or grilling, and it is often served with a sauce. Smoked salmon is a traditional way of treating the fish. Fresh or frozen salmon is available from most fish shops and specialty food stores. Smoked salmon is often sold presliced in packs, either vacuum-sealed or frozen. Salmon is also sold in cans.

Wine Notes

A dry white wine, well favored but not overpowering, would be most appropriate.

FRANCE : An Alsatian Riesling, strong and slightly aromatic, would be a good choice.

USA : Try a crisp Semillon or Semillon-Sauvignon Blanc blend from Washington State.

AUSTRALIA : Choose a Verdelho, in particular one from Margater River in Western Australia or from the Hunter Valley in New South Wales.

NEW ZEALAND : Select a top-quality Sauvignon Blanc such as the outstanding Cloudy Bay from the South Island.

KOTLIETY PO-KIEVSKY

Chicken Kiev

The relationship of this dish to the Ukrainian city of kiev is unclear. Some food historians believe it was created by the French chef Antonin Careme at the court of Russia's Alexander I. Today it is well known in international cuisine for its delicate flavors. Some early recipes used boned and stuffed chicken breasts with the wing attached, but modern versions use chicken fillets for ease of preparation and eating.

SERVES 4

To make dry bread crumbs, thinly slice a day-old loaf of French bread and discard the crusts. Place the slices on a baking sheet and toast in a low oven (300°F / 150 ℃) until dry and crisp, about 10 minutes. Place in a food processor and finely crumb. Stored in an airtight container in the refrigerator, the crumbs will keep of 1 to 2 months.

Ingredient

- ⅓ cup (3oz / 90g) unsalted butter, at room temperature
- 4 whole chicken breasts (about 8oz / 250g each), skinned, boned and halved
- 1 ½ cups (60oz / 185g) dry bread crumbs vegetable oil, for frying
- 1 tablespoon lemon juice
- freshly ground white pepper, to taste
- 3 tablespoons all-purpose (plain) flour
- 2 small eggs, beaten

Method

1 Blend together the butter, lemon juice and pepper. Roll the mixture into 1 inch (2.5cm) logs. Cover with plastic wrap and chill for several hours or until quite hard.

2 Pound the chicken breasts gently between two sheets of wax (greaseproof) paper, to flatten without tipping the meat.

3 Place a roll of butter in the center of each fillet, turn in the ends and roll up firmly, ensuring there are no tears in the meat through which the butter could seep out.

4 Dip the rolls lightly in the flour, shaking off any excess. Dip into the beaten egg, then roll in the bread crumbs until well coated.

5 Cover and chill for several hours.

6 Add the oil to a deep fryer, to a depth of 2~3 inches (5~8cm). When the oil is about 350°F (180℃), drop the rolls in batches, allowing plenty of room in the deep fryer. Cook until they are deep golden brown, about 8 to 10 minutes.

7 Place on paper towels and keep warm in a low oven (300°F / 150℃) until the rest of the chicken is cooked.

8 Serve immediately—it is essential that this dish be served piping hot. Be careful when making the first cut into the chicken, as some of the hot butter will spurt out.

Wine Notes

A full-bodied Chardonnay is the perfect partner for this dish.

FRANCE : If the budget permits, select a White Burgundy such as Meursault of Puligny-Monrachet.

USA : Try a Chardonnay form the Monterey—San Francisco Bay area, from producers such as Paul Masson, Chalone and Mirasson.

AUSTRALIA : Try one of the great Chardonnays from the Mornington Peninsula, near Melbourne.

NEW ZEALAND : Excellent Chardonnays, big and strongly flavored, are made in the Hawkes Bay and Gisborne areas.

KOTLIETY POJARSKIE

Cutlets of Ground Chicken

The origins of this dish are more certain than many other recipes. It is believed to have originated in the kitchens of an inn in the small Russian town of Torjzhok. Pojarski's inn was a favorite staging post for people journeying from Moscow to St. Petersburg. While the carriage horses were being changed, the travelers would be served a meal which would include cutlets made from ground venison or other meats, fish, or chicken.

MAKES 6

Serve sautéed mushrooms with this dish.

Ingredient

3 thick slices bread, crusts removed
1 lb (500g) lean, ground (minced) chicken
½ teaspoon salt
¼ teaspoon ground nutmeg
1 egg, beaten
butter, for cooking
4 tablespoons milk
⅓ cup (3oz / 90g) butter, softened
⅓ teaspoon freshly ground black pepper
4 tablespoons flour
dry bread crumbs (see Kotliery po-Kievsky recipe, on facing page)

Method

1 Soak the bread slices in the mlik, then squeeze as dry as possible. Blend together the chicken, butter and bread.
2 Add the salt, pepper and nutmeg and mix well, with lightly floured hands, divide the mixture into 6 portions and form into cutlet shapes.
3 Dust lightly with flour, dip into the egg and then coat well with the bread crumbs.
4 Place on a plate or tray, cover and chill for 30 minutes.
5 Heat sufficient butter to generously cover the base of a large skillet and cook the cutlets for about 5 minutes each side, or until golden brown and the juices run clear when a skewer is inserted into the center.

Wine Notes

A flavorsome dry white wine would help to enhance the subtle flavor of this dish.

FRANCE : Choose a Pouilly-Fume or Sancerr, dry but pungent and definite in flavor.

USA : Select a full-flavored California Chardonnay from Edna Valley or a Sauvignon Blanc; try one from Benziger of Sonoma.

AUSTRALIA : Try a Semillon or Sauvignon Blanc from quality Western Australian winemakers such as Cullens and Cape Mentelle from the Margaret River region and Evans and Tate from the Swan Valley.

NEW ZEALAND : A Marlborough Sauvignon Blanc, with its powerful varietal characteristics, is an excellent choice.

VARYONOYE MIASO

Boiled Beef

Most national cuisines include a classic boiled beef recipe. This was apparently one of Catherine the Great's favorites (she preferred basic cooking to the fancy European styles), and it still enjoys popularity in Russian today. Simple yet filling, this dish is often served with horseradish, mustard. mayonnaise, pickled beets and cucumber. Horseradish sauces are essential to Russian cuisine, and complement plainly prepared meat and fish dishes.

VARYONOYE MIASO

Boiled Beef

SERVES 6

Some cooks like to reserve the marrow from the bone and reheat it gently to serve with the meat. It may also be spread on bread and served with the meat.

Ingredient

1 lb (500g) beef marrow bones, such as shin of beef
1 large onion, coarsely chopped
1 small white turnip, cubed
2 garlic cloves, chopped or slivered
3 lb (1.5kg) beef, rump or round roast (in the piece)
1 teaspoon salt
Goryachliy Sous iz Khrena (see recipe)
8 cups (64 fl oz / 2L) water
1 carrot, thickly sliced
2 celery stalks, with leaves
bouquet garni of 6 sprigs dill, 6 sprigs parsley, 10 peppercorns and 2 bay leaves
fresh dill sprigs, for garnish

Method

1 Combine the marrow bones, water, vegetables, garlic and bouquet garni in a large saucepan. Heat to boiling and skim any froth from the surface as it rises.
2 Add the piece of beef and the salt and return to simmer. Reduce heat to low, cover and continue simmering until the beef is very tender when pierced, about 3 to 3 ½ hours. Skim off any froth from time to time as required.
3 If the beef is to be served hot, remove immediately from the cooking liquid when tender and allow to stand for about 10 minutes. Strain the stock and keep warm; reserve 1 cup for the horseradish sauce.
4 Slice the beef thickly and arrange on a heated serving platter. Spoon a little of the stock over the meat. Garnish with the dill sprigs, and serve sauce separately.
5 If the beef is to be served cold, allow to cool in the cooking liquid to room temperature, then refrigerate for several hours. When ready to serve, slice thickly, garnish with the dill and serve with the sauce.

GORYACHIY SOUS IZ KHRENA

Hot Horseradish Sauce

MAKES ABOUT 2 CUPS

If fresh horseradish is used, choose tender young roots. Peel and grate them finely, then rinse and dry before adding to the sauce. If preferred, prepared horseradish may be used straight from jar.

Ingredient

1 ½ tablespoons butter
1 cup (8 fl oz / 250 mL) beef stock, reserved from Varyonoye Miaso
⅓ teaspoon sugar
1 ½ tablespoons all-purpose (plain) flour
¾ cup (6oz / 185g) sour cream
½ cup finely grated white horseradish root
1 teaspoon white wine vinegar

Method

1 Melt the butter in a small saucepan over moderate heat. Stir in the flour and cook for 1 minute without allowing to brown.
2 Gradually add the reserved stock, stirring constantly. Add the sour cream, horseradish, sugar and vinegar and stir well. Heat for several minutes without allowing to boil, then serve.

DILL Dill(Anethum graveolens) is a pungent, aromatic herb similar to fennel. It originated in the dry, temperate regions of the Mediterranean and Asia Minor, and was popular during the Middle Ages as a cure for flatulence and colic. The feathery green leaves of the dill plant team well with fish dishes, particularly salmon, salads (cucumber with dill is a scandinavian speciality) and vegetables. They are also used as a garnish and to add flavor to soups. If a stronger taste is desired, as for pickles and relishes, the seeds are used. Dill can be grown in a pot or in the garden at home. Fresh and dried dill and dill seeds are readily available at supermarkets. If not using immediately, fresh dill should be kept in water in the refrigerator; use it as soon as possible.

SHASHLYK I PLOV S GRIBAMI

Skewered Lamb and Mushroom and Rice Pilaf

This method of cooking meat, usually lamb or beef, evolved in the Caucasus region, once part of the Russian empire. The meat, often treated with a spicy marinade, was cooked on sticks over open fires. The marinade was probably used when it was necessary to tenderize and flavor meat that was not perfectly fresh. Traditionally shashlyk is served with pilaf, a rice dish which has almost infinite variations.

SHASHLYK

Skewered Lamb

SERVES 4

A good quality broiling (grilling) beef may be substituted for the lamb in this recipe.
1~1 ½ lb (16~24oz / 500~750g) lean lamb, cut into large cubes.

Ingredient

MARINADE

1 onion, grated or finely chopped
1 tablespoon olive oil
⅓ teaspoon freshly ground black pepper
⅓ teaspoon dill seeds
juice of ½ lemon
½ teaspoon salt
½ teaspoon crushed cilantro (coriander) seeds
2 allspice berries, crushed

GARNISH

2 tomatoes, cut into wedges
1 lemon, cut into wedges
4 sprigs fresh bay leaves

Method

1 Mix together all the marinade ingredients in a stainless steel, ceramic or glass bowl. Add the lamb cubes and toss well. Cover and leave for at least 8 hours, turning the meat from time to time.
2 Press the meat cubes onto metal skewers and cook over hot coals or under a hot, preheated broiler (griller) for about 8 to 10 minutes, turning several times.
3 Place the shashlyks on a platter. Garnish with the tomatoes, bay leaves and lemon.
4 Serve with Rice Pilaf.

PROV S GRIBAMI

Mushroom and Rice Pilaf

SERVES 6

Although it is not essential to use dried mushrooms, they do provide a more mature flavor. You may use a few dark-grilled mature field mushrooms instead replace the mushroom soaking water when cooking the rice.

Ingredient

3 dried porcini mushrooms
½ cup (4oz / 125g) butter
1 lb (500g) mushrooms, sliced
2 garlic cloves, finely chopped
1 ½ cups (12 fl oz / 375mL) vegetable stock or water
⅓ teaspoon freshly ground black pepper
¾ cup (6 fl oz / 180mL) cold water
6 onions, finely chopped
⅓ cup (3oz / 90g) sour cream
1 cup (6oz / 185g) short grain rice
½ teaspoon salt
⅓ cup finely chopped parsley

Method

1 Soak the dried mushrooms in the water for several hours. Strain the liquid from the mushrooms through muslin and reserve. Chop the mushrooms finely.

2 Melt one-third of the butter in a large pan and cook the onions over medium heat until golden brown, stirring often. In another pan, melt another one-third of the butter and cook both the dried and fresh mushrooms for about 20 minutes. Add the sour cream and the garlic and heat gently for about 5 minutes.

3 Meanwhile, rinse the rice and drain well. Heat the stock or water and mushroom water to boiling, add the rice and salt and cover the saucepan. Reduce heat and simmer for about 20 minutes, or until the rice has absorbed all the cooking liquid. Stir occasionally while it cooks. Stir in the remaining butter, then add the mushrooms, onion, pepper and parsley and allow to heat through.

4 Serve at once.

ALLSPICE An aromatic spice, allspice is the dried, unripe berry of a West Indian evergreen tree (Pimento dioica), a member of the myrtle family. The first known mention of allspice—somtimes called Jamaican pepper—is in Christopher Columbus' journal. The early settlers of the Caribbean exported the spice to Europe. It is called allspice because when ground its flavor is a combination of cinnamon, nutmeg and cloves. Whole allspice berries are used in pickles and casseroles and in sauces for pork, veal and poultry. The ground spice is used for flavoring fruitcakes and puddings, as well as sausages and stuffings. The berries which resemble peppercorns, can be bought whole or ground. They are readily available. Store them in an airtight container out of the light.

BEF STROGANOV

Beef Stroganov

Well known around the world today, many believe that this dish was named last century after the almost legendary Stroganov family who were financiers, traders and patrons of the arts. Others say it was named for Count Paul Stroganov, a prominent diplomat of the time and a famous gourmet. Quality meat and precise cooking times are the secret to success. Simplicity is the essence of this dish.

SERVES 4

Do not slice the meat too far advance or it will be wet and will stew rather than brown quickly. If necessary, pat dry with paper towels before cooking.

Ingredient

1 ½ lb (750g) tenderloin (fillet) steak
1 small onion, thinly sliced into rings
⅓ teaspoon salt
1 cup (8oz / 250g) sour cream or smetana (see glossary)
⅓ cup (3oz / 90g) butter
8oz (250g) button mushrooms, thickly sliced
¼ teaspoon freshly grated nutmeg
1 tablespoon finely chopped parsley, for garnish

Method

1 Cut the steak across the grain into thin strips about 1 inch (2.5cm) wide.
2 Melt half the butter in a large skillet, and cook the onion over moderate heat until transparent. Raise heat slightly, add the beef and cook quickly for about 5 minutes, ensuring all sides are browned. If necessary, do this in batches, removing strips as they are cooked.
3 Meanwhile, cook the mushrooms in a smaller pan with the remaining butter Season them with the salt and nutmeg and add to the beef.
4 Warm the sour cream, then stir it into the beef and mushrooms. Heat through gently.
5 Garnish with the parsley. Serve at once with rice or noodles.

SOUR CREAM Sour cream is fresh pasteurized cream into which bacteria are deliberately introduced to tum the natural sugar into lactic acid. Its semi-solid consistency makes it ideal as a topping for both jacket potatoes and desserts, as a substitute for mayonnaise, and with dips. Added to sauces and soups, sour cream gives a creamy, slightly tart taste. When adding it to a hot dish, add it at the end of the cooking time, taking care it does not boil or it will curdle. Sour cream is readily available wherever dairy food is sold. It will keep for up to two if stored in a refrigerator.

Wine Notes

It has to be a red wine this dish; a good quality, flavorsome one.

FRANCE : Choose a Bordeaux, preferably a Grand Cru Pomerol or Saint Emilion.

USA : A Cabernet from the Napa Valley in Califonia would be perfect; choose one with four or five years' bottle age.

AUSTRALIA : Try a Cabernet-Merlot blend from Margaret River or the Yarra Valley.

ITALY : Select a Cabernet blend such as San Gilrgio by Lungarotti of Umbria, or Antinon's Solaia from Tussany.

PASHKA

Molded Cream Cheese with Fruits and Nuts

This rich, cheese-based dessert is traditionally served at Easter with kulich, a sweet cake-like bread. There is a bewildering array of recipes for this well-loved dish. Some cooks dictate that it must be cooked: others insist this is unnecessary. Some use hard-cooked egg yolks: others leave the yolks uncooked. Often the Pashka is pressed into an elaborate, pyramid-shaped mold lined with damp muslin. Candied violets are a traditional garnish.

SERVES 8

Some recipes use cottage cheese instead of ricotta; ricotta gives a better texture.

Ingredient

- $2\frac{1}{4}$ cups (12oz / 375g) cream cheese
- $\frac{2}{3}$ cup (5oz / 155g) unsalted butter
- $\frac{2}{3}$ cup (5oz / 155g) superfine (caster) sugar
- 2 tablespoons chopped almonds
- $\frac{1}{2}$ teaspoon vanilla extract (vanilla essence)
- $\frac{1}{2}$ teaspoon grated orange zest
- 1 cup (12oz / 375g) ricotta cheese
- 2 egg yolks
- 3 tablespoons chopped glace fruits
- 2 tablespoons chopped golden rasins (sultanas)
- $\frac{1}{2}$ teaspoon grated lemon zest
- additional glace fruits, for garnish

Method

1. Beat the cream cheese until it is soft, then gradually beat in the ricotta cheese, butter, egg yolks and sugar.
2. Stir in the glace fruits, almonds, raisins, vanilla extract and fruit zests.
3. Line a Pashka mold (or a dampened earthenware flowerpot with a hole in its base) with damp cheesecloth, smoothing out the creases as much as possible. Spoon in the mixture and press down firmly.
4. Cover with plastic wrap and flowerpot in the refrigerator to drain for at least 12 hours.
5. Turn out so that the narrow end is at the top, garnish with glace fruits and serve.

Wine Notes

The ideal choice is a wine or liqueur that echoes this dessert's orange or strawberry flavor.

FRANCE : A white Curacao (or Triple Sec) such as Cointreau would be a perfect choice.

USA : Southern Comfort, served chilled in a small glass, would be excellent.

AUSTRALIA : Choose a fresh, very fruity dessert wine such as Brown Brothers Orange Muscat and Flora.

NEW ZEALAND : Try a fruit wine, such as one of the liqueur–like strawberry wines marketed by Barkers.

KLUBNICHNOYE ROMANOVSKI

Strawberries Romanov

Rich, sweet desserts and pastries were a great favorite of the wealthy in Russia and featured traditional flavorings such as walnuts, honey and crystallized fruit, while fresh fruit was also prized. This simple but delicious dish is attributed to the French chef, Antonin Careme from his time at the court of Tsar Alexander I. It bears the name of the Russian imperial family of the time.

SERVES 4

Choose small, deep red strawberries for greatest depth of flavor. Do not prepare too far in advance, or the berries will lose their texture and become soggy.

Ingredient

3 cups small ripe strawberries
3 tablespoons freshly squeezed orange juice
juice of $\frac{1}{2}$ lemon
2 tablespoons Curaçao or other orange flavored liqueur
1 tablespoon very finely julienned orange zest

CHANTILLY CREAM
1 cup (8 fl oz / 250mL) whipping cream
$\frac{1}{3}$ teaspoon vanilla extract (vanilla essence)
2 teaspoons confectioners' (icing) sugar

Method

1 Wipe the berries with a damp paper towel, remove hulls, pat dry and place in a bowl.
2 Add the orange liqueur, orange and lemon juices and julienned zest. Allow to macerate for about 30 minutes in the refrigerator.
3 To serve, spoon the berries and the marinade into individual goblets and pass the cream around separately.

Wine Notes

The ideal choice is a wine or liqueur that echoes this dessert's orange or strawberry flavor.

FRANCE : A white Curaçao (or Triple Sec) such as Cointreau would be a perfect choice.

USA : Southern Comfort, served chilled in a small glass, would be excellent.

AUSTRALIA : Choose a fresh, very fruity dessert wine such as Brown Brothers Orange Muscat and Flora.

NEW ZEALAND : Try a fruit wine, such as one of the liqueur-like strawberry wines marketed by Barkers.

SPAIN

World Cuisine

SPAIN in its new guise, is as effervescent as a glass of cava, the local sparkling wine. Everything is possible and open for discussion. You can hear the buzz in the expressive talk of Madrid's tapas bars, in the swank outdoor cafés on the Plaza Mayor and in the Barrio de Santa Cruz in Seville. Spain is on show around the clock, erupting with street life in sidewalk terrazzas and bars, with street theatre of all kinds. All Spanish cities are jam-packed with restaurants, cervecerias (beer halls), mesones (inns) and tascas (bistros).

Las Ramblas, Barcelona's great stretch of strolling street life, is best known for charging double the usual rate for a cup of coffee, and the passing parade of "los guapos," as the handsome young men are known. Even between midnight and dawn you can find somewhere to buy a drink or snack. Partygoers, the disco crowd and insomniacs mix with early morning workers, in much the same way as Parisians used to do at the old Les Halles markets in France. But for food lovers, this legendary walking street is also home to the Mercat de la Bouqueria, one of the grandest produce markets in Europe. A great glass and metal construction from the nineteenth-century, Barcelona's Mercat is a daily gathering of Spain's finest meats, fish, fruits, vegetables, cheese and flowers.

The Mercado in Salamanca is another of the great produce markets of Spain–and in Salamanca, situated in the center of Spain's largest wheatbelt, can be found the bread that best accompanies the cornucopia of food avaliable at the Mercado. Spanish restaurants routinely sport the words "pan y vino (bread and wine)" on menus because the two things are seen as obligatory to any Spanish meal.

The best way to get a snap impression of the bone structure of Spain's still largely traditional cuisine is through a journey over the vast plains of the Iberian Peninsula. Huge wheatfields, green in spring, dark yellow in the fall, signal the beginnings of the thick-crusted Spanish bread. Galicia's famous cabbage soup is heartily enjoyed after passing the rows of long-leafed, blue-green cabbages that proliferate throughout this northwestern province. All along the rugged north coast of Spain, restaurant windows showcase teeming heaps of red, black, silver and orange Atlantic fish and shellfish.

A popular eating place in Madrid is the Museo del Jamon—literally, the museum of ham. The waiters simply reach up and pull down individual hams from the long rows above their heads as customers call for favorite delicacies. Spanish hams are a deep rose-pink marbled with weaving lines of fat, and the most prized is jamon serrano from Huelva in the south.

Its other claims to fame notwithstanding, Seville was the first place in Europe where potatoes were grown after their importation from the Americas. Andalusian olives, which are among the fattest and juiciest in the world, also come from the red soil surrounding Seville. In the same region irrigated ricefields produce the thick, highly absorbent grain required for a good paella. Jordan almonds from Valencia are the end product of many acres of pink-blossomed trees.

Since their surge to fashionable popularity in the 1980s, tapas have become the Spanish specialty on everybody's lips, both figuratively and literally. Madrid is said to have the best tapas bars in Spain, pumping out piquant tidbits like Albondigas (meatballs), prawn fritters, small slices of Spanish omelette, marinated squid, salads and eels cooked in garlic and chili-flavored olive oil. Most people drink wine with tapas but many Spaniards prefer horchata, a milky-looking drink made from ground almonds or chufas (tiger nuts). In Spain you can buy horchata in icecream parlor and in milk cartons but the best versions are to be found in tapas bars.

The meaning of the word gazpacho is obscure; not so the widespread taste for this most refreshing of summer soups. Some linguists maintain that the name comes from the Moorish word "kaz" meaning bowl; others trace its lineage back to the old Spanish word indicating the feeling of satiation. Gazpacho comes in two versions—white and red—of which the latter is the most popular. A blend of tomatoes, peppers, garlic, bread crumbs, and vinegar, with a variety of garnishes—well made, it can remain long in the memory as a gastronomic delight.

Paella has the look of a medieval still-life—lavish, multi-colored and diverse. Every Spanish cook claims to have a personal secret way with this most Spanish of dishes but idiosyncratic genius aside, the dish has a few essential ingredients, which include thick-grained Spanish rice and saffron to impart the hint of sweetness. After that, depending on your taste and your budget add chicken, pork, chorizo, fish, mussels, peppers, peas or shrimp. In some regions rabbit is added, and in Valencia, snails are a popular inclusion. Understandably, given its extravagance, paella is seen as a festive dish and you must order it several hours in advance in most Spanish restaurants so as to allow plenty of time for its preparation.

Roasted and boiled meat, almost sixteenth century in presentation, holds sway on the great central plateau of Spain, while sausages are frequently used in composite dishes. The most famous Spanish sausage is the chorizo, of which each region has its own variation—fine or coarse, long or short. Chorizo is eaten like salami, slivered into stews and soups, or used for toppings for tortilla. Morcilla, a sausage made with blood, onions and rice, turns up in boiled meat dishes, fried on its own or in soups. Tocino, cured pork fat, is often chopped and fried with onion to start a hearty soup.

The Spanish use great quantities of eggs and nuts in their desserts, which are consequently very rich. Standing in a Spanish pastry shop with a shot of black coffee and a slice of brazo de gitano—longer and thinner than a jelly roll but made in the same way and filled with custard—is to know true pleasure.

TAPAS

Appetizers

Tapas are the appetizers that are served with glasses of wine in wine bars all over Spain. Tapa is the Spanish word for cover, the name probably comes from the bartender's custom of placing a small dish of appetizers on top of the glass of wine ordered. From the simplest origin–a chunk of crusty bread, a dish of olives–tapas have become a tantalizing array of snacks that often reflect specialties of the regions in which they originated.

ALBONDIGAS

Spicy Meatballs

8 TAPAS SERVINGS

These Spicy meatballs have been a favorite of the Spaniards for centuries.

Ingredient

8oz (250g) lean ground (minced) steak
2 garlic cloves, very finely chopped
1 teaspoon dry sherry
salt and pepper, to taste
1 egg
4 tablespoons olive oil
4oz (125g) Spicy sausage, ground (minced)
1 tablespoon finely chopped parsley
½ teaspoon mixed spice (see glossary)
⅓ teaspoon cayenne pepper
1~1 ½ tablespoons all-purpose (plain) flour

Method

1 Combine all the ingredients except the flour and oil in a large bowl and mix together well. Roll the mixture into small balls and toss lightly in the flour.
2 Heat the oil in a pan over moderate heat, and fry the balls for about 12 minutes, turning them often as they color. Cook until evenly browned and cooked through, then remove from the pan and drain well.
3 Serve in small preheated bowls.

FLAN DE CHAMPINONY QUESO

Mushroom and Cheese flam

8 TAPAS SERVINGS

A hard sheeps'-milk cheese is the traditional choice, but any hard, strongly flavored cheese like Cheddar will work well.

Ingredient

2 tablespoons olive oil
1 garlic clove, finely chopped
4 eggs, beaten
salt and pepper, to taste
4 oz (125g) mushrooms, chopped
1 cup (8 fl oz / 250mL) milk
⅓ cup (1 ½ oz / 45g) finely grated hard cheese

Method

1 Preheat the oven to 350°F (180℃).
2 Heat the oil in a small pan, add the mushrooms and garlic and stir-fry until soft. Pour off any excess oil.
3 Warm the milk in another pan, then remove from heat and stir in the eggs, cheese, mushrooms and garlic. Add the salt and pepper.
4 Pour the mixture into a well-buttered 9 inches (23cm) gratin dish.
5 Place in a baking dish with about 1 inch (2.5cm) water in the base and cook in the oven for 35 minutes, or until the mixture is firmly set.
6 Allow to cool, then carefully turn out of the dish and cut into small portions.

PRINGADAS EXTREMENAS

Fried Bread with Sausage

8 TAPAS SERVINGS

This easy dish from the Extremadura can also be eaten alone as an appetizer. Then the bread squares would be slightly larger.

Ingredient

4 tablespoons olive oil
4 slices chorizo or similar sausage
2 garlic cloves, halved
4 slices fatty ham
4 thick slices dense-textured white bread

Method

1 Heat 1 tablespoon of the oil in a pan and fry the ham and sausage for about 3 minutes. Remove from the pan and keep hot.
2 Remove the crusts from the bread and cut each slice into 2 inches (5cm) squares. Rub the surface of the bread squares with the cut garlic cloves.
3 Heat the remaining oil, add the bread in batches and fry until crisp and golden on each side. Drain well on paper towels.
4 Place a piece of ham and sausage on each piece of bread and serve at once.

GAMBAS AL PIL PIL

Shrimp in Garlic and Oil

8 TAPAS SERVINGS

This standard entry on the tapas menu originated in the Basque region. It is usually served straight from the cooking pot and eaten with wooden cocktail picks. Sometimes a sprinkle of sherry is added at the last minute, which adds a pleasant and interesting flavor.

Ingredient

4 tablespoons olive oil
8 oz (250g) small raw shrimp (prawns), shelled and deveined
2 large garlic cloves, slivered
⅓ cup finely chopped red bell pepper (capsicum)
⅓ teaspoon cayenne pepper

Method

1 Heat the oil in a shallow two-handled pan or an earthenware casserole over high heat.
2 Add the garlic and cook for 1 minute, then add the shrimp and cook for about 2 minutes, or until the flesh begins to turn opaque.
3 Add the red bell pepper and cayenne and quickly stir-fry in the pan.
4 Remove from heat and serve.
5 Sea salt may be passed around separately or sprinkled over the shrimp.

CHORIZO This spicy, dry sausage was first made in Spain where it comes in many different varieties. All chorizos contain pork. Hanging in a fifteenth-century Spanish kitchen, they would attest to the owner's Christianity, serving as a visual proof to the Inquisition that no one of the Jewish or Muslim faith lived there. Paprika, sweet or spicy, is another essential ingredient of chorizo, although other minced meats and seasonings may be added as well. Chorizo contains very little fat. Spanish chorizo is made with smoked pork whereas Mexican chorizo is made with fresh. Chorizo can be eaten raw, thinly sliced and served with bread, wine and olives; or it can be broiled (grilled), fried or cut in chunks and simmered in casseroles and soups.

Wine Notes

In Spain, sherry is served with tapas and seems to marry perfectly with the diversity. Beer is a good all-purpose substitute; if wine is preferred, choose a crisp, flavorsome dry white.

FRANCE : A white Bordeaux would be a successful choice, being dry and not overly grapey.

USA : Choose a Californian Fumé Blanc with a woody, pungent, edgy flavor.

AUSTRALIA : Try a South Australian Colombard or a Semillon from Western Australia.

SPAIN : Manzanilla, from the Sanlucar estuary near Jerez, is the ideal sherry: light, dry and slightly salty; or try a good chilled fino.

GAZPACHO ANDALUZ

Andalusian Gazpacho

This speciality of Andalusia, created by peasants to use up leftovers, has evolved into an international favorite. The ingredients reflect Spain's culinary history: garlic and wine vinegar courtesy of the Romans, and tomatoes and peppers introduced by the conquistadors and explorers who carried them to Spain from the New World. Gazpacho can be served on its own for lunch or as a first course for dinner on a hot slimmer's night.

SERVES 6

Traditional cooks pound the ingredients together with a mortar and pestle; modern cooks, no doubt, prefer to use the food processor. If using a food processor, it is best to puree the ingredients in batches. The finely chopped garnishes can be added before serving or passed around separately at the table.

Ingredient

3 slices stale bread, crusts removed
1 green bell pepper (capsicum), finely chopped
2 garlic cloves, finely chopped
1 large white onion, finely chopped
1 tablespoon chopped mint
2 lb (1kg) very ripe tomatoes, peeled and chopped
1 red bell pepper (capsicum), finely chopped
⅔ cup (5 fl oz / 160mL) white wine vinegar
1 tablespoon parsley
salt and pepper, to taste

GARNISH

1 small onion, finely chopped
1 small green bell pepper (capsicum), finely chopped
1 hard-cooked (hard-boiled) egg, finely chopped
6 sprigs of basil
1 small tomato, peeled and diced
¼ cup diced cucumber
1 lemon, thinly sliced

Method

1 Cover the bread with cold water and leave to soak for 10 minutes, then squeeze out as much water as possible.
2 Place the bread and the other ingredients in the food processor and puree. Process to a smooth consistency.
3 Adjust the seasoning, transfer to a bowl, cover and chill.
4 If the soup is too thick, add sufficient cold water to create the desired consistency.
5 Spoon the soup into individual bowls and divide the garnishes between them.

GARLIC There are conflicting theories as to garlic's place of origin—possibilities include central Asia, the Mediterranean region and the Middle East—but there is no doubt that it goes well back into the culinary history of the world. The ancient Greeks used it as a medicine—Hippocrates described it as "hot, laxative and diuretic." The Ancient Romans believed in the therapeutic qualities of garlic and encouraged their soldiers and athletes to eat it. The Romans are credited with inventing the mixing of garlic with olive oil, the forerunner of the famous Probencçal aïoli and the Catalan alioli. In the Middle Ages in Europe it was thought to protect people from the twm perils of the plague and the devil and also, legends has it, from vampires and witches. The medical school in Salerno set out a "regimen of health" which extolled the virtues of garlic, particularly as a guard against infection, although it did acknowledge the consequence of garlic on the breath. Medieval Europeans would also rub garlic on the skin to ward off stinging insects. Known botanically as Allium sativum, garlic is related to onions and chives. Grown as a bulb, garlic is dug up when its leaves begin to die back. Dirt is shaken from the bulb, and it is hung up to dry. "Fresh" garlic is, in fact, a dry bulb, with about 12 to 16 bulblets, called cloves. In the garden organic gardeners often plant garlic in between rows of vegetables to keep garden pests away. Its pungent flavor is used to great advantage in the cuisines of many countries, particularly in Asia, the Mediterranean region and Mexico. Long slow cooking tends the sweeten its flavor and reduce its strong smell. One of garlic's main roles in the kitchen is in promoting the flavor of other ingredients while losing its own potency. Should any unpleasant odor linger one the breath after eating garlic, chewing fresh parsley should disguise it. Garlic is available in dried from as well as finely chopped in jars but there is really no substitute for the flavor and aroma of fresh garlic cloves. Store garlic in a cool dry spot where air can circulate around it.

Wine Notes

Chilled fino sherry IS the best accompaniment to this fine soup. A tangy white wine could also be served. Sangria is another option.

FRANCE : Choose the lively piquant flavors of a Sancerre or Pouilly-Fumé.

USA : Select a Napa or Sonoma Sauvignon Blanc, or a more unusual Washington State Pinot Gris.

AUSTRALIA : A fine Australian flor fino-style sherry such as Lindemans and Seppelts Reserve and Show labels would be enjoyable.

SPAIN : Try a fino or manzartilla sherry from Domeea Harveys or Gonzales Byass.

HUEVOS A LA FLAMENCA

Eggs Flamenco

The Spanish explorers of the sixteenth century brought back numerous plants from the New World. Among them were tomato plants, which were at first used only as ornamentals, but eventually they worked their way into many Spanish recipes. This dish is Andalusian in origin and was probably created in the city of Seville. It is perfect for a brunch, a light evening meal, or served as a first course to a dinner.

SERVES 4

This dish looks best cooked and served in a cazuela, a flameproof earthenware dish.

Ingredient

¼ cup (2 fl oz / 60mL) Spanish olive oil
1 large onion, chopped
4 tomatoes, peeled and chopped
⅓ cup (1oz / 30g) shelled green peas
salt and pepper, to taste
4 eggs
1 large boiled potato, diced
4oz (125g) prosciutto or similar cured ham, diced
4oz (125g) chorizo or similar sausage, thinly sliced
⅓ cup (2 ½ oz / 75g) string beans, cut into 1 inch (2.5cm) lengths
chopped parsley, for garnish

Method

1. Preheat the oven to 350°F (180℃).
2. Heat the oil in a large pan or earthenware dish, then add the potato and stir-fry until browned. Add the onion and cook for 2 to 3 minutes, then add the ham and stir-fry for several minutes. Stir in the tomatoes and cook an additional 5 minutes.
3. Add the sausage, green peas, string beans, salt and pepper. Cover and cook until the vegetables are tender.
4. Break the eggs over the mixture or divide the mixture among individual heatproof dishes and break an egg into each.
5. Bake until the eggs are just set, about 15 minutes. Serve, sprinkled with the parsley.

Wine Notes

A simple dry red or a full-flavored dry white would suit this dish.

FRANCE : Select a rustic red, such as a Bandol or Fitou; or a white, such as a Bourgogne Blanc.

USA : Choose a light, dry red such as Grenache, or a crisp white such as Sauvignon Blanc or Colombard from the Napa, Sonoma or Russian River Valley areas.

AUSTRALIA : Try a Semillon, Sauvignon Blanc or Colombard from the Hunter Valley.

SPAIN : A chilled dry sherry would be the first choice; or try an export-quality dry wine.

BACALAO CON PATATAS

Salt Cod and Potato Casserole

The Basque provinces form the northern frontier of Spain touching the Atlantic Ocean at the Bay of Biscay. Basques, seafarers throughout history, are thought to be the last survivors of Spain's original Celtic-Iberian inhabitants. Their language and customs are quite different from those of the rest of Spain. Fish features prominently in their diet. Bacalao, or dried salt cod, is said to have originated in Basque region.

SERVES 4

Although it is more usual for the parsley / nut / garlic mixture to be stirred into the casserole a few minutes before it finishes cooking, it can also be sprinkled over the top just before serving.

Ingredient

8oz (250g) piece dried salt cod, soaked for at least 12 hours
1 lb (500g) potatoes, peeled and diced
¼ cup (1oz / 30g) ground almonds
2 tablespoons parsley, very finely chopped
2 garlic cloves, very finely chopped
⅓ cup (3 fl oz / 90mL) olive oil
2 tomatoes, peeled and chopped
1 teaspoon sweet paprika
1 tablespoon (½ oz / 15g) crushed or ground pine nuts
1 teaspoon lemon zest, optional

Method

1 Drain the cod very well, pat dry and cut into small pieces.
2 Heat the oil in a large pan, add the fish and tomatoes and cook for 8 minutes, stirring gently from time to time.
3 Add the potatoes and cook for an additional 8 minutes, stirring often. Stir in the paprika.
4 Add enough water to barely cover the contents of the saucepan, cover and simmer gently for 35 to 45 minutes, until the potatoes are tender.
5 Blend together the almonds, pine nuts, parsley, garlic and lemon zest and stir into the casserole. Cook gently for an additional 5 minutes before serving.

Wine Notes

The nature of this dish calls for a simple, strongly flavored white wine.

FRANCE : Select a white vin de pays from Gard or Hérault in the southern Languedoc region.

AUSTRALIA : The dry slightly lemony flavor of a Semillon or a Semillon-Sauvignon Blanc blend from the Barossa Valley is a good choice.

SPAIN : Try a dry white from the Penedés region, such as Torres Viña Sol, or one of the underrated whites of Aragon and Catalonia.

FAVES A LA CATALANA

Catalan Fava Bean Casserole

Catalonia is very diverse, both geographically and gastronomically. From the Pyrenees to the Ebro delta and the coastal Mediterranean plain come livestock and game, freshwater and saltwater fish, fruits, vegetables and wine. Fava beans, grown between rows of olive trees, play an important part in the local diet. They are eaten fresh in the summer months and dried for winter soups and casseroles.

SERVES 4

The original regional recipe for this dish calls for lard; however, in keeping with current dietary attitudes, olive oil is now a more acceptable alternative.

Ingredient

- 3 tablespoons Spanish olive oil
- 8oz (250g) chorizo or similar sausage, sliced or diced
- 3 garlic cloves, finely chopped
- ½ cup (4 fl oz / 125mL) dry red wine
- bouquet garni of thyme, oregano, bay leaf and mint
- 2 cloves
- 8oz (250g) bacon or speck, cut into strips
- 2 onions, chopped
- 1 large tomato, peeled and chopped
- 4 lb (2kg) fava beans (broad beans), shelled
- 1 cup (8 fl oz / 250mL) chicken or veal stock
- ¾ teaspoon mixed spice (see glossary)
- salt and pepper, to taste

Method

1. Heat the oil in a large casserole or heavy-based saucepan, add the bacon and sausage and fry until lightly colored. Remove with a slotted spoon and set aside.
2. Add the onions, tomato and garlic and fry for 8 minutes or until softened.
3. Add the beans, bacon and sausage and stir in the wine and stock. Add the bouquet garni, spice, cloves and salt and pepper.
4. Cover and cook over low heat for 30 to 35 minutes, or until the beans are tender.
5. Discard the bouquet garni.
6. Serve immediately

FAVA BEANS (BROAD BEANS) Fava beans (Vicia faba) have been eaten since prehistoric times and were cultivated widely by the ancients, particularly the Egyptians. Large, flat beans, they can be green, brown or beige in color, depending on their age, and have a robust flavor and smooth, creamy texture when cooked. Fava beans are best used in purees, soups, stews or bean patties. They are available dried, frozen or canned, particularly in Greek and Middle Eastern food stores.

Wine Notes

A lightish red would be best with this dish.

FRANCE : Try a rustic style from the south, such as a vin de pays from Gard or Nîmes, or perhaps a Côtes-du-Rhône.

USA : A Californian Grenache or Barbera would provide spicy flavors without great heaviness of body.

AUSTRALIA : Choose a Cabernet-Merlot of the “everyday” rather than the “boutique” kind: Tyrrells' Old Winery and Midara's Church Hill are very reliable.

SPAIN : Try a Catalan red produced by Torres, such as their Sangre de Toro or Coronas.

PEPITORIA DE POLLO

Chicken with Almonds

This recipe from Spain's Costa del Sol provides hints, in the form of almonds and spices, of a Moorish presence m the area centuries ago. The Moors planted the first almond groves, bringing the nuts with them from North Africa, and local farmers still maintain them to subsidize their incomes. The Arabs also carried with them saffron, nutmeg and black pepper, which soon became an intrinsic part of local cuisine.

SERVES 6

Saffron threads (the stamens of crocus flowers), the most expensive spice in the world, impart a beautiful and distintive flavor. In this recipe dried saffron may be used as a substitute (about ½ teaspoon) if the threads are not available, but turmeric, which is sometimes suggested as an alternative, is not really satisfactory.

Ingredient

1 roasting chicken, about 3 lb (1.5kg)
freshly ground black pepper, to taste
3 tablespoon olive oil
2 garlic cloves, chopped
1 ¾ cups (14 fl oz / 450mL) chicken stock
1 bay leaf
1 ¼ cups (4oz / 125g) ground almonds
⅓ teaspoon saffron threads, soaked in 1 tablespoon water
spring of bay leaves, for garnish
pinch of salt
2 tablespoon all-purpose (plain) flour
2 onions, finely chopped
¾ cup (6 fl oz / 180mL) dry white wine
bouquet garni
1 ¼ cups (14 fl oz / 450mL) chicken stock
½ teaspoon mixed spice (see glossary)
grated zest and juice of 1 lemon
4 tablespoons chopped parsley, for garnish

Method

1 Cut the chicken into serving portions.
2 Mix together the salt, pepper and flour and sprinkle over the chicken pieces.
3 Heat the oil in a skillet and brown the chicken pieces in batches on all sides. When evenly browned, remove the chicken pieces from the pan with a slotted spoon and arrange in a large shallow saucepan.
4 Sauté the onion and garlic in the remaining oil for about 5 minutes, then spread the mixture over the chicken pieces.
5 Add the wine, stock, bouquet garni and bay leaf to the chicken pieces, then heat to boiling. Reduce heat, cover the saucepan and simmer gently for 25 minutes.
6 Mix together the ground almonds, spice, saffron liquid, lemon zest and juice and blend to a smooth consistency. Stir in a little of the liquid from the saucepan. Spoon the almond mixture into the saucepan, stir lightly, cover and cook gently for 15 minutes, or until the chicken pieces are tender.

7 Remove the bouquet garni and bay leaf, and transfer the chicken pieces to a large, heated serving platter. Keep warm. Heat the liquid to boiling in the saucepan and cook until reduced by half. Spoon over the chicken and garnish with the chopped parsley and the bay leaves.

ALMONDS The almond (prunus dulcis) is one of the most versatile of nuts. It originated in Asia and has been found among Bronze Age relics on the island of Crete, where it was considered a symbol of fertility. There are many references to it in the Bible. In the Middle Ages almonds were used in soups and desserts, Priests from Spain took almond trees to California, and now half the world's supply is grown there (Spain and Italy produce most of the remaining half). The nut itself is the most important product. Almonds are a popular snack food that can be eaten raw (it is hard to equal the flavor of milky sweet almonds straight from the tree) or roasted and salted. They are also used in cooking (whole, slivered, chopped or ground, blanched or toasted) in recipes for cakes, cookies (biscuits), other desserts, and fish and poultry dishes. Toasted almonds have a particularly delicious flavor and aroma. Almond paste (mainly used to cover cakes) is made from finely ground blanched almonds; expensive and delicate almond oil is used in confectionary and in cosmetics. Store shelled container in the refrigerator if they are to be kept for any length of time. Almond paste and almond all should also be stored in the refrigerator.

Wine Notes

This dish would suit a Chardonnay—particularly an oak-matured style.

FRANCE : A white Burgundy would be excellent: try Chassagne-Montrachet or a decent, more affordable Mâcon-Villages.

USA : Choose one of the many well-made Chardonnays from Carneros, Mendocino or Sonoma.

AUSTRALIA : Select a rich, nutty Chardonnay from the Barossa Valley, McLaren Vale or the Hunter Valley.

SPAIN : Chardonnay is not a traditional Spanish variety, but Torres Gran Viña Sol is a good example.

PAELLA

Spanish men tend to regard the making of paella as their job, much as American and Australian men dominate the barbecue ritual. Paella Valenciana, perhaps the most famous of the paellas with its wide assortment of seafood and meats, is considered a "speclal occasion" dish in other parts of Spain. The version given here is more of a family affair, well flavored but simpler in style. Paella takes its name from the pan in which it is cooked, the paellera.

SERVES 6

This recipe lends itself to adaptation: feel free to add diced pork or fish as well as chicken or shellfish, such as crawfish.

Ingredient

- 1 cup (4oz / 125g) green peas
- 4 tablespoons olive oil
- 1 large red bell pepper (capsicum), seeded and cut into strips or chunks
- 1 tomato, peeled and finely chopped
- 2 garlic cloves, chopped
- ½ teaspoon saffron threads soaked in 2 tablespoons water
- 6 scallops, if available
- 7 mussels, scrubbed and debearded
- 1 cup (8oz / 250g) green beans, cut into 1 inch (2.5cm) pieces
- 4 oz (125g) chicken breast fillet, diced
- 1 large onion, peeled and chopped
- 1 ⅓ cups (8oz / 250g) short grain rice
- bouquet garni
- salt and pepper, to taste
- 5 cups (40 fl oz / 1.25L) chicken stock
- 7 shrimp (prawns), shelled and deveined

Method

1 Combine the peas and beans in a saucepan and pour boiling water over them. Reheat the water to boiling, strain the peas and beans and refresh under cold running water, then set aside.
2 Heat the olive oil, add the red pepper and cook for several minutes, until soft. Remove with a slotted spoon and set aside.
3 Add the chicken to the pan, brown lightly, remove and set aside with the red pepper. Cook the onion and tomatoes in the oil until softened. Add the rice, garlic, bouquet garni, strained saffron liquid, salt and pepper and chicken stock. Stir in the chicken and red pepper. Cover and simmer for 10 minutes.
4 Arrange the scallops, shrimp and mussels on top, cover and cook for an additional 10 minutes, or until the rice is tender.
5 Lightly stir in the peas and beans and cook until tender.
6 Serve directly from the cooking pot.

SAFFRON Saffron, the world's most expensive spice, is the dried stigmas of a crocus plant (Crocus sativus). Each flower must be hand-picked, and it takes about 150000 flowers to make 2 pounds (1 kilogram) of saffron. The plant originated in Asia Minor and was later introduced to Spain. In ancient times saffron was used as a medicine, a dye and in cookery. Saffron is intensely aromatic, with a slightly pungent flavor, and gives its beautiful color to any dish to which it is added. It is also available in powdered form, though the powder is considered inferior to the threads.

Wine Notes

This dish calls for a white wine with body, flavor and perhaps a slightly pungent tone.

FRANCE : The character of Pouilly-Fumé and Sancerre would be appropriate here.

USA : Select a Fumé Blanc from Napa, Sonoma or Carneros.

AUSTRALIA : Choose a Semillon-Sauvignon Blanc blend from the Hunter Vallev or Margaret River.

SPAIN : Albarino, the fragrant but slightly acidic wine from Galicta, would be excellent or try a good white from the Rioja Alta region.

CALDERETA ASTURIANA

Seafood Casserole

The wet climate and the inhospitable mountains of the Asturias, in Spain's far northwest, deterred the Moorish invaders. This may explain why the region has a character and a cuisine unlike any other in Spain. Hemmed in by mountains and the Atlantic, its farmlands are nevertheless fertile, yielding grains, vegetables and luscious fruits. The region is especially famous for its cider, which is marketed both nationally and internationally.

SERVES 6

Maize is a major crop of the Asturias. Most of it is ground to make cornmeal or flour. Crusty corn bread is the perfect accompaniment to this dish.

Ingredient

- 1 ½ lb (750g) mixed seafood, such as mussels, clams, scallops and baby octopus
- 1 large onion, chopped
- 2 lb (1kg) firm whlte fish fillets, cut into chunks
- 1 teaspoon coarsely cracked black peppercorns
- ⅔ cup (5 fl oz / 160mL) dry cider or dry white wine
- salt, to taste
- 1 bouquet garni
- ⅓ cup (3 fl oz / 90mL) olive oil
- 1 large red bell pepper (capsicum), chopped
- 2 tablespoons chopped Italian parsley
- ⅓ teaspoon grated nutmeg
- 1 small red chili, seeded
- 8oz (250g) raw shrimp (prawns), shelled and deveined

Method

1. Scrub the clams or mussels, if using discarding any that are not firmly closed. Place in a saucepan with a little water and the bouquet garni and heat to boiling. Strain, reserving the cooking liquid. Any clams or mussels that have not opened should be discarded. If using octopus, tenderize it by pounding with a meat mallet. Discard the skin, eyes and beak.
2. Heat the olive oil in a large saucepan and stir-fry the onion and red pepper until softened. Add the fish pieces and stir-fry until lightly golden, then add the baby octopus.
3. Add enough water to the reserved cooking liquid to make 4 ½ cups (36 fl oz / 1.1L), and add to the pan.
4. Stir in the parsley, peppercorns and nutmeg. Add the cider, chili and salt.
5. Heat to boiling, cover, and simmer for about 30 minutes.
6. Add the remaining mixed seafood and the shrimp and simmer for an additional 10 minutes. Remove the chili.
7. Ladle into individual heated bowls and serve with bread for mopping up the juices.

PEPPER Pepper is probably the most popular and most used spice in the world. It is native to India and is thought to have been taken to Java by Hindu settlers about 2000 years ago. About the same time Arab traders introduced it to Europe, where it quickly became popular with first the Greeks and then the Romans, who regarded it as an "essential luxury." Many of the voyages of the great explorers were made to search for supplies of pepper and other spices. Green, red, black and white peppercorns all come from the same source—the pepper plant (Piper nigrum). Their color shows the state of maturity or type of processing. Green peppercorns are unripe; pink peppercorns are ripe; black peppercorns are produced by sun-drying green peppercorns; white peppercorns are sun-dried ripe peppercorns from which the outer husks have been removed. Black peppercorns are spicy and hot to the palate; green are fruitier and pungent; white and pink are somewhat milder. White pepper is best for pale dishes, such as white sauces, where the flecks of black pepper would stand out. Pepper is at its most aromatic when freshly ground. Black and white pepper can be bought ready-ground. All the various peppercorns are available packed in brine, in cans or jars.

Wine Notes

A dry, rather flinty white wine should complement this dish.

FRANCE : Choose a Muscadet from the Loire Valley. Those labelled sur lie have the most flavor and character.

USA : Sauvignon Blanc would be a good choice; the rariety lends itself to seafoods. Caymus from the Napa Valley and Geyser Peak from Sonoma are well worth trying.

AUSTRALIA : Australian Verdelho is an excellent seafood wine. Western Australia and the Hunter Valley produce the best examples.

SPAIN : Locals would serve a dry cider or "green" wine from Galicia but many Spanish dry whites would be appropriate. Try one from Rueda, such as Marques de Riscal, or one from Valdeorras, both in Spain's northwest.

POLLO AL GEREZ

Chicken with Sherry

The Andalusian cities of Jerez de la Frontera and Cadiz lie among rolling hills of chalky soil at the southern tip of Spain. Covering the hills are green vines bearing the grapes that are used to make the fortified wine called jerez, or sherry, for which the area is world famous. Sherry is produced in many forms, from very dry finos to the sweeter olorosos. It also plays a large part in Spanish cuisine, as this recipe testifies.

SERVES 4

To Insure authentic flavor, make this dish with a Spanish sherry. Because of strict manufacturing standards, all sherries made in Spain, regardless of price, are of high quality.

Ingredient

- 3 lb (1.5kg) roasting chicken
- ½ teaspoon salt
- 2 garlic cloves, finely chopped
- 1 very small red chili, seeded and finely chopped, optional
- 1 bouquet garni
- 2 onions, finely chopped
- 3 small carrots, peeled and diced or sliced
- ⅔ cup (5 fl oz / 160mL) good-quality dry sherry
- 2 tablespoons cornstarch (cornflour), mixed with 3 tablespoons cold water

Method

1. Remove excess fat from the chicken, then cut the chicken into serving portions.
2. Place in a saucepan with the bouquet garni and salt, and add enough water to barely cover.
3. Heat to boiling, then reduce heat and simmer gently for 20 minutes, removing froth as it rises to the surface.
4. Add the onion, garlic, carrots and chili and simmer for an additional 30 minutes, or until the chicken is almost tender. Stir in the sherry and simmer for another 10 minutes or until the chicken is cooked through. Remove the bouquet garni.
5. Stir in the combined cornstarch and water, stirring constantly until the sauce thickens.
6. Serve with plain boiled rice.

SHERRY The making of sherry originated in the town of Jerez de la Frontera. Forified with brandy and made principally from the Palomino grape, all true Spanish sherries are naturally dry when first produced. The sweet, or "cream," sherries were created for the colder climates and markets of northern Europe by adding the Pedro Ximinez grape. There are three main types of Spanish sherry: the very dry fino; the more mature amontillado; and oloroso, usually darker and sweeter (it too is naturally dry, but is then sweetened by the maker).

Wine Notes

A full-bodied dry white would be the most appropriate choice.

FRANCE : Choose a Rhone Valley white, such as Condrieu or White Hermitage.

USA : A chardonnay, perhaps from a warmer district such as the Central Valley, would have the necessary flavor and body.

AUSTRALIA : A wood-aged Hunter Valley Semillon with some bottle age would be ideal.

SPAIN : One of the, wood-aged whites of Rioja with their round, slightly oxidized character would be a good choice.

CARNE CON OLIVAS

Beef with Olives

Aragon lies in northeastern Spain, climbing towards the French border high in the Pyrenees. It is famous for the quality of its fruit and vegetables. It also produces much of Spain's wine, fermented until recently in vats in a process dating back to the Phoenicians who introduced wine to Spain in ancient times. The distinctive flavor of this traditional recipe comes from the generous quantity of green olives; wine too is an important ingredient.

SERVES 6

Top round (topside) and chuck (blade) are two cuts of meat that work well in this recipe. For significantly faster cooking, substitute rump steak and reduce the total cooking time from 90 to 30 minutes.

Ingredient

- 1 ½ lb (750g) roasting beef
- ¼ cup (2 fl oz / 60mL) Spanish olive oil
- 1 red bell pepper (capsicum), chopped
- ¾ cup (6 fl oz / 180mL) dry red wine
- salt and pepper, to taste
- 2 tablespoons all-purpose (plain) flour
- 2 small onions, sliced
- 1 ¼ cups (10 fl oz / 310mL) water
- 2 bay leaves
- 1 cup (5oz / 155g) green olives

Method

1. Preheat the oven to 350°F (180℃).
2. Thinly slice the beef, then lightly dredge in the flour and shake off excess.
3. Heat the oil in a heavy pan and brown the meat lightly on each side. Transfer to an ovenproof casserole.
4. Add the onion and red pepper to the oil in the pan and cook gently until softened. Transfer to the casserole with the meat.
5. Pour in the water, wine, bay leaves, salt and pepper, cover the casserole and bake for 1 hour, then add the olives. Cook for an additional 30 minutes. Stir occasionally.
6. Remove the bay leaves. Spoon onto a platter to serve.

OLIVES Olives and their oil have played an important role in shaping the cuisine of Mediterranean countries since biblical times. All olives, whether green (unripe) or black (more mature), are intensely bitter in their natural state and need extensive processing before they become edible. Varying in color, size and shape, olives are prepared differently from country to country. Spanish-style olives are soaked in brine for up to 12 months with sugar added to aid fermentation. They are sometimes pitted, then stuffed with such ingredients as pimiento, onion or jalapeño pepper. Olives are very versatile and can be used in cooking or eaten on their own.

Wine Notes

A robust but reasonably soft red would complement this dish.

FRANCE : A decent Rhône red such as Crozes-Hermitage would be an appropriate choice.

USA : Choose a medium-bodied Californian Zinfandel or Syrah.

AUSTRALIA : Try a Shiraz from Coonawarra or Central Victoria.

SPAIN : Select a young Rioja red, but avoid Reserva.

TORTADA DE ALMENDRA CON NARANJA

Almond Torte

Valencia is described as the gastronomic center of the Levante, a region on Spain's Mediterranean east coast. Oranges, almonds and sugar, which provide the main flavors in this Valencian speciality, are legacies of the Moorish occupation; indeed the Spanish word for orange—naranja—comes from the Arabic naranj. This dense cake is verv rich, delicious as a dessert, but often served as a snack with strong black coffee.

SERVES 6

For extra flavor, add julienned orange zest to the syrup while it simmers, and offer heavy cream to spoon over the cake at the table. Line the cake pan with wax (greaseproof) paper.

Ingredient

CAKE

6 eggs, separated
2 teaspoons orange zest
$\frac{1}{2}$ teaspoon almond extract (almond essence)
3 teaspoons cinnamon
$\frac{3}{4}$ cup (6oz / 185g) ground blanched almonds
$\frac{1}{4}$ cup (1oz / 30g) all-purpose (plain) flour, sifted
3 teaspoons confectioner's (icing) sugar

SYRUP

$\frac{1}{3}$ cup (3 fl oz / 90mL) water
juice of $\frac{1}{2}$ orange (about 2~3 tablespoons)
$\frac{1}{4}$ cup (2oz / 60g) sugar

Method

1 Preheat the oven to 250℉ (120℃).
2 Beat the egg whites until stiff peaks form, then gradually add the sugar. Fold in the beaten yolks and gradually add the ground almonds, orange zest, flour and almond extract.
3 Spoon into a lined and buttered 15 inches (28cm) round cake pan and bake in the oven for 1 hour, or until a thin skewer comes out clean when the cake is pierced.
4 Cool the cake in the pan, then carefully remove from the pan.
5 Combine the water and sugar in a small saucepan and stir over low heat until the sugar dissolves. Add the orange juice and leave to cool to at least room temperature.
6 Prick the surface of the cooled cake, gently pour the syrup over it and leave for about 10 minutes. Sift together the confectioners' sugar and cinnamon. Sprinkle over the cake and serve.

Wine Notes

This dish calls for a very sweet dessert wine or a rather rich fortified wine.

FRANCE : Sauternes would be ideal; or try one of the cheaper dessert wines from Monbazillac or Loupiac.

USA : Look for a luscious, botrytis-affected Semillon or Johannisberg Riesling from the Pacific Northwest of from Napa-Sonoma.

SPAIN : Malaga is Spain's richest, heaviest wine; try the thick, treacly "Dulce-Negro" style.

BRAZO DE GITANO

Gypsy's Arm

Desserts do not feature prominently in Spain but the many cakes and pastries which are eaten as snacks or at teatime testify to the Moorish legacy of honey, eggs and almonds in sweet baking. The intriguing name of this sponge cake roll derives from its shape which, with a little imagination, resembles an arm. In Andalusia the custard filling is likely to include a little of an oloroso sherry from Jerez.

SERVES 6

This may be served in the afternoon with strong coffee, or as a dessert. It is best eaten on the day it is baked.

Ingredient

CAKE

4 eggs
1 cup (4oz / 125g) self-rising (self-raising) flour or 4oz (125g) all-purpose (plain) flour sifted with ¾ teaspoon baking powder
½ cup (2oz / 60g) superfine (caster) sugar

CUSTARD

⅔ cup (4 fl oz / 160mL) milk
2 tablespoons oloroso sherry or rum
3 egg yolks
2 tablespoons cornstarch (cornflour)
3 teaspoons ground cinnamon
1 vanilla bean, broken into 2 pieces or ¾ teaspoon vanilla extract (vanilla essence)
¼ cup (2oz / 60g) superfine (caster) sugar
2 tablespoons confectioners' (icing) sugar

Method

1 Preheat the oven to 400°F (200℃).
2 Whisk together the eggs and superfine sugar until the mixture is thick and creamy. Sift the flour into the mixture and fold in lightly, using a spatula.
3 Pour into a 14×10 inches (35×25cm) jelly roll (Swiss roll) pan that has been buttered lightly and dusted with flour. Spread to an even thickness; the easiest way is to tilt the tin.
4 Bake for 15 minutes, or until the cake is springy when touched with a fingertip. While the cake is still warm, turn onto a lightly sugared sheet of wax (greaseproof) paper and roll up, starting at one of the long sides. Set aside.
5 To prepare the custard, pour the milk into a saucepan with the vanilla bean or extract, add the sherry and heat to boiling over moderate heat. Set aside to cool. Remove the vanilla bean, if using.
6 Beat together the egg yolks, sugar and cornstarch. Whisk this egg mixture into the milk and cook gently for 5 to 6 minutes, stirring constantly until the custard is thick and free of lumps. Allow to cool.

7 Unroll the cake and discard the paper. Spread the custard filling onto the sponge and roll up carefully. Wrap gently but firmly in foil and chill for at least 1 hour before serving.

8 Sift the confectioners' sugar and cinnamon together, then dust over the cake before cutting into slices.

Wine Notes

A sweet fortified wine would be appropriate to serve as an accompaniment.

FRANCE : Look for a lightly fortified Muscat, either a Beaumes-de-Venise from the Rhône Valley or one of the vins doux naturels from the south.

USA : Select a port-or Madeira-style fortified wine from California's Central Valley district.

AUSTRALIA : Try a fortified Tokay, Verdelho or Frontignac from northeastern Victoria or the Barossa Valley.

SPAIN : Choose an oloroso sherry, rich, sweetish, but not heavy.

THAILAND

World Cuisine

THAILAND is a country of amazing diversity, no single phrase or word can truly encapsulate its essence. Nothing quite conjures up the unique mélange of big city bustle, the beauty of the countryside, the warmth and gentleness of the people, the magnificence of the palaces and temples, the intense excitement of the food. The kaleidoscopic mixture that is one of Asia's leading "Little Dragons" firmly defies all attempts at glib description.

Thailand is a "come back" country—a first visit only serves to whet the appetite for more. Thai food possesses the same magnetic appeal. Exotic, distinctive and virtually irresistible, it is a unique hybrid of Southeast Asian and Indian influences that is still somehow completely individual.

Like most countries, Thailand has two levels of cookery—elegant and everyday. The different regions also have their own distinctive cuisines, but a national thread weaves its way throughout the county. Chiang Mai in the north, for example, has milder food than the central plains. In the south, curries hold sway while the northeast is closest to its gastronomic roots.

Bangkok is one of the great eating cities of the world. Intense traffic fumes notwithstanding, snacking in the streets has been elevated to an art form, and powerfully attractive smells assail the nostrils at every turn. Considering such constant temptation, it's a miracle that the Thais manage to retain their enviably slim figures.

Countless food stalls line the streets of the city. At the colorful weekend markets. peripatetic cooks with their portable stoves serve up expertly prepared and unforgettable meals in three minutes flat. Or, if your fancy is for meals on keels, kitchen boat chefs at the floating market at Damnoen Saduak deftly concoct succulent bowls of noodles richly embellished with the accompaniments in your choice.

What makes Thai food so distinctive is the use of herbs and spices, and in particular, three basic ingredients; cilantro (coriander) root, which is used as an ingredient both in cooking and in marinades; cilantro leaves, which are used for cooking and garnishing; and nam pla, a pungent fish sauce that adds saltiness and helps to enhance the flavors of other foods.

Spices and herbs are the mainstays of Thai cuisine for two reasons. First, they stimulate appetites that fade away under the onslaught of the hot, humid climate, and second, they make everything taste superb.

Apart from cilantro, the most commonly used spices and herbs are turmeric, peppercorns, garlic, cinnamon, cumin, cloves, lemon grass, sweet basil and a ginger-like root called kha (galangal). Chilies are also a mainstay and play a major role in an endless assortment of spicy, hot and very hot curries, dips and salads.

Thai meal revolve around rice, which is eaten three times a day. Thailand is one of the greatest rice-growing nations in the world and its inhabitants mainly prefer the polished long grain variety. Rice is usually cooked to a slightly sticky consistency by the absorption method but in the north where the glutinous type is highly prized, steaming is favored.

A typical Thai dinner comprises rice plus five or more dishes. These would include soup, a steamed or grilled dish, a fried dish, a salad, and hot sauces for flavoring the vegetables, meat and fish. Curries are almost as much a staple as rice and at least one curry dish are served at most dinners. Most of the dishes served are placed on the table at the same time and shared by all.

The Thais do not use chopsticks. In former times, most Thais ate with their fingers, but these days preference is given to a large spoon and fork. China bowls, plates and platters are the most common serving containers in Thailand today. Individual lacquer serving trays, each with Its own conical hood, were formerly used, but these days such elegance is mainly reserved for special occasions and religious offerings.

The main cooking techniques used are stir-frying, boiling, stewing and broiling (grilling). Stir-frying, the most popular method, obviously echoes a Chinese note, and the Thais also use woks and bowl-like pans. As in all Asian cuisines, foods to be stir-fried are slivered or cut to bite-size, and cooking times are brief. Fish and vegetables are boiled, and stewing is mainly employed in the preparation of curries. Broiling (grilling) over charcoal is popular for satay-like dishes of chicken, pork, seafood and meat.

The Thais particularly relish soups. They are served in charcoal braziers resembling Mongolian firepots and do not begin the meal, but are offered with the other dishes. Chicken and eggs enjoy wide popularity and there is an enormous choice of fish and seafood from the more than 3000 miles (4800 kilometers) of mainland seacoast.

The superstar of Thai cuisine is curry. Thai curries come in white, yellow, red, orange and green, each color reflecting a different combination of spices and herbs. Every household has a mortar and herbs. Every household has a mortar and pestle (or food processor or blender if they are affluent) for grinding together the various herbs and spices. The most exquisite Thai curries have a subtle, though spicy flavor.

The Thais are also enthusiastic eaters of desserts and sweetmeats, a predilection said to be the legacy of Portuguese missionaries and trader. The emphasis is very much on the use of fruits, eggs and coconut milk. Foithong, which is enormously popular, is made by cooking beaten egg in simmering sugar syrup. Fried bananas in coconut cream and various custards are other Simple favorites, as is sticky rice cooked in coconut milk.

If Thai sweetmeats are in a class by themselves, so are their fruits. The intensity of flavors simply defies description. Small sweet bananas, luscious perfumed mangoes, custard apples, pineapples, juicy watermelons, mangosteens, deep orange pawpaws, thirst-quenching rambutans, pomelos and rose apples all exhibit a level of sweetness and ripeness virtually unknown elsewhere. It hardly ranks as a deprivation that, in spite of their sweet tooth, most Thais choose to round off a meal with fruit rather than a sticky dessert.

TOM KHA GAI

Chicken and Coconut Milk Soup

Soup is an important component of a Thai meal. It is usually served at the same time as a number of other dishes, rather than as a separate course in the Western way. Diners eat it from individual bowls or spoon it over the rice on their plate, as they wish—either way is acceptable. Coconut milk adds a delicate creaminess to this aromatic soup from Bangkok and the surrounding central plains.

SERVES 4

It Is sometimes possible to buy fresh or frozen kaffir lime leaves from Asian supermarkets, but if these are unavailable, an equal quantity of dried leaves is an acceptable substitute. If necessary, you can use leaves from an ordinary lime tree in the soup, and garnish with cilantro.

Ingredient

- 3 cups (24 fl oz / 750mL) coconut milk
- 4 lemon grass stalks, cut into 2 inches (5cm) lengths and crushed
- 4 small red chilies, seeded and thinly sliced
- ½ teaspoon fish sauce
- 2 kaffir lime leaves, torn into pieces
- 4 kaffir lime leaves, for garnish
- 2 cups (16 fl oz / 500mL) water
- 3 large chicken breasts, boned and cut into bite-sized portion
- ¼ cup (2 fl oz / 60mL) lime juice
- 1 tablespoon thinly sliced galangal
- extra lime juice, optional

Method

1 In a large saucepan mix together the coconut milk and water, then add the lemon grass. Heat to boiling, reduce heat and add the remaining ingredients, except the lime leaves for garnish.

2 Simmer over medium heat for 15 to 20 minutes, or until the chicken is cooked. Taste to check the flavor, and add a little extra lime juice if a tarter flavor is preferred.

3 Ladle into individual bowls and garnish with the kaffir lime leaves.

Wine Notes

This soup could be served with either a fruity Riesling or Traminer.

FRANCE : Select a Riesling, Gewurztraminer or Tokay from Alsace.

USA : Choose one of the delightful but underrated Johannisberg Rieslings of the Pacific Northwest.

AUSTRALIA : Try a Traminer-Riesling blend from the Hunter Valley.

NEW ZEALAND : Choose a dry white, perhaps a Semillon or Semillon-Sauvignon Blanc blend.

TOM YAM KUNG

Hot and Sour Shrimp Soup

Travellers to Thailand will remember this famous soup, which can be searingly spicy to foreign palates. In a City in the east of the country, I once counted in one serving no fewer than seventeen prik kee noo, the incredibly hot little green chilies that give Thai food so much of its character. This delicious soup, encountered throughout Thailand, differs from region to region but the essential hot-sour flavor elements remain constant.

SERVES 4

Though shrimp are traditionally used, chicken or fish chunks may be substituted.

Ingredient

- 4 lemon grass stalks, cut into 2 inches (5cm) pieces and crushed
- ¼ cup (2 fl oz / 60mL) fresh lime juice
- ½ teaspoon salt
- 2 kaffir lime leaves
- 1 cup straw mushrooms
- 2 tablespoons cilantro (coriander) leaves, for garnish
- 5 cups (40 fl oz / 1.25L) water
- 4~5 small fresh red chilies or 3 small green chilies, seeded and very thinly sliced
- 2 tablespoons fish sauce
- 6 thin slices fresh galangal
- 1 lb (500g) shrimp (prawns), shelled and deveined

Method

1 Place the lemon grass and the water in a saucepan and simmer until the lemon grass turns yellow. Add all the remaining ingredients except the shrimp and cilantro leaves, and stir for about 5 minutes.

2 Add the shrimp and cook for only 2 to 3 minutes, or until the flesh turns pink.

3 Ladle into individual bowls and garnish with the cilantro leaves.

Wine Notes

This fierv soup is best served with lemon grass tea. If a wine is to be served, choose a soft, low-acid style with some character or pungency.

FRANCE : Choose a white from the Loire Valley: a Sauvignon Blanc such as Pouilly Fumé or Sancerre or a Chenin Blanc such as Vouvray or Montlouis.

USA : Try a Sauvignon Blanc, or perhaps a good Californian Colombard or Chenin Blanc (avoid the heavier, wood-aged styles).

AUSTRALIA : Choose a Sauvignon Blanc from the Barossa Valley or McLaren Vale.

NEW ZEALAND : Select a Sauvignon Blanc, perhaps blended with Semillon or Chenin Blanc, from the Hawkes Bay area.

YAM KAI DOW

Crisp Fried Egg Salad

The thin, long-legged chickens pecking in the dusty streets of every Thai village contribute both meat and eggs to each family's cooking pot. This particular dish, originally from Bangkok and the surrounding area, is now very popular throughout Thailand. Perhaps the best of all Thai salads, it presents eggs cooked in a way that is unusual for a salad. However, Yam Kai Dow is typical of Thai cuisine in its mix of colors, textures and flavors.

SERVES 4

The dressing may be served separately or spooned over the salad.

Ingredient

DRESSING

1 small onion, finely chopped or grated
2 tablespoons cilantro (coriander) leaves
⅓ cup (3 fl oz / 90mL) fish sauce
⅓ cup (3 fl oz / 90mL) lime juice
6 garlic cloves, finely chopped
3 small green Thai chilies (prik kee noo), or 5 small jalapeño chilies, finely shredded
2 tablespoons palm sugar or brown sugar

lettuce leaves
2 small tomatoes, quartered or cut into eighths
2 small white onion, thinly sliced
⅓ cup (3 fl oz / 90 mL) vegetable oil
2 small carrots, peeled and sliced
½ green bell pepper (capsicum) seeded and cut into strips
4 eggs

Method

1 Combine all the dressing ingredients, mix well and set aside until required.
2 Place the lettuce leaves on a serving platter and arrange the vegetables on top.
3 Heat the oil in a small pan and fry the eggs one at a time until well crisped around the edges of the white, and puffy and golden. Cook until the yolk is set.
4 Drain the eggs on paper towels, cut into pieces and pile on top of the vegetables and serve.

FISH SAUCE Fish sauce, the filtered liquid of fermented fish, is an integral ingredient in many Southeast Asian cuisines. In ranges from amber to dark brown in color and is known by different names in different countries; for example, nam pla in Thailand, and nuoc cham or nuoc mam in Vietnam, Laos and Kampuchea. There is no substitute for its distinctive salty flavor. Look for fish sauce in Asian food stores. It will keep for several months.

Wine Notes

A soft, rounded white wine without high acidity would be best suited to this dish.

FRANCE : Try either Condrieu or the less common White Hermitage from the Rhône Valley.

USA : Choose wines from varieties such as Rousanne and Viognier, grown in California. Their style is fragrant and flavorsome without being overstated.

AUSTRALIA : The Marsannes grown in Victoria's Goulburn Valley produce a soft white with a subtle flavor.

ITALY : Try the soft, somewhat spicy Oriveto from Umbria or Tocai from Friuli.

HAW MOK

Steamed Fish in Banana Leaf

This is a traditional fish recipe from Bangkok and the central plains. While Western cooks may find it more convenient to wrap the fish in foil, the dish will lose something in the translation. Banana leaves have been used in Southeast Asia for centuries to wrap food for steaming. They ensure the succulence of the cooked food by retaining its moisture, and at the same time they impart their own subtle flavor to the dish.

SERVES 6

This dish has a fragrance that wafts through the room as each banana leaf is opened. filling the diners with anticipatory pleasure. The packages may be prepared up to 4 hours in advance and chilled until cooking time.

Ingredient

¾ cup (6 fl oz / 180mL) Yellow Curry Paste.
3 tablespoons fish sauce
1 ½ lb (750g) firm white fish fillets, diced
1 tablespoon palm sugar or brown sugar
3 lettuce leaves, shredded
1 cup (8 fl oz / 250mL) coconut cream
2 jalapeño chilies, sliced and seeded
2 cups (16 fl oz / 500mL) coconut milk
2 ½ tablespoons cornstarch (cornflour)
1 tablespoon lime juice
banana leaves, cut into 6 pieces, each 9 × 9 inches (23 × 23cm)
1 cup sweet basil leaves
⅓ cup cilantro (coriander) leaves

Method

1 In a bowl, mix together the curry paste, coconut milk, fish sauce and cornstarch. Whisk until well blended.
2 Add the fish cubes, lime juice and palm sugar, and marinate in the refrigerator for about 30 minutes.
3 Carefully wipe each banana leaf with a damp cloth.
4 Spoon a portion of the shredded lettuce into the center of each banana leaf square, then top with a portion of the marinated fish cubes.
5 Stir the coconut cream thoroughly and spoon over the fish cubes. Sprinkle with the basil leaves, sliced chilies and cilantro leaves.
6 Wrap each banana leaf to form a parcel and secure with a toothpick or small satay stick.
7 Arrange the packages in the top half of a steamer and steam over boiling water for 15 to 20 minutes.
8 Serve with a bowl of steamed rice.

CILANTRO Cilantro (coriandum sativum) is also known as coriander and Chinese parsley. It is member of the carrot family, and the leaves, stems, roots are all used in the kitchen today. A native of the Mediterranean area, cilantro was being used in Egypt 3500 years ago and in Persia 500 years later, where it was grown in the Hanging Gardens of Babylon. Also, cilantro was one of the first herbs to be grown by the newly arrived American colonists–it was in cultivation in Massachusetts by 1670. Cilantro has a distinctive flavor that defies description and is used extensively in Asian (but particularly Thai), South American and Middle Eastern cuisines, where its flavor and refreshing smell are highly prized. In Western cuisine, the sweet, aromatic seeds, whole and ground, are more likely to be used–they feature in cakes and cookies, breads and pastries, and with baked fruits. Their flavor is quite distinct from the green leaves. Fresh cilantro leaves are generally available, as are dried leaves and whole and ground dried seeds.

Wine Notes

The combination of flavors here suggests a wine with some residual sweetness.

FRANCE : A demi-sec Vouvray, slightly sweet and honey-like, will provide a nice balance of flavors.

USA : Try a Johannisberg Riesling from California.

AUSTRALIA : Choose a late-picked Rhine Riesling with a little bottle age.

GERMANY : Select a Kabinett quality wine from the Rheinhessen or Rheinpfalz, or a Spätlese Riesling from the Mosel.

LAAB

Thai Ground Beef Salad

Thai meals usually include a salad, although with their characteristic hot and sour flavors they differ somewhat from the Western concept of a salad. This is particularly true of Laab, which features spicy cold meat. This dish, originally from the northeast of Thailand, is today served all over the country and is also very popular in the West. Beef is the meat most commonly used, but pork or chicken are also popular choices.

SERVES 4

To prepare roasted ground rice, tip a thin layer of sticky or other rice grains over the base of a heavy pan and cook over moderately high heat until golden brown. Allow the grains to cool then grind them with a mortar and pestle or in a food processor. Ground chicken or pork may be substituted for the beef but then you will need to use about 2 tablespoons of vegetable oil to fry the meat.

Ingredient

8oz (250g) ground (minced) lean beef
2 small white onions, finely chopped
3~5 teaspoons finely chopped red chilies
3 tablespoon finely chopped mint leaves
4 tablespoon lime juice
2 tablespoon roasted ground rice
12 lettuce leaves, washed and patted dry
3 garlic cloves, finely chopped
2 scallions (spring onions), chopped
1 tablespoon finely chopped cilantro (coriander) leaves
3 tablespoon fish sauce
1 teaspoon salt
mint leaves, for garnish

Method

1 Using a nonstick pan, brown the ground beef and garlic over medium heat.
2 Transfer the mixture to a bowl and allow to cool.
3 Thoroughly mix in the onions, scallions, chilies, cilantro, mint, lime juice, fish sauce, ground rice and salt.
4 To serve, spoon the meat mixture onto a lettuce leaf and top with the fresh mint leaves. Wrap the lettuce around the meat and eat with your fingers.

Wine Notes

This informal dish calls for a lightish, simple wine—rosé would be a good choice.

FRANCE : Try a Rosé d'Anjou from the Loire Valley or perhaps a Beaujolais; both are attractive, easy drinking styles.

USA : Choose a lightweight Zinfandel or rosé-style Grenache.

AUSTRALIA : Many light red wines are produced in Australia. Try a Rosé made from Grenache, Malbec or Cabernet, also Shiraz and Pinot Noir are used for fresh young reds in the "nouveau" style.

PORTUGAL : Rosé is something of a Portuguese specialty; it is a pleasant everyday wine.

PAD THAI

Stir-Fried Thai Noodles

This dish is served everywhere in ThaiLand: in restaurants, in homes, and at all hours from the multitude of street stalls, particularly in Bangkok. Like most noodle dishes in Thailand, it is more likely to be eaten for lunch or a light meal than as part of a dinner. In keeping with their Chinese origins, noodles are the only Thai food that is eaten with chopsticks. Most Thai dishes today are eaten with a spoon and fork.

SERVES

To make a chili "flower," choose a smooth, well-shaped, small red chili. Using a very sharp knife or scissors, make two or three cuts from the tip to the base of the chili. Then place the chili in iced water for about 30 minutes, or until the "petals" curl.

Ingredient

- 8oz (250g) dried rice noodles (about ¼ inches / 0.5cm wide)
- 8 shrimp (prawns), shelled and deveined
- 2 large eggs
- 1~2 tablespoons tamarind water (see glossary)
- 2 tablespoons palm sugar or brown sugar
- 2 scallions (spring onions), cut into 2 inches (5cm) pieces
- ½ cup roasted peanuts, chopped
- 3 tablespoons vegetable oil
- 2 garlic cloves, minced
- ½ cup tofu, cut into ¼ inch (0.5cm) cubes
- 10 small dried shrimp (prawns), very finely chopped
- 3 tablespoons fish sauce
- 2 teaspoons sweet paprika
- 2 cups bean sprouts
- scallions (spring onions), red chill "flowers" and cilantro (coriander) leaves, for garnish

Method

1. Cover the dried noodles with warm water and soak for 45 minutes, or until softened. Drain, and discard the water.
2. Heat the oil in a pan until hot, add the garlic and stir-fry for 20 seconds or until just golden. Add the fresh shrimp and stir-fry for 2 to 3 minutes or until pink. Add the tofu and cook, stirring constantly, for about 3 minutes.
3. Push the shrimp and tofu mixture to one side and add 1 egg, stirring constantly for about 1 minute. Push the egg to the side, add the second egg and repeat the process.
4. Add the noodles, chopped dried shrimp, tamarind water, fish sauce, palm sugar and paprika and stir-fry gently for about 2 minutes, until well mixed and heated.
5. Add the scallions and bean sprouts and stir-fry gently for 2 to 3 minutes.
6. Spoon the mixture onto a serving platter and sprinkle with the peanuts.
7. Garnish with the scallions, red chili "flowers" and cilantro leaves.

Wine Notes

This is a tasty, spicy dish in all its incarnations soft, aromatic style of white wine, so suitable with many Asian dishes, is the choice again here.

FRANCE : Choose a Gewurztraminer from Alsace.

USA : Try a Gewurztraminer from the Sonoma district or a Johannisberg Riesling from the Pacific Northwest or any of California's wine districts.

AUSTRALIA : Try a fruity and flavorsome Barossa Valley or Padthaway Rhine Riesling.

GERMANY : Try a middle-of-the-range Spätlese. They are light and not too sweet.

POO PAD PRIK

Chili Crab

Fishing is an important part of life in the south of Thailand and visitors are often amazed at the vast catches brought in by local fishermen who venture out great distances in boats that look hardly capable of crossing the bay. At local outdoor restaurants customers may choose from the fresh catch of the day and specify how their selection is to be prepared. Chili Crab is a famous dish that is often enjoyed by locals and tourists alike.

SERVES 4

For a milder flavor, substitute Red or Yellow Curry Paste for the Green variety.

Ingredient

1 very large whole crab or 2 smaller crabs
3 garlic cloves, finely chopped
3 tablespoons fish sauce
2 tablespoons palm sugar or brown sugar
1 tablespoon sesame oil
2 scallions (spring onions), cut into 1 inch (2.5cm) pieces
3 tablespoons oil
1 white onion, sliced
2 tablespoons oyster sauce
3 tablespoons Green Curry Paste
2 tablespoons cilantro (coriander) leaves

Method

1 Freeze the crab for 1 to 2 hours, then place in a large pot of rapidly boiling water. Cook for 20 minutes, or until the crab is red, then remove it from the pot.
2 Remove the shell from the crab's body and set aside. Detach the legs and claws and break at the joints, then crack their shells.
3 Heat the oil in a large pan over medium-high heat. Add the garlic and onion and stir-fry for 30 seconds. Add the crab pieces and flesh and stir-fry for 2 to 3 minutes.
4 Add the remaining ingredients except the cilantro leaves and scallions. Cover the pan and cook over medium heat for 3 minutes, or until the crab meat is cooked.
5 Spoon into a serving dish, add the reserved crab shell and garnish with the cilantro leaves and scallions.

PALM SUGAR Palm sugar comes from the palmyra palm (Borassus flabellifer), which is native to Southeast Asia. Chinese records show that it was in use there almost 2000 years ago. It is used throughout Asia, and is known as nam taan peep in Thailand, gula Jawa in Indonesia, jaggery in India, Burma and Sri Lanka and gula Malacca in Malaysia. Palm sugar has a strong flavor and gives richness to both sweet and savory dishes. It is sold compressed into round or rectangular shapes (which may need to be grated before use), or in round slightly domed cakes, or as a thick paste. If it is unavailable, substitute soft brown sugar or demerara sugar.

Wine Notes

A lively, young dry white is needed here.

FRANCE : Muscadet goes well with shellfish, but also try Sancerre.

USA : Choose a young style of Sauvignon Blanc from Mendocino, Lake County or Sonoma.

AUSTRALIA : Select a youthful, unoaked Colombard, Chenin Blanc or Semillon from the Riverland.

NEW ZEALAND : Try a Sauvignon Blanc from the Marlborough region.

GAI PAD BAI GRAPAO KAB KHAO NEOW

Chicken with Basil and Steamed Sticky Rice

This beautiful chicken dish, fragrant with basil, is stir-fried, a method of cooking introduced to Thailand by the Chinese. As in China, eating is a communal experience —the dishes are placed in the center of the table for all to share. Rice is served with every meal and is an important part of the Thai diet. Khao Neow, the sticky rice served here, is a variety of rice which is most popular in northern Thailand.

GAI PAD BAI GRAPAO

Chicken with Basil

SERVES 6

If desired a little stirred coconut cream may be spooned over the chicken before serving. If hot basil leaves are not available, sweet basil or Vietnamese mint may be used instead.

Ingredient

- 3 tablespoons vegetable oil
- 4 garlic cloves, finely chopped
- 3 tablespoons hot basil leaves
- 2 tablespoons fish sauce
- 6 red chilies, seeded and finely sliced
- 4 chicken breasts, skinned and cut into bitesized pieces
- ⅓ teaspoon palm sugar or brown sugar

Method

1. Heat the oil in a large pan over moderate heat and stir-fry the chilies and garlic. Do not allow the garlic to bum as this creates an unpleasant flavor.
2. Add the chicken pieces and stir-fry until cooked, about 5 minutes. Add the other ingredients and stir-fry for 1 minute.
3. Spoon into a serving dish and serve hot with Steamed Sticky Rice.

KHAO NEOW

Steamed Sticky Rice

SERVES 6

There is no real substitute for this variety of rice, which is sometimes known as glutinous rice because of its consistency when cooked. It should be available at Asian grocery stores. However, if sticky rice is not available, try serving steamed jasmine rice instead.

Ingredient

- 4 cups (1 ¼ lb / 630g) sticky (glutinous) rice
- water

1 Tip the rice into a bowl and pour in enough water to barely cover. Stir lightly and strain. Continue to follow this procedure until the water that strains off is no longer cloudy.
2 Cover the rice with cold water again and leave overnight.
3 The next day, strain the rice and tip it into the top half of a steamer. Place over boiling water, cover tightly and steam for 25 to 35 minutes or until the rice is quite glutinous.
4 Serve at once.

BASIL Basil is an annual herb with aromatic leaves that add distinctive flavor to many dishes. It is thought to have grown first in tropical Asia and Africa and was known in ancient Egypt, Rome and Greece. The ancient Greeks named it basilikon phyton, the kingly herb (only the sovereign could cut it). There are a number of types of basil, all species of Ocimum. The basil associated with Mediterranean cuisine is sweet basil while the main varieties used in Thai (as well as Laotian and Vietnamese) cooking are hot basil, also known as holy or heavenly basil or hair basil; and purple basil, with the fragrance of cloves. Sweet basil may be substituted if hairy or purple basil are not available. The fresh leaves have a sweet pungent flavor and should be used where possible.

Wine Notes

Look for a Ilhlte with full, aromatic flavor.

FRANCE : Try a wine made from Aligote, the minor white variety grown in Burgundy. Its style is more assertive than the more widely grown Chardonnay.

USA : Select a Semillon, either as a straight varietal or blended with Sauvignon Blanc, from the Napa-Sonoma region.

AUSTRALIA : Choose a Verdelho from the Hunter Valley or from Western Australia.

ITALY : Try a vino da tavola white from Tuscany, particularly one from such producers as Antinori of Frescobaldi.

PAD PO TAEK

Seafood Combination with Lemon Grass

Good fish dishes are popular all over Thailand but by far the greatest number are to be found in the south, which is almost completely surrounded by water. This particularly delicious recipe is made with Green Curry Paste. The predominant flavors are typically Thai: refreshing lemon grass blends with the seafood; the hot chilies are tempered by creamy coconut, and the whole dish is perfumed with basil.

SERVES 4

The striped shrimp of Thailand are particularly large and succulent, but any fresh shrimps work well in this recipe.

Ingredient

2 tablespoons oil
8 mussels, cleaned
4oz (125g) firm white fish fillets, sliced
⅓ cup (3 fl oz / 90mL) coconut milk
1 tablespoon palm sugar or brown sugar
⅓ cup sweet basil leaves
8 shrimps (prawns), shelled and deveined
4oz (125g) scallops
¼ cup (2 fl oz / 60mL) Green Curry Paste
¼ cup (2 fl oz / 60mL) fish sauce
2 lemon grass stalks, cut into 1 inch (2.5cm) lengths and lightly crushed

Method

1 Heat the oil in a heavy pan. Add the seafood and stir-fry 2 minutes over high heat, until the fish becomes opaque.
2 Stir in the combined curry paste, coconut milk, fish sauce and sugar and cook gently for 2 to 3 minutes. Add the lemon grass and basil and toss gently. Cover the pan and cook for an additional 7 minutes.
3 Spoon onto a serving platter and serve at once with steamed rice.

Wine Notes

This dish could be matched with many dry white wine styles.

FRANCE : Try a youthful Petit Chablis: it should be dry, with a lively fruit quality.

USA : Choose an unwooded Chardonnay, a Sauvignon Blanc or a Johannisberg Riesling.

AUSTRALIA : Select a dry Rhine Riesling from the Clare Valley or from Mount Barker in Western Australia.

PORTUGAL : The popular Vinho Verde style with its fresh, vinous character is ideal. Try to find one from Minho, in the north.

NAM PRIK NOOM

Vegetables with Chili Dipping Sauce

This spicy sauce comes from Chiang Mai in northern Thailand, where it is made with large young green chilies. It is usually served as a dipping sauce for raw vegetables, which are available in great variety in Thailand. The choice of vegetables may vary depending on the seasons, but the combination suggested here is a popular one. If preferred, more conventional vegetables, such as carrot or celery, may be substituted.

SERVES 4

Charring the vegetables gives this dish its characteristic flavor.

Ingredient

16 green jalapeño chilies
8 French shallots
1 tablespoon anchovy paste
sprig of mint, for garnish, optional
3 tablespoons cilantro (coriander) leaves, for garnish, optional
12 garlic cloves
2 ripe tomatoes
3 tablespoons fish sauce
2 scallions (spring onions), chopped, for garnish, optional

VEGETABLES

1 medium cucumber, sliced
¼ Chinese cabbage, torn into pieces
1 Japanese eggplant, sliced
12 young green beans or snake beans, cut into 2 inches (5cm) lengths

Method

1. Broil (grill) the chilies, garlic cloves, shallots and tomatoes until the tomato and chili skins are slightly blackened.
2. Combine the broiled vegetables, anchovy paste and fish sauce, and grind in a mortar and pestle or a food processor until a coarse-textured paste is formed.
3. Spoon the paste into a serving bowl and garnish as desired. Serve with the fresh vegetables.

Wine Notes

This dish is usually served with water or tea. However, a soft aromatic white would be the best choice of wine.

FRANCE : Choose a Gewurztraminer, or perhaps the less well known Muscat from Alsace.

USA : Try a Johannisberg Riesling or Gewurztraminer from California or the Pacific Northwest.

AUSTRALIA : Select a Rhine Riesling in the soft, aromatic vein; perhaps a dry botrytis affected style from Padthaway or Coonawarra.

GERMANY : Select an aromatic, softly acid white from the Palatinate region.

MASSAMAN NEUA

Massaman Beef Curry

This rich, mild curry originated in the far south of Thailand, where it borders Malaysia. It is the mildest of Thai curries. The choice of spices, the inclusion of potatoes and the lengthy cooking time all reflect the influence of Indian migrants—the Muslims for whom Massaman Beef Curry was named. This recipe is popular with Thai Muslims, who prefer it to the more typical Thai curries.

SERVES 4

Chicken may be substituted for the beef if preferred; in that case, simply reduce the initial simmering time from 2 hours to 50 to 60 minutes.

Ingredient

4 tablespoons vegetable oil
4 cups (32 fl oz / 1L) coconut milk
4 small potatoes, peeled and cut into chunks
2 onions, sliced
3 tablespoons fish sauce
1 ½ lb (750g) round or buttock steak, diced
2~3 tablespoons Massaman Curry Paste (see recipe)
½ cup roasted peanuts, coarsely chopped
2 tablespoons palm sugar or brown sugar

Method

1 Heat the oil in a large pan over medium heat.
2 Stir-fry the meat for about 5 minutes, then add the coconut milk and heat to boiling.
3 Reduce heat, cover and allow the meat to simmer for about 2 hours, or until tender.
4 In another small pan, over medium heat, fry the curry paste with ½ cup (4 fl oz / 125mL) of the cooking liquid. Mix well.
5 Stir the paste mixture into the meat. Add the remaining ingredients and simmer for 20 minutes.
6 Pour into a serving bowl and serve with steamed rice.

MASSAMAN CURRY PASTE

MAKES ABOUT ⅓ CUP

Refrigerated, this will keep for 12 months.

Ingredient

10 large dried red chilies
6 French shallots, finely chopped
1 teaspoon caraway seeds
6 cloves
1 teaspoon salt
2 tablespoons vegetable oil
4 bay leaves
8 garlic cloves, finely chopped
1 teaspoon finely chopped galangal
⅓ small lemon grass stalk, finely chopped
1 teaspoon cinnamon
⅓ teaspoon ground nutmeg
6 cardamom pods
1 teaspoon shrimp paste

Method

1 Prepare the chilies by soaking in hot water for 20 minutes. Seed them, then mince or chop finely.

2 Brown the garlic and shallots in a dry pan over low heat for about 3 minutes. Add the seeded and chopped chilies and stir-fry over low heat for about 3 minutes, being careful not to allow ingredients to burn.

3 Transfer to a mortar and pestle or a food processor, add all ingredients except the last four, and grind them together to form a paste.

4 Heat the oil over low heat, then add the cardamom pods, bay leaves and shrimp paste, and cook for 2 minutes. Add the prepared paste and cook for 1 minute, stirring well.

5 Store in the refrigerator in a tightly sealed container. Remove the cardamom pods and bay leaves before using.

STAR ANISE This beautiful and exotic spice is the fruit of a long-lived evergreen tree (Illicium verum) that is native to China and Vietnam. Botanically it is no relation to anise, although it has a similar flavor. Although it has been known in Europe for at least 300 years, it is used mainly in Chinese and other Asian cuisines. In India the seeds are chewed as a breath freshener; and in Japan the ground bark is burned for perfume. It has a strong flavor and should be used with care. Star anise is combined with cloves, cinnamon, fennel and Szechwan (anise) pepper to make Chinese five-spice powder. Star anise is generally available in dried form in its natural star shape, or ground. Store ground star anise in an airtight container.

Wine Notes

A dry red would be best with this curry. Avoid a style which has too much astringency.

FRANCE : Try an "everyday" style from the Saint-Emilion region of Bordeaux. Look for Saint-Emilion, Fronsac or Côtes de Castillon.

USA : Choose a Californian Merlot with supple fruitiness and good body. The Monterey-San Francisco Bay area produces some excellent examples.

AUSTRALIA : Select from the many good blends featuring Shiraz, Merlot and Cabernet; they offer generous flavor with well-rounded structure.

ITALY : The north-eastern districts produce some lovely soft, fleshy Merlot wines.

GAENG MOO KAB NAM PRIK

Pork Curry and Curry Pastes

Pork is used less often than chicken, seafood or beef in Thai cuisine, but this pork curry is popular in the Bangkok region. Traditionally curry pastes were made with a pestle and mortar—a laborious task for the cook, especially as some of the old mortars were 3 feet (1meter) across, their pestles almost too heavy to lift. The heat factor in Thai curry pastes ranges from green at the hot end, down through red, yellow and Massaman, which is the mildest.

GAENG MOO PHED GAI

Red Pork Curry

SERVES 4

Swamp cabbage is a "leggy" creeper-type vegetable with small green leaves. It is often available fresh in Asian grocery stores, but, if unobtainable, spinach leaves may be used instead. If using dried kaffir lime leaves, soak them in hot water for 5 minutes.

Ingredient

2 cups (16 fl oz / 500mL) coconut milk
1 teaspoon salt
2 tablespoons fish sauce
2 tablespoons tamarind water (see glossary)
2 cups coarsely shredded swamp cabbage
2 tablespoons Red Curry Paste (see recipe)
1 lb (500g) lean pork, diced
1 tablespoon palm sugar or brown sugar
3 fresh or dried kaffir lime leaves, shredded

Method

1 Blend half the coconut milk together with the curry paste and salt and cook in a large saucepan over moderate heat for 2 minutes, stirring continuously.
2 Add the pork and simmer until tender, about 40 minutes (depending on the tenderness of the meat). Add the remaining ingredients, including the rest of the coconut milk, and bring slowly to a simmer. Cook for 3 minutes, stirring occasionally.
3 Transfer to a serving dish.

NAM PRIK DANG

Red Curry Paste

MAKES ABOUT ⅓ CUP

This will keep in the refrigerator for 12 months.

Ingredient

14 large dried red chilies
2 teaspoons caraway seeds
2 tablespoons finely chopped cilantro (coriander) roots
1 teaspoon cilantro (coriander) seeds
1 teaspoon salt
1 / 2 teaspoon dried kaffir lime leaves, crumbled

1 tablespoon finely chopped galangal
5 garlic cloves, finely chopped
6 black peppercorns, crushed
4 tablespoons vegetable oil
4 French shallots, finely chopped
2 tablespoons chopped lemon grass
1 tablespoon shrimp paste

Method

1 Soak the dried chilies in hot water for 20 minutes, then seed.
2 While the chilies are soaking, dry-fry the cilantro and caraway seeds in a small pan, over low heat, for about 5 minutes.
3 Combine the chilies and salt in a mortar and pestle or food processor and grind to a puree.
4 Add the caraway and cilantro seeds and grind. Add the remaining ingredients except the shrimp paste and oil, and puree. Stir in the shrimp paste and oil to make a smooth paste.
5 Store in the refrigerator in a tightly sealed container.

NAM PRIK GAENG KEO WAN

Green Curry Paste

MAKES ABOUT ½ CUP

The seeds are the hottest part of the chili. Handle both fresh and dried chilies carefully and wash your hands after touching them. This curry paste will keep in the refrigerator for up to 12 months.

Ingredient

10 fresh green chilies, with seeds
2 tablespoons finely chopped lemon grass
1 teaspoon cilantro (coriander) seeds, ground
1 teaspoon finely chopped galangal
1 teaspoon salt
2 tablespoons finely chopped French shallots
4 tablespoons vegetable oil
6 garlic cloves, finely chopped
2 tablespoons finely chopped cilantro (coriander) roots
1 teaspoon caraway seeds, crushed
6 black peppercorns, crushed
1 teaspoon shrimp paste

Method

1 Dry-fry all the mgredients except the shrimp paste and oil over low heat until brown, about 5 minutes. Then place the mixture in a mortar and pestle or food processor and grind to puree.
2 Add the shrimp paste and oil and mix to a smooth paste.
3 Store in the refrigerator in a tightly sealed container.

NAM PRIK GAENG KARIE

Yellow Curry Paste

MAKES ABOUT ¼ CUP

This will keep in the refrigerator for 12 months.

Ingredient

7 large dried red chilies
1 teaspoon caraway seeds
1 tablespoon finely chopped lemon grass
3 garlic cloves, finely chopped
1 teaspoon finely chopped galagal
1 teaspoon dried mustard
3~4 tablespoons vegetable oil
1 tablespoon cilantro (coriander) seeds
1 teaspoon salt
5 French shallots or 1 white onion, finely chopped
1 teaspoon grated ginger root
1 tablespoon curry powder
1 tablespoon shrimp paste

Method

1 Soak the chilies in hot water for 20 minutes, then seed.
2 While the chilies are soaking, brown the cilantro seeds and caraway seeds in a dry pan for about 5 minutes.
3 Combine the seeded chilies and salt in a mortar and pestle or food processor and grind. Add the cilantro and caraway seeds and grind to a powder.
4 Add remaining ingredients, except the shrimp paste and vegetable oil, and mix together well.
5 Add the shrimp paste and oil and mix to a smooth paste
6 Store in the refrigerator in a tightly sealed container.

THAI CHILIES Native to the America, chilies were taken back to Europe by early explorers and by the mid-fifteenth century were being used (and grown) in Europe, Asia and Africa. In Thailand there are small red, small green, long red and long green varieties, as well as others that are a little fatter. Generally the smallest ones (prik kee noo) are the hottest, and they are fiercest when green. The larger jalapeño chilies (prik chee fa) are used either green or ripe when a milder heat is required. Remember to discard the seeds if you wish to reduce the heat of chilies and to wash your hands immediately after handling chilies as their oils can irritate the skin and also the eyes. If fresh chilies are not available, dried and powdered forms can be used.

Wine Notes

A soft fruity wine—red or white—would best suit this curry. A hint of sweetness in the wine will temper the typical Thai hot-sweet-sour flavors.

FRANCE : Choose a Beaujolais to serve with this dish.

USA : Try a Zinfandel, either in the light red or "blush" (pale pink) from. The spicy aromatic quality of the variety should be perfect.

AUSTRALIA : Choose a light and spicy Grenache Rosé.

GERMANY : Select from the many attractive whites and light reds from the southern wine-growing regions. Weissherbst (a rosé style) and such whites as Rülander and Traminer from Baden-Wurttemberg would be good.

KHTA NEOW MAMUANG

Mango with Sticky Rice Pudding

In Thailand, as in most of Southeast Asia, everyday meals traditionally conclude with fresh fruit. Desserts, like this famous one from the northern region, are reserved for special meals. Many dessert recipes are based on sweetened rice and coconut cream, slightly salted to maintain the balance of flavors. This dish is usually served at room temperature and is often varied by using different exotic fruits such as rambutans, longans or lychees.

SERVES 4

Choose the ripest fruit you can find. The sweetness of the mango is complemented by the slightly salty coconut cream sauce.

Ingredient

2 cups (10oz / 315g) sticky (glutinous) rice
¼ cup (1oz / 30g) palm sugar or brown sugar
1 cup (8 fl oz / 250mL) coconut cream
3 cups (24 fl oz / 750mL) water
2 large ripe mangoes
⅓ teaspoon salt

Method

1 Rinse the sticky rice twice, then drain well in a colander. Place the rice in a medium-sized saucepan with the water. Heat to boiling, then cook, uncovered, until the rice is soft, about 20 minutes. Stir in the sugar, and cook for an additional 5 to 10 minutes, or until the sugar is dissolved.
2 Remove from heat and allow to cool.
3 Peel the mangoes and slice the flesh.
4 To serve, spoon the rice onto a serving dish. Whisk together the coconut cream and salt and spoon over the prepared rice. Arrange the mango slices with the rice.

Wine Notes

A dessert wine is delectable with the fruit in this dish.

FRANCE : Choose one of the highly fortified Muscats of the Rhône Valley or southern France, notably Minervois.

USA : Try a late-picked dessert-style Johannisberg Riesling from California.

AUSTRALIA : Select one of the very aromatic dessert styles featuring such varieties as Lexia or Orange Muscat.

GERMANY : A good choice would be the sweet, rather heavy Spätlese from the Rheinpfalz, made from Muscat, Traminer or, more rarely, Riesling.

FOITHONG

Golden Threads

This decorative favorite, originally from the central area around Bangkok, is very fiddly to make. However. it is well worth the effort because it tastes delicious and look delightful with its golden "threads" of egg yolk. In Thailand it is traditionally made with a cone of banana leaf or a special brass funnel. Foithong is usually served as a snack with coffee, or sprinkled over rice desserts. Its sweetness help to balance the spiciness of the main meal.

SERVES 4

Handsome brass funnels for making Golden Threads are readily available in the market places of Thailand. It is just as easy (or not more difficult!) to use a funnel made of aluminum foil or cooking parchment. To do this, roll a sheet of foil or parchment into a funnel shape, then make a small hole at the base and use It to create the fine threads needed.

Ingredient

3 cups (24 fl oz / 750mL) water
12 egg yolks
3 cups (24oz / 750g) sugar

Method

1 Heat the water to a slow boil in a large saucepan, add the sugar and keep the liquid simmering.
2 Gently whisk the egg yolks and pour through a strainer into another bowl or jug.
3 Slowly pour the yolks through a traditional brass funnel (or a funnel made from foil or cooking parchment) into the rapidly simmering water. Move the funnel from side to side so that as the egg yolk meets the water fine golden threads are formed. Add the egg yolk in small batches.
4 As the threads cook. carefully remove them with long satay sticks or skewers.
5 Fold the drained threads into neat little bundles and arrange on a serving plate.
6 Serve barely warm or cold. They can be eaten with your fingers or with a fork.

Wine Notes

Serve with coffee and a small glass of fortified wine or a dessert wine.

FRANCE : Choose a Sauternes, Lopiac or Monbazillac from the Bordeaux region.

USA : Try a fortified white perhaps from the Central Valley around Madera, or a late harvest Semillon.

AUSTRALIA : A fortified Frontignac would be a suitable choice, North-eastern Victoria produces many fine examples.

PORTUGAL : Portugal produces many outstanding sweet wines. Moscato de Setúbal would be ideal with this dish, or choose a good Tawny Port.

GLOSSARY

There are 90 ingredients which have been featured in separate boxes throughout the text. Please refer to the Index for the relevant page numbers.

AGAR-AGAR

A setting agent obtained from seaweed, agar-i)gar has no taste of its own and does not need refrigeration to set. These properties make it popular with the food industry. Desserts made with agar-agar hold their shape well, and can be cut with scissors into decorative shapes. Agar-agar is available as a powder or in strands from health food shops and Asian groceries. It will keep indefinitely if stored in a dry, airtight container.

ARROWROOT

Arrowroot is a powder obtailled from the underground stem of the Maranta plant, which grows in the tropoics. It is particularly useful as a thickening agent because it dissolves to a clear liquid and cooks at a lower temperature than other starches. It is also flavorless, and easily digestible. It can be bought in powder form from any supermarket, and should be stored in an airtight container out of direct light.

CREME FRAICHE

Creme fraiche means literally fresh cream in French. However, today the term is applied to a heavy cream which has acquired a sharp tangy flavor through the introduction of lactic bacteria. It is somewhat sweeter than sour cream. Creme fraiche is available commercially, but it can also be easily made at home. Mix 1 cup of heavy cream with 1 tablespoon of buttermilk and leave in a warm place for at least 4 hours. The longer the mixture is left the sharper the resulting tang. Once prepared, creme fraiche should be kept in the refrigerator and used within a week.

DAIKON

A giant white radish that can grow to over 2 feet (60cm) long, daikon is widely used in Asian cuisines. In Japan it is eaten raw in salads, shredded as a garnish or grated as an accompaniment to fish dishes. It is also pickled as a relish, simmered in soups and broths or cooked as a vegetable. It is sold by Asian food stores. Choose small daikon, which will be more tender and juicy than the larger ones. Daikon will keep in the vegetable compartment of the refrigerator for up to 2 weeks.

EPAZOTE

Epazote is an herb that grows wild in both America and in Europe. Its unique flavor partners well with beans, and It is often included in Mexican bean dishes. It is not readily available, but can be grown at home from seed.

FIVE-SPICE POWER

The five spices which are combined to make this powder are star anise, Szechwan pepper, fennel, cloves and cinnamon. A favorite in Chinese cooking, it is strongly aromatic and pungent and should be used sparingly. It is available from most supermarkets and Asian groceries.

JICAMA

Native to Mexico, the jicama is a large bulbous root with juicy white flesh. Often eaten raw in salads, or with a dip of dressing, it can also be cooked. Its texture lends interest to a dish. A good substitute would be water chestnuts. Available in vegetable markets of Asian food stores, jicamas will keep in the refrigerator for several weeks.

JUNIPER BERRIES

The berry of the juniper tree is widely used in cooking, especially in Scandinavia. The piquant spiciness of the juniper berry marries well with rich game meats, and is often found in marinades and cabbage dishes. The juniper berry also gives gin its characteristic taste, and is included in different flavored brandies and schnapps. The dried berry is widely available in food stores, and should be crushed before use.

KAFFIR LIME LEA VES

The kaffir lime, known as magrut to the Thais, is a similr size to the common lime, but has a rough, knobbly and dark green skin. The leaves, the peel and the Juice are "idely used in Asian cuisine. While fresh leaves are not always available, frozen or dned leaves are often sold by Asian food stores. If dried leaves are to be used, they will require soaking in water first. Lemon can be substituted for kaffir lime, but its flavor is not as strong nor as sharp.

KOMBU

Also known as konbu, this variety of dried Japanese seaweed is an essential in the making of Dashi, the quintessential Japanese fish stock. Greenish black in color, and sun-dried, it is sold in strips. Before use it should be lightly wiped to remove any powdery salt deposits, and then scored to help release its characteristic sea flavor. After cooking, kombu can be retrieved from the stock. wiped clean and stored in a dry, cool place for reuse. However, its flavor will decrease with subsequent use. Kombu can also be cooked as a vegetable, or pickled as a relish. It is available from Asian food stores, and should be stored in an airtight container.

LEMON GRASS

Also known as citronella, lemon grass is an aromatic herb that grows in most tropical countries. Its bulbous base is cut up and used in curries. The lower, more tender part of the stem is pounded to release its strong lemon flavor. This is then used to give a dish the sharp freshness that is so characteristic of Thai and other Asian cuisines. Lemon grass can be bought in jars, dried or in powder form, but the flavor is not so intense.

The lemon grass stalks are readily available fresh from Asian food stores, and should be kept in the refrigerator.

MIXED SPICE

Traditionally the spices used in this prepared mixture are cinnamon, cloves and nutmeg. However, different blends may also include ginger, allspice or coriander. Mixed spice should be stored in a dry area, away from the light. It is available in jars from supermarkets.

NIBAN DASHI

Niban Dashi is a milder, more dilute version of Dashi, the classic Japanese fish stock that is made from dried bonito shavings and kombu (see recipe). To make Niban Dashi, use the drained kombu and kelp from the Dashi and simmer in a second lot of water for 20 minutes. Dashi is the basis for soups, sauces, sweet-and-sour dishes and vegetables, and is best when freshly made. However, it can be purchased from Asian food stores as instant granules or as dried cubes, or in a paste form, to which liquid must be added.

NORI

Non is a type of seaweed which in Japan is used dried to wrap sushi, or crushed and used as a garnish over soups, noodles and rice. It is sold in strips, and is best lightly toasted before use. It is also a widely used ingredient in Korean cuisine where It is known as keem. Available from Asian food stores or health food shops, nori needs to be kept completely dry, otherwise mildew will develop.

ORANGE FLOWER WATER

Also known as orange blossom water, it is distilled from the flowers of the bitter Seville orange. Widely used for centuries in the Middle East for flavonng confectionery, desserts and cakes, it is also used in the perfumery industry. Orange flower water is widely available from Greek or Middle Eastern food stores, and should be kept tightly sealed in a cool area away from direct sunlight.

PANDANUS LEAF

The pandanus tree is found throughout tropical Asia and its bright green leaves are used in Malaysia and Indonesia to flavor deserts, and occasionally rice dishes. The fresh leaf gives the best flavor, but it may be difficult to obtain. The pandanus extract, which is strong and should be used sparingly, is available from Asian food stores.

PHYLLO PASTRY

Sometimes spelled filo or fillo, these paper-thin sheets of pastry are widely used in Greek and Middle Eastern cooking. Made with a high-gluten flour and little fat, the pastry is very pliable and thus lends itself to wrapping ingredients into packets. It is used to make both savory and sweet dishes. Phyllo pastry is difficult to make, but it can be purchased chilled or frozen from most supermarkets.

PROSCIUTTO

Prosciutto is also known as Parma ham, after its place of ongin in Italy. It is a delicately flavored raw ham which has been cured with a mixture that includes salt, pepper, sugar and allspice. Often served in very thin slices with fruit such as melon, figs and peaches, prosciutto is available from specialist food stores.

RICE

Although there are a number of intermediate types of rice, the two main types of rice are short grain and long grain. Short grain rice has grains that are almost round, and these tend to be more moist and gold together well when cooked. Short grain rice is used in croquettes and molds as well as in desserts. Long grain rice is about four times longer than its wide and the grains remain separate after cooking. It is served as a side dish, or combined with meat, fish of vegetables in hot or cold dishes. Both brown and white rice (a more processed form) come in long and short grain varieties. Arborio rice is a special variety of short grain rice, originally grown near Arborio in northern Italy. The term is now applied to the rice that is used in risotto and which has the ability to absorb a lot of liquid quickly while remaining firm. Arborio rice is also used in soups, and in sweet dishes. It can be found in most large supermarkets and Italian grocery stores. Wild rice is not really rice, but the seed of a water grass native to North America. It is much more expensive than white or brown rice.

SALAM LEA VES

The salam tree is found throughout Indonesia, and its tough aromatic leaves are used in both Indonesian and Malaysian cuisine. Its leaves are larger than curry leaves, but are used in a similar manner, and curry leaves make a good substitute if salam leaves are unavailable. Salam leaves can be bought either fresh or dried, and are used to add flavor to rice dishes, soups, sauces and curries if they are bought fresh they should be kept in the refrigerator; dried leaves need to be stored in an airtight container. Salam leaves can be purchased from Asian food stores.

SAVOIARDI

Ladyfingers, sponge fingers or boudoir biscuits are other names for these elongated sponge cookies which are perfect as an accompaniment to desserts. They are also used to form layers in cream—or custard—based desserts and in refrigerated desserts such as iced charlottes. Most supermarkets will stock them, and they should be stored in an airtight container to prevent them from going soft.

SEA SALT

Basically there are two types of salt—rock salt, which is found in the ground, and sea salt, which is removed from sea water by evaporation. Sea salt has more flavor than rock salt. It is usually formed in small flakes or chunks and can be served in that form or in a grinder like a pepper grinder, to be ground at the table. It is available from specialist food stores and health food stores, and should be stored in a dry place.

SMETANA

This is a soured dairy cream which is a favonte of Russian and Eastern European cooks. Smetana is often added to soups, mixed into dressings and gently heated in sauces. It partners horseradish, a Russian favorite, particularly well. It should be kept in the refrigerator and used within a few days as it does not keep for long. Sour cream is an acceptable alternative.

TAMARIND WATER

The tamannd tree was originally a native of India and now also grows in other tropical countries. Its pods contain a sour, even bitter, pulp that is widely favored in Asia as a condiment. Tamarind water is made from tamarind pulp by soaking 1 tablespoon of pulp in ½ cup of hot water for 10 to 15 mmutes. The pulp is then squeezed and the liquid strained. This process can be repeated to extract more juice, after which the pulp is discarded. The unused pulp and the resulting water should be stored in the refngerator and used within 2 weeks. The tartness of the tamarind water makes it a popular thirst-quenching drink, while it is considered an essential ingredient in many curries. Tamarind pulp can be bought by weight in most Asian food stores.

ZEST

Zest is the name given to the colored thin outermost peel of oranges, lemons and other citrus fruit. It contains fragrant oils and is strongly flavored. To obtains the zest use a potato peeler, a very sharp krufe or a special zester to separate it from the pith (the white part of the skin). Zest is used as a flavoring in both sweet and savory dishes and also as a garnish. Oranges and lemons are the fruits most often used.

INDEX

T

V

X

Y

Z

저자소개

유상훈 Sanghun Yoo

학력

University of Santo Tomas(B.S Tourim / 관광학 학사)
University of the Philippines(Master of Food Service Administration / 외식경영학 석사)
세종대학교(Doctor of Food science / 식품공학 박사)
The Culinary Institute of America, New York, USA(Associates degree in Culinary Arts 졸업)

경력

Harbin University of Commerce, Chinese Cuisine study, Harbin, CHINA 수료
Center for Culinary Arts, Short Course study, Manila, PHILIPPINES 수료
Baipai Thai Cooking School, Thai cuisine study, Bangkok, THAILAND 수료
Trung Tam Day Nghe Hoan Kiem, Vietnam Cuisine study, Hanoi, VIETNAM 수료
김포대학 외래교수
경희대학교 외래교수
리츠칼튼호텔 조리팀
쉐라톤워커힐호텔 조리팀
Buddakan, New York, USA(Externship)
KAI Restaurant, New York, USA(Externship)
ServSafe Certification(USA): 미국 NRA 식품안전관리사
한국직업능률원 "특성화고 조리서비스영어" 집필위원
2006 전국육류창작대회, 준비위원장
2006 서울세계관광음식박람회(SIFE 2006), 팀감독(단체전: HOT 부문 금상, COLD 부문 은상)
2011 Culinaire Malaysia, 말레이시아, WACS 한국대표 심사위원
2012 Philippines Culinary Competition, 팀감독(Silver Medal 6, Bronze Medal 6)
2012 FHC China Culinary Arts Competition 상해 · 중국, 팀감독(Bronze Medal 8)
2012 대전세계조리사대회, WACS 심사위원
2012 TUCC 태국, WACS 한국대표 심사위원
2012 IKA(독일조리올림픽), 최초 WACS 한국대표 심사위원
2012 FHC China Culinary Arts Competition 상해 · 중국, 최초 WACS 한국대표 심사위원
WACS(세계조리사회연맹) 심사위원
동양조리학과 초대학과장(2003~2006년, 2009~2012년)
Shanghai Institute of Tourism, Guest Professor
현재 영산대학교 동양조리학과 교수

세계조리학
World Cuisine

2012년 12월 20일 초판 인쇄
2012년 12월 27일 초판 발행

지은이 유상훈
펴낸이 류제동
펴낸곳 (주)교문사

전무이사 양계성
편집부장 모은영
책임편집 정혜재
본문디자인 에바다에딧
표지디자인 이혜진
제작 김선형
영업 이진석 · 정용섭 · 송기윤

출력 현대미디어
인쇄 동화인쇄
제본 한진제본

우편번호 413-756
주소 경기도 파주시 교하읍 문발리 출판문화정보산업단지 536-2
전화 031-955-6111(代)
팩스 031-955-0955
등록 1960. 10. 28. 제406-2006-000035호

홈페이지 www.kyomunsa.co.kr
E-mail webmaster@kyomunsa.co.kr
ISBN 978-89-363-1303-6 (93590)

값 17,000원

* 잘못된 책은 바꿔 드립니다.

본 저서는 영산대학교 교내연구비지원으로 출판되었습니다.